Sport in the ... ty

General Ed ... an

THE FUTURE OF FOOTBALL

14

SPORT IN THE GLOBAL SOCIETY

General Editor: J.A. Mangan

The interest in sports studies around the world is growing and will continue to do so. This unique series combines aspects of the expanding study of *sport in the global society*, providing comprehensiveness and comparison under one editorial umbrella. It is particularly timely, with studies in the cultural, economic, ethnographic, geographical, political, social, anthropological, sociological and aesthetic elements of sport proliferating in institutions of higher education.

Eric Hobsbawm once called sport one of the most significant practices of the late nineteenth century. Its significance was even more marked in the late twentieth century and will continue to grow in importance into the new millennium as the world develops into a 'global village' sharing the English language, technology and sport.

Other Titles in the Series

Football Culture
Local Contests, Global Visions
*Edited by Gerry P.T. Finn and
Richard Giulianotti*

France and the 1998 World Cup
The National Impact of a World Sporting
Event
Edited by Hugh Dauncey and Geoff Hare

The First Black Footballer
Arthur Wharton 1865–1930:
An Absence of Memory
Phil Vasili

Scoring for Britain
International Football and International
Politics, 1900–1939
Peter J. Beck

Sporting Nationalisms
Identity, Ethnicity, Immigration and
Assimilation
Edited by Mike Cronin and David Mayall

Shaping the Superman
Fascist Body as Political Icon:
Aryan Fascism
Edited by J.A. Mangan

Cricket and England
A Cultural and Social History of the
Inter-war Years
Jack Williams

**Flat Racing and British Society,
1790–1914**
A Social and Economic History
Mike Huggins

The Games Ethic and Imperialism
Aspects of the Diffusion of an Ideal
J.A. Mangan

The Race Game
Sport and Politics in South Africa
Douglas Booth

Making the Rugby World
Race, Gender, Commerce
*Edited by Timothy J.L. Chandler
and John Nauright*

Rugby's Great Split
Class, Culture and the Origins of Rugby
League Football
Tony Collins

THE FUTURE OF FOOTBALL

Challenges for the Twenty-First Century

Editors

JON GARLAND, DOMINIC MALCOLM and MICHAEL ROWE

University of Leicester

FRANK CASS

LONDON • PORTLAND, OR

First published in 2000 in Great Britain by
FRANK CASS PUBLISHERS
Newbury House, 900 Eastern Avenue
London, IG2 7HH

and in the United States of America by
FRANK CASS PUBLISHERS
c/o ISBS, 5804 N.E. Hassalo Street
Portland, Oregon 97213-3644

Website: www.frankcass.com

British Library Cataloguing in Publication Data

The future of football : challenges for the twenty-first century. –
(Sport in the global society)
1. Soccer – Great Britain 2. Soccer – Social aspects –
Great Britain 3. Soccer – Economic aspects – Great Britain
I. Garland, Jon II. Malcolm, Dominic III. Rowe, Michael, 1967–
306.4'83'0941

ISBN 0-7146-5068-4 (cloth)
ISBN 0-7146-8117-2 (paper)
ISSN 1368-9789

Library of Congress Cataloging-in-Publication Data

The future of football: challenges for the twenty-first century/
editors, Jon Garland, Dominic Malcolm, and Michael Rowe.
    p. cm. – (Sport in the global society, ISSN 1368-9789; no. 17)
    "This group of studies first appeared as a special issue of
Soccer and society (ISSN 1466-0970), Vol. 1, No. 1, Spring 2000"
– T.p. verso. ISBN 0-7146-5068-4 (cloth) – ISBN 0-7146-8117-2 (pbk.)
    1. Soccer – Social aspects. 2. Soccer – Economic aspects. 3. Soccer
– Forecasting. I. Garland, Jon, 1967 – II. Malcolm, Dominic, 1969 –
III. Rowe, Michael, 1967 – IV. Soccer and society. V. Cass series – sport
global society; 17.

GV 943.9.S64 F89 2000
7966.334–dc21   00-029442

This group of studies first appeared as a special issue of *Soccer and Society*
(ISSN 1466-0970), Vol.1, No.1, Spring 2000, published by Frank Cass

Printed in Great Britain by Antony Rowe Ltd., Chippenham, Wilts

To Karen, with love, Jon

To Liz, Lucy, Lottie and Monica, with love, Dom

To Liz and Ken Rowe, with love and thanks, Mike

Contents

Tables and Figures

Foreword

Football is a nostalgic business. Most of us know of fans who can happily spend hours engaged in heated debate over the respective merits of players from different eras, comparing George Best with Ryan Giggs, Pele with Ronaldo, or Michael Owen with Gary Lineker. Newspapers and television programmes occasionally produce league tables that attempt to rank the performances of clubs throughout the twentieth century, or to select sides composed of the greatest players of all time. Such reflections are often accompanied by complaints that the game has somehow lost its soul or neglected its traditions. Players, it is often stated, have become over-paid and separated from the working-class communities they used to represent, and changes to the spirit and the rules of the game have reduced football to a pale shadow of its former self. Many of these grumbles often fail to stand up to much scrutiny, and perhaps say more about those who repeat them than they do about the reality of the situation. Just as we recall the summers of childhood as hot and ever-lasting, we tend to look back on the 'good old days' of football through rose-tinted spectacles.

This does not mean, of course, that there have not been major changes in the nation's favourite sport during recent decades. My professional career began when I signed for Arsenal in 1969 and in the years that followed I played with Cambridge United and then West Bromwich Albion, before retiring in 1984. During the 15 years I played full-time there were tremendous changes within the game. Commercial development in the form of sponsorship and the general increase in the celebrity status of top footballers have brought tremendous benefits to individuals and to the sport as a whole. Other features of that era had a terrible impact on football and hooliganism and racism reared their ugly heads in ways that disfigured the sport for many years.

Comparing the game during my playing days with the sport of today, though, makes one realize the enormous upheavals that have occurred in the last decade or so. Football may have been developing throughout its long history but it seems that the pace of change has increased dramatically. The advent of the Premier League, the influx of foreign players into the British game, particularly following the *Bosman* judgment, increasing revenues from television companies, and the huge impact that events such as Euro '96 have had on the national stage have meant that the many aspects of the game have changed almost beyond recognition. The consequences of these changes are open to debate, of course. For every supporter who welcomes the success and glory that has come their way there are others who feel that their club has been unfairly excluded from the party. I do not intend to comment on these controversies here. However, the chapters contained in this collection provide great food for thought for all of those interested in the current state of the national game. From time to time it is worthwhile standing back from the day-to-day business of football and reflecting on longer-term developments. This collection provides a fascinating overview of many aspects of contemporary football and offers a glimpse of the various directions that the game might take in the future.

BRENDON BATSON
Deputy Chief Executive
Professional Footballers' Association

Series Editor's Foreword

In 'this dawn' of the New Millennium, the *Sun* with its sardonic recording of the historic defeat of Glasgow Celtic by Inverness Caledonian Thistle in the third round of the Tennents' Scottish Cup – 'Super Caley Go Ballistic, Celtic Were Atrocious'! – has provided one of the most eye-catching newspaper headlines since 'Pope Elopes' ran the rounds in the United States following a national competition for the most gripping banner headline. In the 'afternoon' of the Old Millennium Celtic romantics, escapists and patriots slumped in gloom in the bars behind the Barrows while highly paid officials, a gregarious club 'Social Convener' and 'gob smacked' fans tottered about in shock in and around Parkhead. It was not only the parrots that were sick in Celtic's gloomy 'dawn' of the twenty-first century! Nevertheless, as Peter Rafferty, Secretary of the Association of Affiliated Celtic Supporters' Clubs observed – albeit with reference to the appointment of Kenny Dalglish as interim manager: 'At least we are keeping continuity in the club.' Exactly. The shock of defeat and the euphoria of victory captures the continuity in club soccer.

However, as *The Future of Football*, the launch number of the new Cass journal *Soccer and Society* as well as a volume in the rapidly expanding Cass Series Sport in the Global Society, makes very clear, there is now considerable change in the world of British soccer as a whole.

The chapter titles trumpet this to the heavens – to select several at random, to make the point: '"Heads above Water": Business Strategies for a New Football Economy' (Barry Pierpoint), 'Football and European Law: Who's in Charge?' (Ken Foster), 'Democracy and Fandom: Developing a Supporters' Trust at Northampton FC' (Brian Lomax), 'Exploring Future Relationships between Football Clubs and Local Government' (Sean Perkins) and 'Racism in Football: A Victim's Perspective' (Richie Moran).

Oh brave new soccer world that has such subjects in it!

Many of the topics in *The Future of Football* were to be found in the excellent earlier volume on the soccer World Cup in the series Sport in the Global Society edited by Hugh Dauncey and Geoff Hare, *France and the 1998 World Cup: The National Impact of a World Sporting Event*. As both *France and the World Cup* and *The Future of Football* reveal, the future is not only full of challenges, it is clearly replete with problems, but as Brendon Batson suggests in his foreword to this collection, there is little doubt that nostalgia will triumph and in time soccer will be the richer (in all senses).

The Future of Football offers a *soi-disant* 'platform for discussion' for *all* fascinated by football. There is no doubt whatsoever given soccer's extraordinary popularity across the globe that the platform will be crowded. One reason for this is the splendidly broad representation of views in the collection: policy-makers, professional football club personnel, pressure group leaders and administrators bring their experience and sometimes expertise to bear on the extensively aired, and little aired but very topical 'myriad problems and challenges' of soccer in the third millennium.

It would be remiss here not to mention *Football Culture* edited by Gerry P.T. Finn and Richard Giulianotti also published this spring as a Special Issue of *Culture, Sport, Society* and as a volume in the series Sport in the Global Society. In many ways with its wider global coverage of soccer's problems and challenges across the world it complements superbly *The Future of Football*.

With *Football Culture* and *The Future of Football*, Sport in the Global Society is serving up, metaphorically, laden platters for those crowding the global 'platform for discussion'. With an appropriate nod of agreement in the direction of G.K. Chesterton who once wrote, 'digestion exists for health, and health exists for life, and life exists for the love of music or beautiful things' (like soccer, of course), with these new Cass publications they can 'tuck in' to a tasty two–course menu.

J.A. MANGAN
International Research Centre for Sport, Socialisation, Society
University of Strathclyde

March 2000

Introduction

Collectively the essays in this volume reveal the contrary and complex state of 'the nation's favourite game' at the end of the twentieth century. They are not intended to provide a comprehensive review of contemporary developments, nor necessarily to outline solutions to the myriad problems and challenges that football faces as it enters its third century as a professional game. Attempting to provide a 'doomsday book' cataloguing the trajectory of twentieth-century football might be an interesting task – it would certainly be a demanding one – but the ambition of this volume is more modest. What we have sought to do is provide a platform for discussion of a wide range of topics relating to the game from as many different perspectives as we could elicit. Together these studies provide diverse but not exhaustive reflection on the future of football in the twenty-first century.

One of the main features of the collection is the variety of its contributors and subsequently the breadth of subjects covered. Contributors are drawn from an extensive scope of academic disciplines, including cultural studies, economics, geography, law, politics and sociology. If, however, this is a collection solely of interest to academics and students interested in the game, then the editors will have failed. A central preoccupation behind this book has been to represent as many of those directly involved in the game as possible. We have tried to include a broad representation of policy-makers, professional football club personnel, pressure group leaders and administrators. Subsequently, a comprehensive range of issues is covered with football providing the core theme which ties the disparate parts together. That there are contradictions and inconsistencies in what follows should be no surprise: the 'brief' given to our contributors was deliberately relaxed and there is no single argument that all the pieces seek to address.

Moreover, the subjects covered in this volume seem set to remain highly topical. Where more established subject issues are broached, such as hooliganism, racism and international politics, contributions develop and update the existing literature. Many new issues, which have not been extensively aired before, are also included. Specifically essays reviewing the changing role of referees and match officials, problems of player migration and the impact of European law on the sport seek to break new ground. The various contributions have been organized into five sections covering the main issues facing the game at the current time. They are presented in no particular order of importance and it will not take more than a cursory glance through the table of contents to realize that there is considerable overlap between them.

Perhaps the range of topics addressed is actually the key theme of the collection. As contributor Sean Perkins indicates, a decade or two ago discussion of the state of the game would have been dominated by the spectre of hooliganism, especially in the English context. Once consideration of policing and public order issues had been completed, few except the most committed supporters would have remained to reflect on any broader significance that the game might have. By the end of the twentieth century the political, social, economic and cultural significance of football was so widely championed that the game seems ubiquitous. International conferences on the sport attract business sponsors, policy-makers, politicians and media pundits, as well as academic interest from diverse disciplines and perspectives. What this renaissance means for the game and its supporters is, of course, much harder to determine, and no definitive answers are provided by this collection. It does seem valuable, and important, that the discussion is being held and this volume both reflects and contributes to these continuing debates, while not claiming the last word on any of them.

The first section of the collection, on football economics and law, reflects on what has become a major concern for élite professional teams in England: whether the renaissance that has been widely identified in recent years will prove to be sustainable. Chris Gratton charts the changing economic fortunes of English professional football over the post-war period, concentrating on the differences between the main English professional team sports' league and its counterparts in the United States. Gratton argues that for most of the post-war period the key features of English professional football differed substantially from those of United States professional team sports leagues, most notably in the objectives of the owners, the number of teams and mechanisms to maintain 'uncertainty of outcome', the latter being a key feature of the literature on the economics of professional team sports. Despite the improved economic fortunes of English Premier League clubs in the 1990s, and the belief that this is due to a more American approach taken in the management and marketing of English professional football, Gratton contends that certain key features of the American model have still not been implemented. Moreover, such is the 'peculiar' nature of English football, the case for their introduction, Gratton argues, is not proven.

Barrie Pierpoint provides a practitioner's perspective on this discussion by arguing that many top-flight clubs find themselves in a precarious financial situation – barely managing to keep their heads above water. The dangers of being over-reliant on television revenue are addressed, and the need to attract new communities to watching live football illustrated. In particular, Pierpoint stresses the necessity for clubs to develop marketing strategies to entice previously excluded communities, such as minority ethnic groups and women, to watch live football, and evaluates some of the methods that clubs can employ by highlighting the initiatives devised by Leicester City FC. The essay concludes by warning that the nature and amount of revenue generated through television rights will soon change, and that this may cause severe problems for all but a handful of the richest clubs. One of the fascinating dimensions of Pierpoint's case is that those seeking to encourage marginalized supporters to attend live football matches might be able to frame an argument that will appeal to the financial interests of directors and shareholders. The relation of football clubs to diverse communities is re-examined later in the collection and Pierpoint suggests that it may even be centrally important to the financial health of teams at the highest levels.

The section finishes with Ken Foster's reflection on the impact that European law continues to have on the game, which suggests that the unusual position of football means that – despite its economic power – it is unlike other industries. Foster, like Gratton, argues that the best sporting competitions are created by leagues, acting as a cartel of businesses, which promote a single product and exclude rival competitions or organizations. Moreover, football is administered by governing bodies, both national and international, that are monopoly regulators. This inevitably brings football into conflict with European competition law and its promotion of a free market. Foster critically examines these areas of conflict, namely restrictions on players' freedom to move, the legality of measures by regulatory bodies to prevent breakaway leagues, the right of clubs rather than leagues to own and exploit broadcasting rights, the freedom of clubs to locate outside the national boundaries of a league, and the powers of UEFA to allocate places in European competitions on a national basis.

The second section explores the political nature of football, a game which has often been presented as 'above' politics yet has always been closely related to more fundamental relations of power and control. The nature of this relationship is addressed by Alan Tomlinson who considers the politics and personalities that have dominated the administration of the game on a world level. Tomlinson explores the role and global development of FIFA and looks at the individuals who have held key positions of power within the game's administrative network. Additionally, particular attention will be paid to the politics of world football and the relation between FIFA, national FAs and other national and international political bodies. In particular Tomlinson reflects on the likelihood of African footballing nations enjoying an increasingly important position at world level.

The essay that follows provides a reflection on the state of the game from the perspective of a leading football administrator of the late 1990s. Pat Day reflects on likely trends in the administration of football in the twenty-first century. In particular Day considers the English FA's attempts to rid the game of hooliganism, and the resulting change to the relationship between football authorities and the government, the changing role of supporters in the running of the game, the development of Centres of Excellence, and managing the demands of club and national playing success. The significance of staging major international football tournaments is also examined from this 'insider' perspective.

Standing in contrast to preceding discussions of politics and football at élite levels is Brian Lomax's perspective on democracy and fandom in the local context. Lomax's insight reflects his highly unusual experience gleaned as a democratically elected director of a football club, Northampton Town FC. He outlines the development of the Supporters' Trust at Northampton Town and the work undertaken by the anti-racist forum based at the club, and places this in the context of contemporary debates surrounding the governance of football. At a time when the 'Northampton model' has been widely heralded as an example for others to follow, Lomax demonstrates that fans can develop a proper, proactive role for themselves within the structure of clubs, and can become empowered through the development of specialist organizations. As with other contributions to this collection, Lomax touches on the nature of the relation between clubs and communities and the role that local authorities can play in the professional game. Whereas Tomlinson's contribution focuses on macro-level politics, Lomax is more concerned with micro-level developments. Neither is a priori more significant that the other, and both are crucial to the successful running of the game.

The third section of the book concentrates on the complex nature of the relation between football clubs and communities. The game has self-confidently paraded itself as a major repository of the hopes and aspirations of local communities for many decades. Critical consideration of this relationship has been a much more recent development, and is one that is greatly advanced through the discussion contained in this collection. A crucial aspect of the renewed fortunes of professional football has been the establishment of a range of super-stadiums that have replaced the 'cattle sheds' of old with new state-of-the-art manifestations of contemporary architecture. A common argument in support of these new stadiums has been that they remove at a stroke many of the parking, noise and other hassles faced by communities who have lived in the shadow of traditional stadiums. John Bale explores the nature of the nuisance which large crowds pose to communities located in close proximity to football grounds. Research findings indicate that the actual problems as experienced by those living closest to grounds are quite different from the potential problems perceived by people in remote communities. Bale relates the significance of these findings to the increasing trend towards stadium relocation to green- and brown-belt areas.

In many of the cases where clubs have developed either a new stadium or relatively strong links with communities, local authorities have been involved – and it is these relations that Sean Perkins analyses in his contribution. It is suggested that the link between football clubs and local authorities is likely to increase in significance in the twenty-first century. For the major 'global' clubs it will be a means of anchoring themselves to their immediate community as they seek to expand their support in overseas markets. For smaller professional clubs, whose very survival is, at best, uncertain, effective local partnerships will contribute to ensuring their day-to-day existence. There are several examples of effective multi-agency partnerships which have tackled issues of education, community involvement, sports development, racism, drug abuse and other social concerns. However, Perkins argues that these models are relatively few in number, and that most clubs and local authorities have failed to see the benefits of such links.

In the following piece, Neil Watson provides a fascinating insight into the types of relationship developed by 'football in the community' schemes, the diverse programmes funded independently of clubs that can foster imaginative initiatives seeking to harness the potential that football offers in so many spheres. The development of 'football in the community' schemes is charted, their impact assessed and possible future strategies are suggested. In particular, Watson examines methods by which successful initiatives can be developed within a strained financial climate. A self-funding community sports programme model is outlined which minimizes 'host' club input and maximizes the prominence and scope of the football in the community scheme.

The fourth section of the collection, which examines football crowds and their policing, begins by challenging the notion that football has wholly transformed itself and now attracts a more diverse 'family' audience to the national game. Dominic Malcolm, Ian Jones and Ivan Waddington take a longitudinal perspective on the history of football crowd surveys and attempt to draw some conclusions about discernible patterns of change. In particular they challenge claims that increasing numbers of women are now watching live football and question the notion that football is increasingly becoming a middle-class spectator sport. The authors argue that the nature of fandom, its unquestioning loyalty and its centrality to an individual's identity mean that football spectators do not easily or unproblematically change their behaviour. Consequently crowd composition may not change quite so rapidly as many have recently assumed.

Jon Garland and Michael Rowe critically assess another area often associated with football that is widely held to have been diminished in recent years: crowd violence. The experience of hooliganism, stadium disaster and the provision of substantial funds to redevelop grounds has meant that British football has been the focus for a wide range of initiatives designed to improve public order and safety. Although the private sector has been involved in the game for many years, the debate surrounding its role in society more generally has largely been absent. Furthermore, many technological innovations which might be of wider societal application were first introduced in football grounds. Garland and Rowe explore these developments and consider whether they have been as successful in tackling problems such as hooliganism and racism as those involved in the game have claimed.

The following study provides an interesting critique of the strategies introduced to improve the policing of the game in recent years. Carlton Brick argues that, even within the context of dramatic changes that have characterized football during the last ten years, the transformation in the image of the fan has been one of the most significant. Society has become increasingly football-friendly and politicians are keen to present themselves as fans and as a 'friend of the fan'. The central paradox which Brick considers is that while football-related violence has decreased dramatically and the fan is now centred 'positively' in cultural and political discourse, the behaviour of those who follow football has never been under so much scrutiny and regulation as it is today. In the new millennium we are likely to see an increase in the control of fan behaviour through the exercise of moral condemnation rather than through an extension of 'the long arm of the law', Brick argues. A culture of regulation that does not require the formal demands of legislation and legal norms, the contemporary excursus of 'moral condemnation' is as authoritarian and as intrusive as that which preceded it.

The fifth and final section focuses directly on the business of the game itself, analysing as it does various issues relating to playing and refereeing the game. Part Five begins by exploring the rarefied world of élite professional footballers. Joe Maguire and Bob Pearton examine the composition of the 32 national teams which participated in the France 1998 World Cup tournament and highlight the distinct pattern of élite player career development. These patterns, Maguire and Pearton argue, are related to the power and control which European soccer enjoys relative to other global soccer regions. They adopt a multi-causal approach which stresses that while economic processes strongly influence the movement pattern of players this alone provides only a necessary, not a sufficient, explanation. An economic analysis must be combined with an understanding of the historical, social, cultural and political processes which structure the movement of élite players. This study is compared and contrasted with other work conducted on élite labour migration both within soccer and in other sports and should be seen as a contribution to the wider study of global sport.

The following essay provides a distinctive personal insight into what has come to be a major issue of concern within the British game in recent years: racism in football. While others have written on trends and developments of the problem and have considered the effect of initiatives designed to counter the problem, relatively little has been written directly on the experience of racism in the game. Richie Moran reflects on his career as a professional footballer, a career largely curtailed by the racism he faced. Moran charts the forms of racism he experienced, including verbal and physical abuse, and the prejudice and discrimination he encountered. These personal experiences are discussed within the context of the development of recent anti-racist initiatives within the game, and it is argued that, despite some successes, there is still a long way to go in the quest to rid football of racist attitudes.

In bringing the collection to a conclusion, Sharon Colwell reflects on the status and position of the most consistently controversial figure in the sport: the referee. Colwell considers the debate surrounding the changing role of referees in football with specific reference to the complex relationship between the 'letter of the law' and the 'spirit of the law'. The implications of technological innovations such as goal-line cameras and the use of video replays of critical incidents are discussed in relation to the contemporary pressures on players, managers and referees. Colwell argues that even though such developments might seem to offer a 'quick fix', the inherent nature of the referee's role is such that controversy is unlikely to be wholly eliminated.

This collection in large part stems from a conference organized by the editors under the heading 'Football 2000: Challenges for the New Millennium'. The editors owe a great debt to all of those who spoke, helped to organize and participated in the proceedings. Special acknowledgement must be given to all of the contributors, most of whom stuck to deadlines and word-limits, even when the editors had given only the flimsiest guidance in either respect. The experience of working with and discussing these essays has proved to the editors that the original remit of the conference, as reflected in the over-arching title of the proceedings, was too ambitious, and our sights have necessarily been lowered. At the beginning of the twenty-first century, though, it does seem opportune to consider the state of the game, in all of its complexity. There are no easily identifiable themes that emerge from this book, which touches on matters ranging from the movement of global capital to the lack of movement caused by traffic congestion around football grounds. The richness and diversity of the experiences reflected by the contributions gathered together here perhaps represent the strength of the game and one reason why it will endure. If, by any slight chance, this volume came to be interred in a time capsule and discovered a thousand years from now, it would be fascinating to know what delegates to Football 3000 would make of it!

JON GARLAND
DOMINIC MALCOLM
MICHAEL ROWE

Leicester, January 2000

PART 1
Football Economics and Law

1

The Peculiar Economics of English Professional Football

CHRIS GRATTON

The literature on the economics of professional team sports has grown rapidly since articles first started to appear in the 1950s. Most of the literature has been generated in North America and deals mainly with issues of restriction of competition in the product and labour markets that characterize American football, basketball, ice-hockey and baseball. Much of the analysis developed in North America has also been applied to UK professional team sports, in particular to football and cricket.

The economics of professional team sports has become particularly relevant over the last decade because of the changes that have taken place in both UK and European professional team sports: the setting up of the Premier League in English professional football in 1992; the move to Super League in rugby league in 1996; the professionalization of rugby union in 1996; and the restructuring of the European Champions' League in football in 1999. The strength of this trend is such that it is likely to continue to be a defining feature of sport in general, and football in particular, in the twenty-first century.

This essay will focus particularly on English professional football. Firstly, however, it will analyse the 'peculiar' economics of professional team sports[1] as developed in North America leading to a definition of 'the American model' of a professional sports league. Secondly, it will discuss the extent to which English football reflects this American model. Finally, it will examine the hypothesis put forward by T. Hoehn and S. Szymanski that the present structure of English professional football is unsustainable and that the natural equilibrium for the English and other European countries' league systems would be the formation of an American-style European Superleague.[2]

COMPETITIVE BALANCE

One of the key features that makes the economics of professional team sports 'peculiar' is that demand for the product (i.e. the game) is positively related to the uncertainty of outcome. As M. El-Hodiri and J. Quirk state: 'As the probability of either team winning approaches one, gate receipts fall substantially, consequently, every team has an economic motive for not becoming too superior

11

in playing talent compared to other teams in the league.'[3] Economists have highlighted this as the crucial feature of the professional team sport industry that distinguishes it from all other industries. The conventional textbook firm in economic theory has an interest in increasing its market power and ultimately it maximizes its own interest (and profit) when it achieves maximum market power as a monopolist. In professional team sports once a team becomes a monopolist, revenue would disappear altogether; output would be zero since it would be impossible to stage a match.

One major function of the league is to ensure that no team achieves too much market power, or excessive dominance. The league therefore aims to restrict competition. This explains why price competition between clubs is effectively prevented. Other non-competitive characteristics of professional team sports' leagues include labour market restrictions giving clubs property rights in players and the pooling of revenues so that poorer clubs are cross-subsidized by the richer ones. As R. Noll points out, in American team sports, 'Nearly every phase of a team or league is influenced by practices and rules that limit economic competition within the industry. In most cases government has either sanctioned or failed to attack effectively these anti-competitive practices.'[4]

Despite almost universal acceptance by economists writing in this area that uncertainty of outcome and competitive balance are the key to demand analysis in professional team sports, J. Cairns *et al.* point out the lack of conclusive empirical evidence in support of this contention:

> it is unfortunate that not only has empirical testing of the key relationship between demand and uncertainty of outcome been limited, but also that the discussion of this central concept has been unmethodical, if not confused. Inadequate attention has been paid to determining the appropriate empirical specifications of the underlying theoretical notions.[5]

They go on to point out that at least three distinct versions of the uncertainty of outcome hypothesis have appeared in the literature: uncertainty of match outcome, uncertainty of seasonal outcome, and uncertainty of outcome in the sense of the absence of long-term domination by one club. J. Quirk and R. Fort incorporate all three aspects of the uncertainty of outcome hypothesis in their measure of competitive balance in American professional sports leagues. They focus on,

> the dispersion ('spread') of W/L percentages in a league and the concentration of championships and high W/L percentages among league teams. A league in which team W/L percentages are bunched together around .500 displays more competitive balance than does a league in which team W/L percentages are widely dispersed; and the more concentrated is the winning of championships and high W/L percentage among a few teams, the less competitive balance there is in a league.[6]

The approach Quirk and Fort take is based on the work of Noll.[7] Effectively, this approach compares the actual performance of a league to the performance that would have occurred if the league had the maximum degree of competitive balance (that is, all teams had equal playing strengths). The degree of competitive balance is greater the smaller the deviation of actual league performance from that of the ideal league. They carried out this analysis for all the five major American professional team sports leagues (National Football League (NFL), National Basketball Association (NBA), National Hockey League (NHL), and the two baseball leagues, the American League (AL) and the National League (NL)) for each decade from 1901 to 1990. Quirk and Fort found that all five leagues operated with a significant degree of competitive imbalance. The NFL had the most competitive balance, and the NBA the least, but even the NFL fell a long way short of the ideal league. They concluded that,

> none of the leagues comes close to achieving the ideal of equal playing strengths. There is ample evidence of long-term competitive imbalance in each league, despite the league rules that are supposedly designed to equalise team strengths. On the other hand, with all their flaws, the leagues have not only survived but have flourished, with growth in numbers of teams, in geographic coverage, in attendance and public interest, and in profitability.[8]

One interpretation of their conclusion would be that uncertainty of outcome and maintenance of competitive balance are not as important to the success of professional team sports leagues as the previous economic literature has suggested. Another interpretation would be that the various restrictions on competition imposed by American sports leagues have achieved sufficient competitive balance to make the leagues successful. It is to this restriction that we now turn.

RESTRICTION OF COMPETITION IN PROFESSIONAL TEAM SPORTS

Although uncertainty of outcome may be a major determinant of attendances at a whole league over a season, each individual club is mainly concerned about its own home gates. One determinant of this is the size of the local market, in terms of population. Furthermore, the number of clubs competing in the local catchment area will influence the size of each club's attendances. However, a major determinant of any one club's demand will be playing success. In general, other things being equal, the more successful the club, the higher the attendance. This is an obvious conflict with the uncertainty of outcome hypothesis discussed above. Whereas each club can maximize its attendances by maximizing its number of wins, the league as a whole may suffer by a reduced uncertainty of outcome. This conflict is a major feature of the supply-side of professional team sports.

Sloane stresses the need for the league to operate strong anti-competitive controls so that the league is not dominated by one or a few teams:

> The more the uncertainty of the results of the games, the higher the public demand for the sport. The more equal the quality of competing teams, the more the uncertainty of the result. Uncertainty of result is threatened by the tendency of wealthy clubs to enjoy a virtuous circle of playing success and rising revenue, and others to be caught in a vicious circle of relative poverty and playing failure. To diminish this possibility sports league organisations claim justification for operating as cartels, redistributing revenue among member clubs, restricting price competition between them, and limiting their property rights in players.[9]

There are several such restrictions in force in American professional team sports. Leagues operate revenue sharing arrangements where television and some sponsorship revenues are negotiated centrally by the league and revenues shared equally between clubs. The draft system operates so that the weakest teams from the previous season get first choice of the college players coming through to the professional league for the new season. Salary caps prevent the richest and most successful clubs bidding up players' wages to attract them.

Yet perhaps one of the most controversial restrictions is the reserve clause that restricts players' bargaining rights in the labour market by keeping the player tied to the club that holds his registration. In Britain, an equivalent scheme, the retain and transfer scheme, operated in British professional football up until 1978. Owners of clubs in North America have consistently argued that the reserve clause was essential for maintaining competitive balance. However, it has increasingly caused disputes between clubs and players and was abolished in 1976 in baseball and basketball. In their historical analysis Quirk and Fort analysed the level of competitive balance in both these sports pre-1976 and post-1976. They concluded that,

> the argument of owners that the reserve-option clause is needed for competitive balance is offered no support at all by microeconomic theory ... (rather) there will be the same degree of competitive balance in a league with a reserve-option clause and unrestricted sale of players as there would be in a league with a free competitive labour market ... there are no indications that introducing competitive labour markets into baseball and basketball has had any measurable impact on competitive balance in those leagues.[10]

Despite this conclusion, it is generally accepted that the role of the league is to operate as a cartel to restrict open competition between clubs in both the product and labour markets so that no one club becomes too dominant.[11] The cartel model as a representation of the sports league is based on the assumption of profit maximization of both the club and the league. In order for the league to secure profit maximization for the group of clubs that form the league, it is necessary for the league to impose restrictions on the profit maximization of individual clubs.

The role of the league in managing the collective interests of all clubs is in direct conflict with the individual profit maximization interests of the most successful clubs which, without restrictions, would be more profitable. The league has the objective of ensuring uncertainty of outcome and competitive balance but each individual club has the objective of maximizing sporting success and the consequent economic benefits of television, sponsorship and gate money revenue. This conflict of interest between the objectives of the cartel and those of individual members of it is the classic scenario of the economics of cartels. Normally, the cartel's role is not only to impose product and labour market restrictions on members, but also to restrict output in order to keep the price high. In American team sports, in the NFL for instance, this restriction of output is exhibited by no team playing more than one game a week, the length of the season being restricted to one-third of the year, and the number of teams being strictly limited (currently to 30).

BROADCASTING DEMAND

Traditionally clubs in professional team sports have earned income primarily from sales of tickets to games. Hence the theory, put forward earlier, that to maximize profits and revenue (paying spectators, for example), the league must maintain uncertainty of outcome and competitive balance. However, in recent years other sources of revenue and profit have become much more important (although revenue from sales of tickets to games still remains the single most important element of total revenue). Whilst sponsorship has become an increasingly important source of income in professional team sports, the most important factor in recent years has been the sharp rise in the economic value of broadcasting rights to professional team sports. In early 1998 American broadcasters agreed to pay $18 billion for the rights for the National Football League for eight years. The previous deal, for 1995–98, was for $1.58 billion and was with Fox, owned by Rupert Murdoch's News Corporation, also owners of BSkyB. This deal projected Fox to be one of the big four broadcasters in the United States together with NBC, CBC and ABC.

The economic value of sport is based on its popularity. The top eight television programmes in the United States are sports events. Around 130 million watch the Super Bowl on television. The result is that advertising rates are at a premium during the televising of such events. Thirty seconds of advertising during the Super Bowl costs over $1 million, and it is the large sports companies such as Nike, Adidas and Reebok who want to attach their advertising slots to this and other major televised sports competitions.

One reason for these revenues is that in America these games are broadcast on free-to-air channels and attract massive audiences; half the American population in the case of the Super Bowl. Moreover, because games typically last two or three times longer than their European equivalents, and are broken more frequently by commercial breaks, television companies can accrue particularly large advertising revenues.

The relationship works both ways, as was illustrated in an article in *The Financial Times* (17 January 1998). Discussing the sale of NFL broadcasting rights, the article indicates how no major network television station can afford to be without football:

> CBS learnt that lesson in 1993 when it allowed Fox ... to outbid it in the previous auction of broadcast rights for football. With the loss of the sport, the network plunged from first to third in the rankings, where it languishes. The fledgling Fox was promoted overnight, and the Big Three which had hitherto dominated viewing became the Big Four.

> CBS ... attempted to restore its fortunes by paying $4 billion (twice the old price) to show some American football games. Fox stumped up $4.4 billion for another package of games, and Walt Disney, which owns ABC and the ESPN cable sports channel, followed with a $9.2 billion deal, a grand total of almost $18 billion. That left NBC, the top-rated network, with no football on its schedule for the first time in decades. Time Warner's TNT, the most popular cable channel in the US was also pushed out of the game.

> The NFL, which started the decade earning $500 million a year from TV rights and last year collected just over $1 billion, will enter the next century with annual small-screen revenues of $2.2 billion.

This escalation in the sale of broadcasting rights to the games of major professional team sports is a phenomenon that started in the United States but, as we will see, was quickly imported into Britain.

THE AMERICAN PROFESSIONAL TEAM SPORTS MODEL

We can identify, therefore, certain characteristics of the American professional team sports model:

- both clubs and leagues clearly have profit maximization as the priority;

- the conflict between the behaviour required to ensure profit maximizing behaviour by the league as a whole and maximization of profits for the most successful clubs in the league, requires that the league acts as a cartel to impose restrictions on output. In addition, the leagues have traditionally employed revenue sharing arrangements so that the economic gap between the richest and the poorest clubs is narrowed;

- these restrictions on competition in both the product and labour markets is accepted by the competition (anti-trust) regulators in the USA as necessary to maintain the competitive balance (or uncertainly of outcome) that is a necessary condition for the successful operation of professional team sports leagues;

– the sale of broadcasting rights has become an increasingly important source of revenue to professional team sports leagues and clubs.

These are the critical aspects of the economics of professional team sports in the USA that we need to bear in mind when we analyse the situation in Britain and the rest of Europe, both now and in the future.

Before leaving the North American scene, however, one other issue needs to be noted. It is the issue raised by Crompton:

> Cities do not use public money to build skyscrapers and then hand them over gratis to IBM or telecom, even though such businesses are likely to have positive economic impact on a community. However, in the US they do use public money to build stadia for professional football and baseball teams, and arenas for professional hockey and basketball teams, and then give them to the millionaire owners of those teams. This largesse is particularly remarkable given the conditions of financial crises and infrastructure deterioration that prevail in major cities ...

> In 1997 there were 113 major league professional franchises in the four sports listed above. Between 1989 and 1997, 31 of them had a new stadium or arena built; and in 1997, an additional 39 teams were actively seeking new facilities, finalising a deal to build one, or waiting to move into one. All of these were built with public money or leased to the owners for either no rental fee or nominal sums which do not approach the amount needed to cover the debt charges involved.[12]

The rationale for local governments providing these massive subsidies to profit maximizing sports businesses is that it is argued that local businesses will benefit from the spending of spectators attracted to the games that take place in these stadiums and arenas. For the moment, it is sufficient simply to note that it is a rather unusual situation for a profit maximizing business to receive such a huge subsidy from local government. Another significant effect of this phenomenon of cities willing to build new stadiums and arenas for American professional sports teams is that these teams move around from city to city, dependent on which city gives the best offer in terms of facilities. As we shall see, this is a major difference from the situation for European football.

THE ECONOMICS OF ENGLISH PROFESSIONAL FOOTBALL

Up until the late 1980s there seemed little relationship between the American professional team sports model described above and the way the major professional team sport in England – football – operated. One major area of difference was in the objectives of clubs. In North America, profit maximization is the clearly established objective. A similar statement would not be true for British football, or other British professional team sports, prior to the 1990s. Sloane regarded utility maximization as the objective of most clubs.[13] He suggested that supporters and directors were willing to outlay money without regard to pecuniary rewards, playing success being the ultimate objective of the clubs. His theory was that clubs strove to maximize utility, subject to financial viability or a maximum security constraint. Cairns, however, argued that 'it is not clear that we are capable in principle of empirically distinguishing utility and profit maximizing behaviour', and therefore differences in objectives would not necessarily result in differences in behaviour.[14]

Whatever the objective of the clubs, the reality was that neither the profit maximizing nor the utility maximizing objective was achieved by the majority of clubs prior to the 1990s. Figure 1.1 shows the long decline in attendances from the peak of 41.3 million in the 1948/49 season. Except for a brief revival following England's World Cup success in 1966, attendances fell steadily from then until reaching their lowest point at just over 16 million in the 1985/86 season. May 1985 proved to be a particularly low point for English professional football. In that month 55 people were killed in the Bradford fire disaster, and a 15-year-old boy died during rioting by Leeds United and Birmingham City supporters. On 30 May 1985, 38 Juventus supporters died at the European Cup Final against Liverpool in the Heysel stadium, Brussels. The result was the banning of all English clubs from European competitions.

Whilst many questioned whether English football would survive,[15] 1985 proved to be the end of English football's long decline. Since then attendances have risen consistently as have revenues to the major clubs (see Figure 1.2). It is not that easy to explain why the long decline changed around in this way in the mid-1980s, particularly since before the 1980s had finished, the Hillsborough disaster (in 1989) seemed to sink another nail into the coffin of English professional football.

However, it is easier to explain why the economics of English professional football more generally became much healthier in the 1990s. Several factors contributed to this. Firstly as a direct result of the Hillsborough disaster, the Taylor Report recommended that all the football grounds in the top league become all-seater stadiums by the start of the 1994/95 season.[16] This resulted in the highest level of new investment in British football grounds in the twentieth century taking place in the first four years of the 1990s. Secondly, the top 22 clubs in the country broke away from the Football League and formed the FA Carling Premier League which began life on 15 August 1992. Thirdly, a few clubs floated on the Stock Market and became publicly quoted companies with a clear responsibility to shareholders to operate on normal commercial grounds (i.e.

FIGURE 1.1

LEAGUE ATTENDANCES 1947–1985

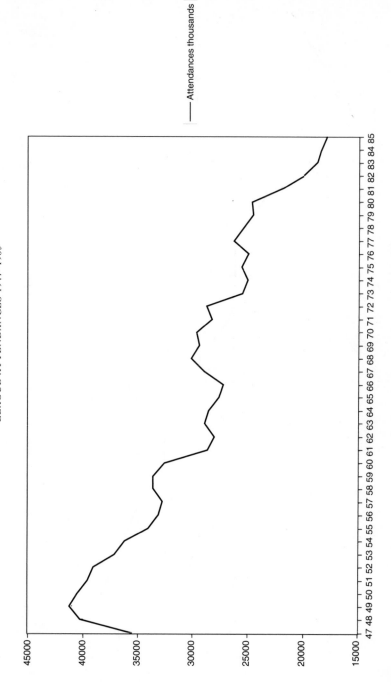

Sources: Rothmans Football Yearbook.

FIGURE 1.2

LEAGUE ATTENDANCES 1986–1998

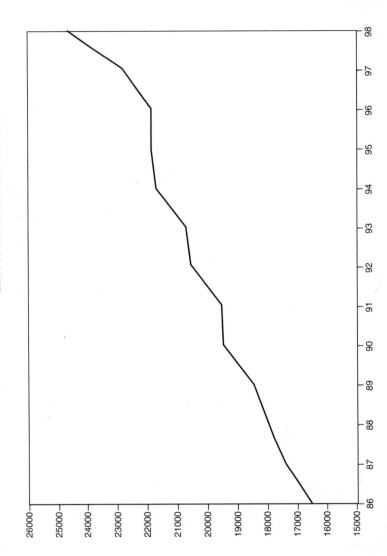

—— Attendances thousands

Sources: Rothmans Football Yearbook.

profit maximization). Prior to 1995 only four clubs, Millwall, Preston, Tottenham Hotspur and Manchester United had taken this route and only the latter could claim it to be a successful move. However in 1995 and 1996 many more clubs followed and certainly in 1996 football club shares were very popular in the City. However, the single largest change to English professional football was the increasing importance of revenue from broadcasting rights.

THE ESCALATING REVENUE FROM THE SALE OF BROADCASTING RIGHTS FOR FOOTBALL

TABLE 1.1

THE COST OF THE RIGHTS TO LIVE LEAGUE MATCHES FROM THE TOP DIVISION IN ENGLAND, 1983–97

Start date of the contract	1983	1985	1986	1988	1992	1997
Length of contract (years)	2	0.5	2	4	5	4
Broadcaster	BBC/ITV	BBC	BBC/ITV	ITV	BSkyB	BSkyB
Rights fee (£m)	5.2	1.3	6.2	44	191.5	670
Annual rights fee (£m)*	2.6	2.6	3.1	11	38.3	167.5
Number of live matches per season	10	6	14	18	60	60
Fees per live match (£m)	0.26	0.43	0.22	0.61	0.64	2.79

* Based on the rights fee divided by the number of years in the contract. There have been variations in annual rights fees. For example, the annual rights fees for the 1992 Premier League contract were £35.5 million in 1992/93, £37.5 million in 1993/94 and £39.5 million in each of the last three years of the contract. The payments in the current four-year contract for rights to the Premier League are £50 million paid when the offer was accepted, £135 million in 1997/98, £145 million in 1998/99, £160 million in 1999/2000 and £180 million in 2000/01.

Source: Monopolies and Mergers Commission (MMC) (1999).

Table 1.1 shows the history of the contracts for televised football from 1983, when the first televised live Football League matches were shown, until 1997 when BSkyB signed a four-year deal for £670 million for the broadcasting of Premier League matches. Deals for 1983/85 and 1986/88 were joint deals with both the BBC and ITV with the annual rights fee rising slightly from £2.6 million in the 1983–85 period to £3.1 million in the 1986–88 period. The major escalation came when ITV pushed up the annual fee to £11 million in 1988–92 for its exclusive coverage with a large increase in the number of live televised matches to 18 per year. This 250 per cent increase over the previous level of fees for televised football was matched again in 1992 when BSkyB, now negotiating with the Premier League, won the rights for 60 live matches at a cost of £38 million per year. When the deal was negotiated in 1997 there was a further 337 per cent rise in the annual rights.[17]

Table 1.2 shows the distribution of television revenues over the Premier League clubs from 1992 to 1998. It shows how the leading five clubs, Manchester

TABLE 1.2

THE PROPORTION OF TOTAL TV PAYMENTS, 1992/93 TO 1997/98

Club	1992/93	1993/94	1994/95	1995/96	1996/97	1997/98	Average for 1992/93 to 1997/98
Arsenal	4.83	5.30	4.19	5.54	6.85	7.52	6.31
Manchester United	6.85	7.24	7.42	7.81	7.58	7.38	7.41
Liverpool	5.66	5.30	5.71	6.49	6.95	6.79	6.42
Chelsea	4.68	3.75	4.31	4.53	5.59	6.45	5.37
Leeds United	4.17	5.83	5.08	4.47	4.71	5.82	5.18
Blackburn Rovers	5.78	6.82	6.86	5.25	4.44	5.61	5.58
Aston Villa	6.44	4.81	3.78	5.81	5.49	5.20	5.26
West Ham United	—	4.06	4.39	5.18	4.52	5.01	4.26
Derby County	—	—	—	—	4.38	4.95	2.78
Newcastle United	—	5.82	5.29	8.11	6.76	4.73	5.26
Coventry City	3.84	4.42	4.11	3.87	3.71	4.66	4.19
Leicester City	—	—	3.24	—	4.73	4.61	3.0
Tottenham Hotspur	4.84	4.56	4.95	5.68	5.24	4.52	4.89
Southampton	3.55	3.34	4.35	3.74	3.85	4.38	4.00
Everton	4.08	3.63	3.87	5.54	4.21	4.25	4.25
Wimbledon	3.96	4.82	4.24	3.84	5.31	4.00	4.39
Bolton Wanderers	—	—	—	3.09	—	3.82	1.69
Sheffield Wednesday	4.53	4.89	4.43	3.94	4.99	3.61	4.27
Crystal Palace	3.32	—	3.34	—	—	3.37	1.89
Barnsley	—	—	—	—	—	3.30	1.18
Others	33.48	25.40	20.42	17.11	10.70	0.00	12.31
Total TV payments (£m)	35.25	36.05	39.59	38.27	83.04	129.11	361.32

Source: MMC (1999).

United, Arsenal, Liverpool, Chelsea and Leeds accounted on average for over 30 per cent of total television payments over this period. This can be contrasted with the revenue-sharing arrangements that are seen in American team sports.

It is also notable that most of the revenue from the sale of broadcasting rights is distributed back to the Premier League clubs as shown in Table 1.2. In 1998/99 less than 14 per cent of this television revenue went to other football-related bodies, mainly the Football League, the Professional Footballers' Association and the Football Trust. In 1998–99 various youth development schemes received a total of £200,000 and the English Schools FA received £25,000 out of total television revenue to the Premier League of £168 million.[18]

The importance of television revenues to individual Premier League clubs can be seen from Table 1.3 which shows that although Manchester United received the largest television payment in 1996/97, it accounted for a smaller percentage of the overall turnover of Manchester United than any other Premier League club. The reason for this is shown in Table 1.4 which indicates the considerable variation in the level of turnover between Premier League clubs. Manchester United had the highest turnover in 1996/97 at £88 million, but this was over

TABLE 1.3

THE PROPORTION OF REVENUE ACCOUNTED FOR BY BSKYB'S COVERAGE OF
THE PREMIER LEAGUE, 1996/97

Club	%	Club	%
Wimbledon	42.3	Aston Villa	20.6
Southampton	34.6	Chelsea	19.6
Derby County	34.0	Notts Forest	19.3
Sheffield Wednesday	28.9	Everton	18.5
Blackburn Rovers	25.8	Leeds United	17.9
Coventry City	25.1	Tottenham Hotspur	15.6
West Ham United	24.6	Liverpool	14.7
Leicester City	22.7	Middlesbrough	13.8
Sunderland	22.3	Newcastle United	13.6
Arsenal	20.9	Manchester United	7.2

Total (£m) 83.0

Source: MMC calculations based on data in the *Deloitte & Touche Annual Review of Football Finance*, August 1998.

TABLE 1.4

REVENUE EXCLUDING TRANSFER FEES IN 1996/97 AND 1992/93

	1992/93 revenue (£m)	1992/93 Growth in revenue (%)	1996/97 revenue (£m)	1996/97 Growth in revenue %	Total Increase %
Manchester United	25,177	13.6	87,939	19.0	249.3
Newcastle United	8,743	4.7	41,134	8.9	370.5
Liverpool	17,496	9.4	39,153	8.4	123.8
Tottenham Hotspur	16,594	9.0	27,874	6.0	68.0
Arsenal	15,342	8.3	27,158	5.9	77.0
Chelsea	7,891	4.3	23,729	5.1	200.1
Middlesbrough	3,968	2.1	22,502	4.9	467.1
Aston Villa	10,175	5.5	22,079	4.8	117.0
Leeds United	13,324	7.2	21,785	4.7	63.5
Everton	7,994	4.3	18,882	4.1	136.2
Leicester City	4,775	2.6	17,320	3.7	262.7
West Ham United	6,571	3.5	15,256	3.3	132.2
Notts Forest	7,651	4.1	14,435	3.1	88.7
Sheffield Wednesday	12,806	6.9	14,335	3.1	11.9
Blackburn Rovers	6,305	3.4	14,302	3.1	126.8
Sunderland	3,806	2.1	13,415	2.9	252.5
Coventry City	4,592	2.5	12,265	2.6	167.1
Derby County	4,183	2.3	10,738	2.3	156.7
Wimbledon	3,556	1.9	10,410	2.2	192.7
Southampton	4,307	2.3	9,238	2.0	114.5
Total	185,256	100.00	463,949	100.00	150.4

Source: MMC calculations based on data in the *Deloitte & Touche Annual Review of Football Finance*, August 1988.

twice that of the next club Newcastle United, at £41 million. The lowest turnover for 1996/97 was Southampton at £9.2 million with Wimbledon the second lowest. However, Wimbledon tops Table 1.3 with 42 per cent of its turnover coming from television revenues and Southampton are second at 35 per cent. Manchester United, on the other hand, are bottom of Table 1.3 with only 7 per cent of its total turnover coming from television revenue because it had the highest gate receipt revenue (£30 million) of any club, although this accounted for only 34 per cent of total revenue in 1996/97. Sponsorship and advertising accounted for a further 13 per cent, conferences and catering 6 per cent, and 'merchandising and other' a massive 33 per cent, almost equal to gate receipts.

This considerable increase in revenue from the sale of broadcasting rights to the Premiership has been the single largest factor affecting the economic fortunes of Premiership clubs. However, little of this money trickles down to those clubs in the Football League, many of which had not seen a change in economic fortunes from the 1980s, even though BSkyB currently has a five-year contract to show Football League games for a total fee of £125 million. The escalation in the fees for broadcasting rights for Premiership football has only served to widen the gap between the richest and poorest clubs. Whereas each Premier League club receives around £8 million a season from television revenue, each First Division club receives around £0.5 million.

THE AMERICAN MODEL AND ENGLISH PROFESSIONAL FOOTBALL

The development of the Premier League in British football in the 1990s, together with the floatation of clubs on the Stock Market, and greatly increased revenues from sports sponsorship, merchandising and the sale of broadcasting rights has led some commentators to argue that this commercialization of British football is an indication that the American model has been adopted in British professional team sports.

There are certainly greater similarities with the American model now than was the case in the 1980s. As already noted, one of the major discussions in the literature in the 1970s and 1980s was the differences in clubs' objectives in American and British (and European) professional team sports (namely profit maximization as opposed to utility maximization). This has effectively changed for many Premier League, and some Football League, clubs by the flotation of the clubs on either the London Stock Exchange or the Alternative Investment Market (AIM). In the 1998/99 season eight Premier League clubs (Aston Villa, Burnden Leisure (Bolton), Leeds Sporting (Leeds United), Leicester City, Manchester United, Newcastle United, Southampton Leisure and Tottenham Hotspur) were quoted on the London Stock Exchange and a further two (Charlton Athletic and Chelsea Village) were quoted on AIM. A further four clubs from other divisions (Heart of Midlothian, Millwall, Sheffield United and Sunderland) were quoted on the London Stock Exchange and six (Birmingham

City, Celtic, Loftus Road QPR/Wasps, Nottingham Forest, Preston North End, West Bromwich Albion) were quoted on AIM. Of these 20 quoted clubs only Manchester United (1991), Millwall (1989), and Tottenham Hotspur (1983) were quoted prior to 1985.[19] Thus, this is a new development in the financing of British (in particular, Premier League) clubs that puts increasing emphasis on stronger commercial management. Flotation automatically involves greater emphasis on profits in the objectives of clubs, and results show that profits of some clubs have improved tremendously in the 1990s.

A quote from the Deloitte and Touche analysis of financial results for 1996/97 indicates both the increased profitability of (mainly) Premier League clubs but also the growing gap between the Premier League and the Football League:

> Turnover grew significantly for the Premier League (34 per cent), Division One (26 per cent), and Division Two (32 per cent), although turnover fell 1 per cent in Division Three. The Premier league now accounts for 68.7 per cent of football revenues ... The top five finishers in the Premier League (Manchester United, Newcastle United, Arsenal, Liverpool, and Aston Villa) had a combined turnover greater than that of all the 72 Football League clubs.[20]

The Deloitte and Touche report goes on to indicate that the aggregate profits of all clubs in the Premier League in 1996/97 increased to £86 million from £52 million in 1995/96. On the other hand, aggregating profit and loss for all clubs in each of the Football League divisions yields a net loss for each division.

This evidence suggests that the Premier League has, at least in some ways, started to exhibit the characteristics of the American professional team sports leagues with increasing revenues from sponsorship, merchandising, and the sale of broadcasting rights. However, one crucial difference between the American model and British professional football is the lack of restriction of output in terms of the number of clubs and number of games. The NFL in the USA has 30 clubs for a population of 260 million. England and Wales have 92 Premier and Football League clubs with a further 40 clubs in Scotland for a total population of 56 million. Whereas clubs in American professional sports leagues play once a week for three months of the year, clubs in British football begin in August and finish in May. Also, international competition, at either club or country level, for most of America's professional team sports is not an important factor. The World and European Championships in football, however, mean that every two years international football goes on into July and, in the intervening years, qualifiers for these tournaments are played in June. Within these long seasons, clubs will often play twice a week. The reorganization of the European Champions' League in 1999 continues the trend of increasing the number of games for Europe's élite players.

Another characteristic not evident in English football has been the movement of franchises from one city to another, often on the basis of incentives such as a new stadium provided out of taxpayers' money, that has been so common in

North America. There is a stronger history of community attachment to clubs in Britain that makes it much more difficult for clubs to move cities.

There are two other major differences, however, between what has happened in British football and the American professional team sports model. Firstly, neither the Premier League nor the Football League has imposed the restrictions on competition (for example, revenue sharing, a draft system, salary caps) regarded as essential in the American model to generate uncertainty of outcome and competitive balance. In the NFL, 90 per cent of revenues are shared and gate receipts are split 60:40 in favour of the home team. In the Premier League and the Football League, the home team takes all the gate receipts. This favours the bigger clubs with larger capacity grounds and good support. Even in the Premier League, commentators have suggested that there are two or three different leagues operating within one league since only a small number of richer clubs stand any realistic chance of winning the Championship or the major cup competitions, another group battle for mid-table positions, and a third group struggle to stay in the Premier League at all with a sub-group of them yo-yoing up and down between the First Division and the Premier League.[21] This lack of attention by the league to its role in maintaining competitive balance is a major difference between Britain and America in its major professional team sports. The success of the Green Bay Packers, a small city team, in recent years is evidence that measures to ensure competitive balance can allow smaller clubs to achieve success. Green Bay's success would be the equivalent in Britain of, say, Port Vale winning the Premier League title or the FA Cup; hardly imaginable in the current economic climate of British professional football.

The second major difference between Britain and America in the economics of professional team sports, however, has not been well recognized. Britain has followed America in the escalation in the fees for broadcasting rights for the major professional team sports. There is a clear difference, however, between the motives of the American broadcasters competing for the rights to the NFL and the motives of BSkyB for acquiring the rights to Premiership football. American broadcasters bid up the rights to the NFL because of its importance in winning them market share, and also because of the ability to increase advertising revenues during football games. BSkyB bids for Premiership rights to increase revenue from subscriptions to its pay-per-view channels.

Whereas in the American scenario there is correspondence between the objectives of clubs, broadcasters, the league, advertisers and major sponsors (since they all get maximum exposure to the country's largest television audiences), in the British case there is conflict between the objectives of the broadcaster (maximum subscriptions) and those of the league, clubs, advertisers and major sponsors (maximum exposure). To some extent, this conflict is reduced in British football by the coverage provided by the BBC's *Match of the Day* highlights programmes and by ITV's the European Champions' League coverage; matches which achieved the highest television audiences of any sports programmes in the

1998/99 season. Whereas audiences for BSkyB's live Premiership matches vary between 1 and 2 million with the odd key match getting slightly more than 2 million, *Match of the Day* viewing figures average around 6 million but often exceed 10 million. ITV's live coverage of Manchester United versus Bayern Munich in the European Champions' League Final in May 1999 attracted an audience of 15.6 million in Britain (with a peak of 18.8 million).

THE AMERICANIZATION OF EUROPEAN FOOTBALL?

The lack of competitive balance in the English Premier League (and most other domestic European leagues) combined with the lack of introduction of restriction of competition, revenue sharing, and salary caps, has led at least one group of commentators to argue that only a European Superleague provides the potential for a true American sports league model in European football:

> Moving from the current European system to a more American structure should be beneficial to clubs. The big clubs will be able to focus on the competition that generates the greatest proportion of their income. Smaller clubs in the top domestic league would lose by no longer competing against Superleague teams that may bring with them large groups of supporters, but this loss is likely to be offset by the improvements in competitive balance in the domestic competition.[22]

However, there seems to be a basic flaw in this argument. The argument for an American-style sports league rests crucially on economic returns to clubs and leagues being dependent on the maintenance of competitive balance, the argument with which this essay began. However, Quirk and Fort showed that all American sports leagues throughout this century had operated with a considerable degree of competitive imbalance and yet had still managed to flourish with a growth in the number of teams, in geographic coverage, in attendance and public interest, and in profitability.[23] The same is true of English professional football in the 1990s; since the formation of the Premier League competitive balance has certainly deteriorated. Hoehn and Szymanski's argument is based on an assumption which is simply not supported by the facts. Manchester United's success in the Champions League in 1999 was not accompanied by any reduction in interest in either the Premier League or the FA Cup, rather exactly the opposite. Current evidence from English football lends no weight to the argument that the future Americanization of European football leagues would increase the economic returns to clubs and leagues.

CONCLUSIONS

Economists studying American professional sport pointed out over 30 years ago the 'peculiar' nature of the economics of team sports and the need for leagues to control competition in order to maintain competitive balance or uncertainty of outcome. Research by economists since then has notably failed to establish any strong evidence in favour of this proposition. Although it is possible to identify an American model of a professional sports league, it remains the case that English football is still a long way from such a model. The economics of English professional football has proved to be even more 'peculiar' than that of American sports leagues. Despite other worries and reservations concerning the state of English football as we enter the next century, economically football is experiencing its strongest period for a generation and there is no reason to suggest that a future move to the American model would be economically beneficial.

NOTES

1. W. Neale, 'The Peculiar Economics of Professional Sports', *Quarterly Journal of Economics*, 78 (1964), 1–14.
2. T. Hoehn and S. Szymanski, 'The Americanisation of European Football', *Economic Policy*, 28 (1999), 205–40.
3. M. El-Hodiri and J. Quirk 'An Economic Model of a Professional Sports League', *Journal of Political Economy*, 79 (1971), 1302–19.
4. R.G. Noll (ed.), *Government and the Sports Business* (Washington DC: Brookings Institution, 1974).
5. J. Cairns, N. Jennett and P.J. Sloane, 'The Economics of Professional Team Sports: A Survey of Theory and Evidence', *Journal of Economic Studies*, 13 (1986), 1–80.
6. J. Quirk and R.D. Fort, *Pay Dirt: The Business of Professional Team Sports* (Princeton, NJ: Princeton University Press, 1992).
7. R. Noll, *Professional Basketball* (Stanford University Studies in Industrial Economics, Paper No 144, 1988).
8. J. Quirk and R.D. Fort, *Pay Dirt*.
9. P.J. Sloane, *Sport in the Market* (London, Institute of Economic Affairs, 1980).
10. J. Quirk and R.D. Fort, *Pay Dirt*.
11. J. Cairns, N. Jennett and P.J. Sloane, 'The Economics'.
12. J. Crompton, 'Ethical challenges and misapplications of economic impact studies undertaken by and for professional sport franchises in the USA', Paper given to Sport in the City, Sheffield Hallam University, July 1998.
13. P.J. Sloane, 'The Economics of Professional Football: The Football Club as a Utility Maximiser', *Scottish Journal of Political Economy*, 18 (1971), 121–46.
14. J. Cairns, 'Economic Analysis of League Sports – A Critical Review of the Literature' (University of Aberdeen, Department of Political Economy Discussion Paper No. 83–01, Aberdeen, 1983).
15. See, for example, C. Crichter, 'Professional Football in Britain: Reading the Signs', in E. Meijer (ed.), *Everyday Life: Leisure and Culture* (Tilburg: Tilburg University Press, 1985).
16. Lord Justice Taylor (Chairman), *The Hillsborough Stadium Disaster: Final Report* (London: HMSO, 1990).
17. Monopolies and Mergers Commission, *British Sky Broadcasting plc and Manchester United PLC: A Report on the Proposed Merger* (London: The Stationery Office, 1999).
18. Ibid.
19. Deloitte & Touche, *Deloitte & Touche Annual Review of Football Finance* (Manchester: Deloitte & Touche, 1998).
20. Deloitte & Touche, *Deloitte & Touche*.
21. Deloitte & Touche, *Deloitte & Touche*.
22. T. Hoehn and S. Szymanski, *The Americanisation*.
23. J. Quirk and R.D. Fort, *Pay Dirt*.

2

'Heads above Water': Business Strategies for a New Football Economy

BARRIE PIERPOINT

Over the last five to ten years the football industry has changed beyond all recognition.[1] Indeed, to talk of football being an 'industry', or even a recognized business sector, ten years ago would have seemed slightly preposterous. With few exceptions, clubs were largely structured along amateur lines, and administered by staff who were often poorly trained, or by non-executive directors whose involvement went little further than enjoying the membership and privileges of an exclusive 'matchday club'.

There are clubs which continue to operate in this fashion, though they are becoming fewer in number. Perhaps more perplexing is that even among the top two leagues of English professional football, acceptance of business and, in particular, marketing-led practices continues to vary widely between clubs.

More rigorous sociological accounts of the sport's development can be found elsewhere,[2] but for the purposes of charting the professionalization of football clubs, the key defining events (in no particular order of relevance) can be identified as: the tragedy at Hillsborough and subsequent Taylor Report[3] into safety at sports grounds; the creation of the FA Carling Premier League in 1992 and its ability to attract national brand sponsors; British Sky Broadcasting's (BSkyB) acquisition of exclusive pay-TV rights to the FA Carling Premier League; independently organized 'fan power', including the fanzine movement and anti-racist initiatives; and substantial capital investment initiatives, including numerous stock market flotations by clubs in the Premier League and First Division of the Football League during the mid-1990s.

These developments – some of which are connected, some which are not – have led the industry to a financial situation where, according to Deloitte & Touche's 1998 review of England's top clubs, the 20 in the FA Carling Premier League posted a combined operating profit of £100.5 million for the 1997–98 season, a 17.5 per cent increase on the previous year.[4] Turnover, meanwhile, grew 23 per cent to £569m in the same period. Moreover, of the world's top 20 richest clubs ranked by turnover, five are from the English Premiership, whilst the only non-European club to make the 20 was Flamengo of Brazil.[5]

Evidently, and as a by-product of recent trends, there now exists a pronounced uneven distribution of wealth between, on the one hand, England's Premiership clubs, and, on the other, those in the lower professional football leagues. More complicated is that even within the Premier League there now exist 'leagues within a league', where clusters of clubs demonstrate very different sets of priorities and expectations. In my view, at the top of this list of 'leagues within a league' is an élite 'A List' of clubs, consisting of those competing for the League Championship and/or places in the European Champions' League. Below these clubs are the 'UEFA-Chasers': clubs who are consistent Premiership members and whose aim is to qualify for European competition through a top-six finish, whilst rarely challenging the élite. Below this set are the 'Survivors': a set of clubs whose season will have been deemed to have been successful providing relegation to the Nationwide League is avoided.

These three broad sets of priorities and expectations are reflected in each club's support base, annual turnover, player wage costs, operating profits and pre-tax profits. Occasionally, clubs can find themselves competing outside of their expected category, but the potential for upward mobility appears to be growing ever slimmer.

The subject of wealth distribution and its implications for the future of football is deserving of a fuller investigation.[6] However, the purpose of this essay is to explore wealth creation using the types of business strategies clubs like Leicester City have adopted, or are in the throes of generating, to maintain their competitiveness. Following an analysis of the changing demographics of football spectatorship and the role of marketing, this study will detail the key marketing initiatives that Leicester City have developed in the 1990s in response to the financial demands that affect top flight football clubs.

FOOTBALL CLUBS AND THEIR CUSTOMERS

More strongly than at any time in its past, the football industry is influenced by market forces. An increase in competition, not just between England's professional clubs but from alternative providers of leisure and entertainment products and services, has highlighted the need for football clubs to adopt more professional approaches to the way they operate in the modern business environment. Non-football leisure activities – from multiplex cinemas and themed restaurant dining to multi-purpose leisure venues – have developed rapidly in the United Kingdom over the last decade. Promoted by the previous government's *laissez-faire* attitude towards out-of-town development, these leisure facilities have an accent on customer service, quality and value for money and both reflect and have helped to change consumers' leisure patterns and their expectations.

Football clubs, whether they wish to accept this or not, operate on similar territory to these providers of new leisure activities. To varying degrees, all professional football clubs are involved in retailing through their merchandising and ticketing activities. This can range from operating a club store on-site, to the supply and distribution of an own-brand range of leisurewear and first-team strips sold through a chain of retail stores, which is Leicester City's approach.

Most clubs are also in the hospitality business to varying degrees. This can range from offering corporate hospitality on matchdays only (often out-sourced to a contract caterer), to selling function suites, conference, exhibition, restaurant and bar facilities seven days a week, 52 weeks a year, with a team of in-house catering, conference and sales staff, again as Leicester City does.

Non-football leisure and entertainment businesses practise a market-led approach which focuses on customers' needs, and an almost scientific approach to understanding patterns of consumption and consumer behaviour. Generally, football has been slow to follow, though more and more clubs are beginning to appreciate that marketing has a role to play as a means of remaining competitive. Findings from a 1997 study[7] provide telling insights into the level of marketing development in the football industry, suggesting that, for example, only 53 per cent of senior marketing executives surveyed saw identifying customer needs as a marketing priority within the club. The report also discovered that just one-fifth of these executives stated that marketing was a guiding philosophy for the whole club, and that a quarter perceived the marketing function to be lower in status to club administration. Similarly, the study revealed that marketing is represented at board level in just 38 clubs; that 13 per cent of clubs carry out little or no marketing planning; and that over a quarter of clubs attach no importance to targeting customers using direct mail for their promotional strategies and nearly half of clubs attach no importance to telemarketing. These findings tend to support the view that whilst marketing is beginning to figure more and more prominently within the football industry, many clubs still have much to do if they are to survive and prosper in a fiercely competitive leisure industry.

Quite why so many clubs continue to attach so little importance to marketing is again a matter for further investigation. It appears that football clubs' traditional view of supporters as captive and unquestioning consumers of their product still prevails. It is for the most part true to categorize football clubs as 'passion brands', or brands to which consumers show a uniquely unerring loyalty. Too often, however, clubs have used this notion to absent themselves from treating spectators as customers, or adopting proactive marketing tactics.[8]

However, football is about to move into a new stage in its development as a mass spectator sport. All clubs currently encounter impacts on their matchday trading activities when regular patterns of spectatorship are broken. At the moment these occurrences are kept to a minimum by UEFA rules governing competitive fixture scheduling for television. Both the launch of full pay-per-view football and the prospect of an increased commitment by the top clubs to European competition seem likely to blow away these self-regulatory measures, and for the clubs and their spectators this will bring about radical changes to patterns of trading and consumption. At the same time, increased pressures are being made on clubs to meet players' spiralling wage demands, and, as a direct result of the *Bosman* ruling, to secure players on expensive and long-term contracts.

Traditionally, football clubs have tended to assume that their supporters will remain a captive audience regardless of how fan demographics are changing, or even the quality of product that is offered. We have long recognized at Leicester City, however, that our fans are our customers, with the ability to spend their hard-earned leisure time and 'leisure pounds' on or at a variety of competing attractions and venues.

The demographic profile of football spectators too is shifting. One in five, or 19 per cent, of football supporters earn over £30,000 per annum, while Leicester City has one of the highest ratios of female season ticket-holders in the Premier League at 16 per cent.[9] Ten, even five years ago, the picture would have been very different.[10] This is not to say that football has been gentrified. Rather, modern supporters are more discerning and their patterns of consumption more variable and unpredictable than they were, say, ten or even five years ago.

Many clubs are clearly ill-equipped with the basic tools of marketing to adapt to football's developing climate and supporters' changing habits. Unless clubs update their outlook on customers and embrace a more market-led approach, their wealth-creating potential threatens to diminish.

THE IMPACT OF PAY-PER-VIEW TELEVISION

Pay-per-view football seems to be an inevitable consequence of the technological and commercial development of television. So far there has been a good deal of hype about pay-per-view football's arrival in the UK, but very little solid information on which to base assumptions. Nevertheless, there are indicators for some of the likely features of a pay-per-view football market in the UK.

Turnstile income for the Premier League's clubs continues to grow at a much slower rate compared to television revenues. Deloitte & Touche[11] predict that, in the medium term, ticket prices will continue to grow faster than inflation before, in the longer term, levelling off and then falling to ensure that grounds remain full when pay-per-view is implemented.

In the summer of 1998, BSkyB submitted a proposal to the FA Premier League to introduce pay-per-view during the 1998/99 season. Among the reasons why the offer was rejected by the clubs was the potential impact on attendances. According to the experts, if there had been an attendant decrease in turnstile income of 30 per cent or more, Sky's offer would not have proved economically viable.

Premier League pay-per-view may have only been temporarily delayed, but such concerns suggest that the future adoption of pay-per-view by the clubs must be weighed against the impact on turnstile income. The relationship between live match transmissions and attendances is not straightforward as certain types of matches are more affected than others. Indeed, there are some clubs for which live television has no impact whatsoever on attendances. Demand for these clubs' home and away match tickets tends to be upheld regardless of the opposition.

Most clubs, however, do not operate under such luxurious conditions. At the moment, losses in gate revenue over the course of a season tend to be less than the clubs receive from BSkyB for the transmission of the match. The impact is likely to be more significant with the arrival of pay-per-view, when it is expected that every game will be screened live.

A variety of measures could be introduced to protect clubs' gate income, including:

- offering 'electronic season tickets' for away matches and to subscribers in the club's local market only;

- redistributing pay-per-view revenue to compensate clubs for lost gate revenue;

- agreeing not to sell individual pay-per-view tickets for matches between clubs whose gate revenue is most affected by live television coverage;

- resisting scheduling matches throughout the week. For some clubs attendances to mid-week matches can be reduced by as much as 20 per cent.

The worst-case scenario for non-'A List' clubs would be a decline in both television and turnstile income resulting from the end of collectively-negotiated television deals, and the introduction of pay-per-view leading to a market-led reduction in ticket prices. Even under less onerous conditions, including the adoption of some or all of the protective measures outlined above, the least most clubs can expect is for their normal matchday trading and consumer patterns to be transformed by the arrival of pay-per-view.

RISING OPERATING COSTS AND FUTURE PROFITABILITY

Already over half of all Premiership clubs' total wages and salaries bills exceed 50 per cent of turnover. According to Deloitte & Touche, at least one Premiership club's wage and salary bill is currently equal to, if not greater than, its annual turnover.[12] Further wage growth is expected as *Bosman* begins to have its effect, with clubs offering improved remuneration to players in a bid to retain them on long-term contracts.[13] Although one immediate effect of this could be a reduction in squad sizes, after a few years this measure is likely to be insufficient to protect clubs' profitability. Increasing the length of players' contracts protects a club's squad for several years, but it comes at the expense of players securing substantial increases and signing-on fees for renewing their contracts. Any savings made on transfer fees under *Bosman* are now being passed on to players who are demanding higher wages.

The agreement by the FA, Premier League and Football League allowing players over the age of 24 and out of contract to move freely between English clubs may have harsh consequences for the UK's smaller professional clubs. These clubs are unlikely to be able to meet the costs which longer-term contracts demand, but risk losing their players as they fall out of contract to clubs better equipped to pay higher wages. The bigger the club, the more likely a player is to sign a longer-term contract.

Pay-per-view television and rising player costs are just two of the challenging situations with which clubs are currently confronted. Professional football clubs can either sit back in the hope that sanity prevails over worst-case scenarios, or they can equip themselves with market-led and wealth-creating strategies to lessen the impact of these factors. Leicester City Football Club does not profess to have all the answers to football's current dilemmas, but it has for some time recognized the value of a market-led approach, of being responsive to the needs of its customers, of practising professional marketing tactics to better understand and serve its customers and, most importantly, to help create wealth for the organization.

Historically, Leicester City Football Club has been categorized among football's 'yo-yo' clubs, bouncing between the top two divisions. In 1990–91 the club narrowly avoided relegation to the Third Division (now Second Division) of the Football League. In less than ten years the club has returned (twice) to the FA Premier League, and is now consolidating its position among English football's top-flight. The 1999/2000 season is Leicester City's fourth consecutive season as an FA Premier League club, during which the club won the Coca-Cola sponsored League Cup and with it entry, for the first time in over 30 years, to the UEFA Cup. Against most expectations, the club claimed successive top-ten finishes for the three seasons to 1999, attracting capacity attendances of 21,500, and made a further Wembley Worthington Cup Final appearance in March 1999.[14]

The brush with relegation to the old Third Division – a league in which Leicester City has never played – is perhaps the point at which the club began to evaluate the role for a more professional business and marketing approach. My own appointment to the newly-created post of Marketing Director in 1991 marked a departure for the club, which previously relied almost entirely on dwindling gate receipts for its income, and was infamous for selling its best players to survive. In subsequent years, Leicester City has pioneered initiatives in the field of marketing, several of which have been adopted by other football clubs. These operations, together with the success enjoyed by Leicester City's improved performances on the pitch, have helped the club to increase its annual turnover from £2m in 1991 to an expected £24 million in 1999. All of these activities will be improved upon when, subject to planning permission, the club relocates to a new, higher capacity stadium equipped with enhanced facilities and a state-of-the-art infrastructure.

DATABASE MARKETING

Leicester City Football Club was one of the first clubs in the football industry to install an in-house database and direct marketing system. This enables the club to centralize information on all of its season ticket holders, adult members, Pepsi Junior Foxes Club members, corporate clients and local businesses, customers of the club's *à la carte* restaurant, conference, banqueting and catering facilities and Fox Leisure merchandise customers, to name but a few. The database is the platform for all of the club's marketing initiatives, and facilitates direct communication with known and regular customers of the club.

Whilst many of the mail-outs are sales-led, containing offers or alerting customers to the hundreds of events held at the club's stadium during each week of the year, the marketing database is also used to develop customer loyalty and affinity. Each of the club's core customer groups – members and season ticket-holders, junior members, corporate clients and retail partners – receive regular newsletters with information about Leicester City activities specially tailored and designed to meet the needs of the customer group. These information brochures in turn are income-generating because of their ability to offer prospective advertisers and sponsors access to a highly targeted and repeat customer base.

FAMILY NIGHT FOOTBALL

Leicester City Football Club's Family Night Football (FNF) concept was pioneered in 1994 to create a family entertainment event around the club's second-team fixtures. The guiding principle has been to introduce live football to people and groups within the local community who, perhaps, would not otherwise attend. The event is supported by dedicated marketing activities, to the extent that operations now mirror those of home first-team matchdays. When once Leicester City was fortunate to attract several hundred to its reserve team fixtures, average attendances have risen to between 5,000 and 6,000 and have reached as high as 17,000.

FNF has created an additional 12 trading matchdays for the club, which allows the club to engage in ticket sales, sponsorship opportunities, merchandising, catering, matchday magazine sales, providing children's birthday parties, maximizing usage of the club's Fosse Restaurant, and more. So successful has FNF been that Leicester City fans have become among the strongest watchers of reserve team football in the Premier League, with our marketing research showing that around one-third attend these matches during the season.

Our research also reveals that one-third of Leicester City fans also have mothers who follow football, and are very likely to live in households with increasing female interest in the sport. FNF has both helped to create and capitalize on these trends by creating a non-hostile and family-friendly environment in which to watch live football. FNF has also become an important platform for Leicester City to promote its credentials as a 'corporate citizen' by showing a commitment to families, youth and community groups and developing relationships with differing sections of the local communities.

Family Night Football has proved popular as a vehicle to promote live football to audiences who might not otherwise attend matches. Whilst the national average for Asian spectatorship at Premier League matches is around one per cent,[15] Leicester City research indicates that ethnic minority spectators at Family Night Football matches regularly exceed 25 per cent of the total gate.

Anti-racist initiatives developed for Family Night Football in conjunction with local community groups, the local authority and amateur African-Caribbean and Asian football clubs in Leicester have blossomed into high-profile programmes at first-team level. These schemes aim to encourage Asian youth's known appetite for football in the hospitable and non-intimidatory environment of Family Night Football, in the hope that this will develop into a lifetime's habit for watching live, first-team matches.

In order to remain competitive, the challenge all football clubs must meet is to cater for greater numbers of women, families with children, excluded groups and others who traditionally have not been attracted to football. Unless this challenge is met, and unless the live game markets itself effectively by making matches accessible to a broader mix of people, the football industry risks becoming over-exposed to rising costs it cannot meet, and of being over-dependent on income from television.

OTHER MARKETING INITIATIVES

The Season Ticket Swipe Card

Leicester City is the first Premier League club to introduce stadium-wide electronic swipe card entry for season ticket holders. This will eventually develop beyond matchday access control into a cash-replacement card for season ticket holders and other regular customers of the club's products and services. Eventually, Leicester City will own a centralized database capable of delivering information on the purchasing habits of corporate and consumer customers, allowing the club's in-house marketing team to segment and target specific groups with a high degree of accuracy and relevance.

Branded Business Diversification

A further important element of Leicester City's market-led strategy is the diversification of its related business activities. These are owned and operated by the club, employing around 150 full-time staff, and are actively marketed to generate wealth for the company to plough back into its core operating area of football. The club's medium to long-term business strategy is to reduce any over-dependence on income streams outside of its control – television income, central sponsorship agreements and so on – to activities which it can control.

Leicester City now has a well-established business base, and is the market leader in its local area and even outside of Leicestershire in conferencing. Since the opening of the Carling Stand in 1994, Leicester City's turnover from conference, banqueting and catering has increased from under £500k a year to over £3m per year, with a net contribution of £500k. Non-matchday sales in this area of operating activity now account for 75 per cent of sales and profits. Leicester City has some nine different function suites with capacities to host parties of ten to 400 people at any one time. The Premier Centre facility can take up to 400 people and is utilized on non-matchdays as a trade show and exhibition venue.

This operation has also sprouted an executive catering brand, Fox Executive Catering, whose external clients include National Power, Alliance & Leicester Bank, Pepsi Co., Bass, Mitchells and Butlers, Barclays Bank and the club's main sponsor Walkers Snack Foods. This entire operation is controlled and operated by the club – not by outside contractors – to guarantee quality, service, standards, value for money and food safety.

Leicester City's own brand, Fox Leisure, is a widely known brand because this is the name borne on the club's first-team and replica kits. Fox Leisure is also active in the wholesale market, supplying football strips to superstores, national sports retail chains, independents and amateur teams and schools. Similar principles are also applied to other Leicester City business ventures – Fox Design to Print, Ticket Sales for external venues and events, publications and Internet, personnel and training. All are in-house and operated with a professional staff.[16]

Operating these activities effectively and running a football club as an entrepreneurial business require investment in professional off-the-field staff and training, which Leicester City has not been afraid to do, whilst acknowledging that our core activity of football ultimately drives the business forward.

CONCLUSION

Football has undergone an enormous transition over the last five to ten years, from being a sport which was governed at club level by largely 'amateur' boards, to a sector which is run along increasingly professional business lines. There are signs that clubs are at last beginning to adopt professional responsibilities towards their customer bases. Even since the research on the role of marketing in professional football clubs cited above was published there has been a noticeable new emphasis on acquiring and developing the standards which are commonplace in other parts of the leisure industry. At least one Premier League club now has International Organization for Standardization (ISO) status, several are applying for Investors in People (including Leicester City), meaning that benchmarks are beginning to be set against which the rest of the industry can be measured.

It is important that football clubs begin to absorb the responsibilities which have long been accepted practice in other business sectors. Government is taking an increasing and keener interest in how clubs run their affairs and how they act in the market, to the extent that an industry regulator first mooted by the government's Football Task Force has already been discussed with the FA and the FA Premier League.

The new football economy has undeniably created enormous opportunities for those fortunate enough to be close to the top. But there are risks ahead. Unless clubs begin to take action by limiting their dependence on revenue streams outside of their direct control – and in particular unless they begin to adopt a more market-led and professional approach towards their customers and trading activities – many professional clubs risk becoming severely exposed and ill-equipped to compete in a changing environment.

Barrie Pierpoint left Leicester City Football Club in January 2000. This essay contains the personal views of Barrie and are not those of the club.

NOTES

1. A. Fynn and L. Guest, *Out of Time: Why Football Isn't Working* (London: Simon & Schuster, 1994).
2. See, for example, A. Brown (ed.), *Fanatics! Power, Identity and Fandom in Football* (London: Routledge, 1998); S. Redhead, *Post-Fandom and the Millennial Blues: The Transformation of Soccer Culture* (London: Routledge, 1997).
3. Lord Justice Taylor (Chairman), *Inquiry into the Hillsborough Stadium Disaster: Final Report* (London: HMSO, 1990).
4. Deloitte & Touche, *Deloitte & Touche Annual Review of Football Finance* (Manchester: Deloitte and Touche, 1998).
5. G. Boon, A. Philips and M. Tench, '20 Richest Football Clubs in the World', *FourFourTwo* (March 1997).
6. See Chris Gratton's essay in this volume about the disparity of football wealth distribution.
7. D. Hudson, *The Position and Role of Marketing in Professional Football Clubs* (Leicester: De Montfort University, 1997).
8. See the piece by Lomax in this volume for an examination of the 'political' role that fans can play within the football clubs they support.
9. Sir Norman Chester Centre for Football Research, *FA Premier League National Fan Survey 1996/97: Summary* (Leicester: Sir Norman Chester Centre for Football Research, 1998).
10. For an alternative view of the demographics of football crowds, see Malcolm, Jones and Waddington in this volume.
11. Deloitte & Touche (1998).
12. Ibid.
13. Gordon Bennett, then Chief Executive at Norwich City, reported in August 1999 that the total wage bill for players at the club had doubled from £2 million in 1996/97 to £4 million in 1998/99. Norwich City FC website: http://www.canaries.co.uk/firstnews/index.htm.
14. Leicester City's average attendance for 1997–98 was 20,615. G. Rollin and J. Rollin, *Rothmans Football Yearbook 1998–99* (London: Headline, 1999), p.576.
15. J. Bains with R. Patel, *Asians Can't Play Football* (Birmingham: Asian Social Development Agency, 1996).
16. Other operations run by the club include Fox Fast Foods – matchday spectator catering; Fox Travel – away supporter travel, holidays and other services.

3

European Law and Football: Who's in Charge?

KEN FOSTER

Bosman is the one legal case that every football player and fan knows. The judgment of the European Court of Justice in 1995 ended an age of innocence when football blithely assumed that it was immune from the intervention of law.[1] Post-*Bosman* footballers are free to move at the end of their contracts. Restrictions that prevented this, such as a transfer fee to the old club, were decreed an infringement of a worker's right of free movement under Article 48 of the Treaty of Rome.[2]

But *Bosman* had a sting in its tail. The Court considered the possibility that football was operating in an anti-competitive manner contrary to Articles 85 and 86 of the Treaty.[3] The final judgment in the *Bosman* case was not based on these grounds but, subsequently, the European Commission, which has enforcement powers against anti-competitive practices, ordered UEFA to comply with the judgment by using these Articles.[4] In future, football would, for legal purposes at least, be a business.

This response by the Commission – that European competition law could apply to football – opened up a Pandora's box. A literal application of that law could make most aspects of the control and regulation of European football by UEFA subject to legal challenge, and consequently this is exactly what happened. A flood of complaints reached the offices of the European Commission. The Commission is, at the time of writing, investigating over 50 cases, ranging from the relocation of clubs to the arrangements for ticket sales at the last World Cup. Football feared for its autonomy and its systems of governance in the face of this barrage of complaints. UEFA (Union Européenne de Football Association) and FIFA (Fédération Internationale de Football Association) became so alarmed that they began to argue and lobby for immunity from European competition law hoping to regain control of their affairs.

The declaration on sport accompanying the Amsterdam Treaty in 1997 ushered in a more measured and less confrontational approach.[5] Although restricted to three brief points, it emphasized the need to recognize the unique features of sport and to avoid the automatic application of European law to the commercial aspects of football. Effectively it ordered the Commission to tread lightly by calling upon 'the bodies of the European Union to listen to sports associations when important questions affecting sport are at issue'.[6]

After these preliminary skirmishes, the Commission is now formulating the ground-rules which will apply in the twenty-first century. Important discussion papers were prepared for the major conference on sports at Olympia in May 1999.[7] Four principles have emerged as guidelines for future legal intervention.

1. The fundamental freedoms for players and clubs to be free to move and operate anywhere within the European Union should not be limited. The only exception is when desirable 'sporting' objectives cannot be reached by any other route.

2. National identity is a key element of sport and thus sporting federations can have a legitimate interest in preserving it. The Amsterdam declaration emphasizes the 'social significance of sport ... in forging identity'. Although discrimination on the grounds of nationality cannot be justified when it interferes with the fundamental legal right to move, post-*Bosman* fears that national distinctions in sport were under threat proved unfounded. Some degree of national difference can still, legally, be recognized.

3. European competition law applies to professional football but sport has unusual features that mean it is not always possible to treat it as any other business. Football authorities can take decisions even if they restrict economic opportunities. However, when they do so they must justify them in sporting terms, such as the need to produce equal sporting competition.

4. Sporting federations, such as UEFA, are monopolies and as such have a 'dominant position' under Article 86 of the Treaty. Their powers can be legally controlled if this position is abused. But football federations are not to be equated to commercial trade associations representing their members. That they deal with amateur as well as professional clubs was explicitly recognized in the Amsterdam declaration. But, some of their activities may again be judged differently because they are acting for the greater good of the game even when the economic interests of professional clubs are damaged.[8]

This essay discusses the continuing problems post-*Bosman* with players' right to move clubs freely, the reciprocal right of clubs as businesses to move wherever they wish within the European Union, and the extent to which these basic freedoms can be curtailed by football's governing bodies for the good of the game or to preserve national identity in sport. It then discusses how far leagues, national or Europe-wide, are subject to European competition law and how the private autonomy of governing bodies is challenged by European Commission intervention acting in the name of the consumer and the public interest.

POST-*BOSMAN*

The *Bosman* judgment left a number of unanswered questions in its wake concerning the footballer's right to move clubs freely. The key finding in *Bosman* was that Article 48 of the Treaty – granting all workers the freedom to move anywhere within the European Union to take up employment – applied to footballers in the same way as it applied to other workers. Therefore, the rule requiring a transfer fee on the expiry of a footballer's contract with his old club when he moved to a new club in another Member State was illegal. Such rules, the Court said, directly affected and limited the player's access to the labour market in another Member State.

But there are limits to the judgment in *Bosman*. Being an international transfer and dealing only with the legality of transfer fees claimed at the end of a player's contract, certain issues remain. First, what is the legal position of domestic transfers that do not involve cross-border moves? On one view domestic transfers between clubs in the same country are outside the scope of European law.[9] Yet to have one rule for 'overseas' players within the European Union and a less favourable rule for home players cannot be justified. It would distort the European labour market in footballers by giving 'overseas' players an advantage. As this advantage is based on the footballer's nationality, it would fall foul of that part of the *Bosman* judgment that outlaws discrimination between workers within the European Union based on nationality. For these legal reasons, the English Football Association (FA) quickly amended its rules to bring domestic transfers into line and abolished transfer fees for players out of contract.[10]

A second problem not solved by *Bosman* was the position of transfers between clubs within the European Union but involving a non-European Union player. An example was the transfer in 1997 of the Croatian, Goran Vlaovic, from Padova in Italy, to Valencia in Spain. Padova claimed a transfer fee of £3.3 million even though the player was at the end of his contract. Had he been a citizen of a European Union country, he would have been able to move freely. FIFA supported Padova's claim and ordered Valencia to pay the fee. Valencia lodged a complaint with the European Commission. The club accepted that it could not rely upon Article 48 which was only applicable to European Union citizens but rested its case on the argument that FIFA's ruling was a restrictive business agreement under Article 85.[11] A similar but reverse case is that of John Collins. Collins, a British citizen, moved to Monaco from Glasgow Celtic. Celtic demanded a fee even though the player was out of contract. The complication in this case is that Monaco is outside the European Union, even though the football club plays under the jurisdiction of the French FA.

The post-*Bosman* challenges have been based on the arguments that charging transfer fees for any player, whatever their nationality, distorts the market between European Union clubs for players and is illegal for that reason. This makes the national location of the clubs the key factor. The logical conclusion of this line of argument then appears to be that any transfer to or from a club within the European Union that involves a fee for an out-of-contract player is an illegal distortion of competition. This has forced the European Commission to suggest to both FIFA and UEFA that the whole international transfer system, at least in so far as it requires fees for out-of-contract players, could be illegal.[12]

Does *Bosman* apply when a player already under contract wishes to move? This is a more complex issue. On the one hand, it could be argued that to demand a transfer fee in these circumstances is just as restrictive of a player's freedom to move as it is to demand a fee at the end of his contract. On the other hand, this is a restraint that the player has freely and contractually agreed and so he should be legally held to his promise. Most legal systems make it difficult to stop workers from moving jobs; players can still leave but their old club may be entitled to compensation. Yet the following questions still await a clear legal answer. Can footballers jump contract whilst still under agreement? If they do so, can they be restrained from playing in all or some of their new club's games? And if they do jump contract, can their old club demand a transfer fee or other form of compensation?

Bosman recognized that there may be justifiable reasons for restricting the free movement of players without compensation. The two main ones discussed in the judgment were the need to compensate clubs for the training and development of young players, and the need to equalize sporting competition by rules that reallocate resources to weaker or poorer clubs. However, in *Bosman* the European Court of Justice decided that these justifiable sporting goals could be achieved by means other than the transfer system. Nevertheless, these two 'sporting' reasons are important. They are the limits within which the football federations and the European Commission have been trying to negotiate guidelines for the future.

FREEDOM OF ESTABLISHMENT

Corresponding to the worker's right to move freely is the right of a business (under Article 52) to establish itself anywhere in the European Union without restrictions based on 'national origin'.[13] This freedom presents problems for the football authorities in Europe. Professional football leagues are normally organized by the national football federation, or at least are under its jurisdiction. Qualification for European competitions is based on performance in national competitions and there are national quotas for entry into Europe. National teams are selected from citizens of the country or people otherwise qualified by some 'national' link such as parentage or residence. All these elements of national identity in football are in opposition to the fundamental freedoms underpinning the European Union which aim to eliminate rules based on national origins. The second main limb of the *Bosman* judgment was that nationality rules in football as to the number of 'foreign' players allowed in a team were illegal in so far as they discriminated against players from countries within the European Union.

The potential operation of Article 52 was well illustrated by the Mouscron case. Royal Excelsior Mouscron are a small Belgian cub who qualified in 1997 for the UEFA Cup. The capacity of their own ground was restricted for safety reasons to 4,500 so they moved their first game, against Limassol of Cyprus, to Lille in France, just across the border from Mouscron. The Lille stadium was larger with a capacity of 21,000. This cross-border transfer was sanctioned by UEFA, who presumably felt unable to object because of European law. However, in the next round Mouscron were drawn against Metz, a French club. The club again asked to transfer their home tie to Lille assuming that this request would be a formality. However in this instance UEFA objected, arguing that this arrangement would give Metz the unfair sporting advantage of playing an 'away' game in their own country. This case shows how economic interests – that of Mouscron in a larger gate revenue – can be over-ridden by sporting interests (presumably those of other teams who felt that Metz were gaining an advantage). However, without such sporting justification UEFA was not prepared to stop such a cross-border transfer in the first game.[14]

Whether or not UEFA can legally prevent the transfer of a club across national borders is also a current issue. Two clubs, Wimbledon of the English Premier League and Clydebank of the Scottish League, have shown an interest in relocating to Dublin – reputed to be the largest European city without a major professional football team. In both cases, the Irish football authority (FAI) has opposed the moves and will not grant permission for them. This raises two linked questions. One, can a national governing body legitimately claim exclusive jurisdiction over professional football in its own territory and exclude foreign clubs? Two, can a national league prevent its clubs from relocating outside its 'territory' by having a rule or a policy as to where clubs can play their games? The answer to the first question appears to be no. FAI's objection is economic; it believes that Wimbledon's presence in Dublin will damage attendance at its own clubs' league games if they are in direct competition. However, this reasoning is merely that of one economic undertaking, the FAI, trying to enforce an exclusive right to organize an economic activity via a 'national territory' agreement. Such agreements are normally treated by European law as being anti-competitive. FAI's objection is backed by UEFA and FIFA. Their power means that they can indirectly enforce the FAI ban by pressurizing the English FA into disciplining Wimbledon if it were to move. But again such manoeuvres are legally dubious. At an economic level, this looks like an international boycott organized by economic undertakings to protect their own interests. Such a boycott would be clearly anti-competitive under Article 86. There appears to be no sporting justification to FAI's objection.

The other side of the issue is whether the English Premier League can legally enforce a policy that its clubs must play all or some of its games within England. Initially, this also seems to be an infringement of Article 52, although it may be possible to argue that there is a consumer interest to be protected.[15] The ultimate purpose of European competition law is the protection of consumers. To move Wimbledon FC to Dublin would seriously prejudice their fans, most of whom are presumably based in London. These consumers would face greater expense in supporting their team in Ireland. It may therefore be possible for the English Premier League to enforce its policy of preventing Wimbledon from going, even if the FAI legally cannot prevent them from coming.[16]

A further variant on the national dimension of sport and the legal complications that can be caused is illustrated by the *Deliège* case.[17] In this case, a professional judo athlete claimed that her federation's selection policy for international competition was circumscribed by international regulations that limited to three the number of athletes the national federation could nominate. This meant that selection for important international competitions, such as the Olympics, was based in part on nationality rather than on merit. The case has not yet been decided by the European Court of Justice, but the Advocate-General has given his opinion. He argues that European law gives only a limited power of self-regulation to sporting federations even where the rules are solely related to sport. He accepts that these rules have the main sporting objective of ensuring a wide representation in international competitions and that these are in the public interest. The implications for European football could be far-reaching if the Court were not to decide in favour of the athlete. This would mean that qualification for European competitions based on national quotas, or at least performance in national leagues, could not be defended. UEFA would have to devise an alternative system of qualification for European competitions, unless it could be shown that there were good sporting reasons, such as encouraging minor football nations who would not otherwise qualify on merit, for their current quota system.

Defences based on national identity in sport have previously succeeded. It was decided in 1976 that choosing a national team based on citizenship was not objectionable under European law;[18] otherwise the whole concept of national sporting teams would be at risk. A similar argument may be feasible for the Champions' League – that teams are national representatives and not solely competing in their own right. However, this argument looks thin with major footballing nations having three or four teams in this competition. In the longer term though there is an increasing emphasis in European policy-making on preserving and encouraging cultural identity. The distinctiveness of sport as part of this process may make the European Commission more responsive to the arguments of football authorities that sport is a vital component of national identity.

'MONOPOLY' LEAGUES

A further issue for European competition law in the twenty-first century will be the threat of breakaway organizations and competitions such as a European Superleague. Essentially such breakaway structures can be seen either as healthy economic competition or as the creation of rival centres of governance that threaten the organizational structure of European football.

The application of competition law without modification in this area is complex. Sport is now seen as both a socio-cultural phenomenon and an economic activity. As an economic activity it is clear that the rules of the EU Treaty should apply even if it is necessary to address the specific requirements of sport. On the other hand, the European Commission's policy on enforcing competition rules has recognized the autonomy of sport as a cultural practice that needs to be preserved.

It was the fear, post-*Bosman*, that the general and immediate application of the Treaty's competition policies could cause serious difficulties and this led to the annexe to the Treaty of Amsterdam in 1997. This emphasizes the need to take into account the impact on sport of these policies and it prompted the Commission to consult sporting organizations before taking actions affecting them. In December 1998 the Vienna European Council further asked the European Commission to prepare a report on 'safeguarding current sport structures'. In preparation for this, the Commission has restated the general principles behind the application of European competition law to sport, and defined four categories of sporting rules.[19] These are:

1. *Rules to which Article 85 of the Treaty does not apply*
Article 85 broadly prohibits any agreement or decision by 'an economic undertaking', in which category sporting organizations clearly fall, which inhibits or prevents competition. There are, however, exceptions now recognized by the Commission where the rules are inherent and necessary to the sport, or where they are necessary for the organization and regulation of the sport. One recent example is the claim in the Lehtonen case.[20] Here a sporting federation had a rule that players who signed for a new club towards the end of a season could not play for that club until the season ended. The Advocate-General's opinion argues that this can be justified in sporting terms despite being a restriction on the player's freedom to work. That is to say, the Advocate-General accepts that this prevents clubs buying players towards the crucial end of season thereby distorting the sporting outcome of the league.

2. *Rules which clearly breach Article 85 because they are anti-competitive*
Such rules must significantly affect cross-border trade to warrant Commission action. This means that UEFA's regulatory regime will be of more interest to the Commission than those of national or local federations of sport. Such rules must also have a significant rather than minor effect on cross-border trade. In addition, there are four authorization criteria established in Article 85(3) by which the Commission can grant an exemption or clearance of an agreement. Agreements to pool revenues, as with UEFA's Champions League, are a clear example. Although these are restrictive, UEFA has recently applied for clearance.[21]

3. *Rules which are initially anti-competitive but whose aim is to preserve or encourage sporting equality*

The Commission appears ready to accept the justifications rehearsed in *Bosman* that the mutual interdependence of competitors or teams in sport is a key element of it. The total economic value and sporting interest is diminished if a small minority of teams begin to monopolize success. Similar arguments have had a strong influence on American anti-trust law, where equalization of sporting competition has been a cardinal principle of the attempts by sporting authorities to combat the regulatory authorities. This has justified such highly restrictive practices as the draft system and the collective pooling of all merchandising revenue in American football. The proposition that sporting monopoly in a league leads to economic ruin is treated as self-evident in these legal cases.[22] Thus, sporting bodies can legitimately attempt to redress the balance. Corrective mechanisms can take a number of forms but four main, non-mutually exclusive routes can be described. Rules can reallocate economic resources from the richer to the poorer clubs so that money is not allowed to buy success (rules which pool resources, for example). Rules can encourage recruitment of new talent in an even manner so that richer clubs do not take the best emerging players. Rules can aim at an even distribution of the best players to enable more equal sporting competition. (Such rules however must not infringe a player's right to move freely under the *Bosman* ruling and are therefore difficult to construct and enforce. However, an example might be salary caps – used for instance in rugby league and ice hockey – which, in part, are designed to prevent the richest clubs monopolizing all the best players.) Finally, rules designed to make results uncertain both in individual games and in season-long competitions. (For example, two-legged cup matches may increase the total of output of games. This presumably brings economic benefits, but makes a sporting upset less likely.)

4. *Rules which are illegal under Article 86 of the EC Treaty because they are an 'abuse of a dominant position'*

Sporting federations are especially vulnerable under this Article. They operate as monopolies of sporting regulation. The Commission nevertheless has affirmed its view that the effective institutional governance of sport may require single national federations. This may lead to the conclusion that a single federation can legitimately take monopoly powers of regulation from its constituent members as the most practicable structure of authority without abusing its dominant position. However, that power must not be exercised in an anti-competitive manner (for instance, by using its superior power to hamper the establishment of another federation could well be illegal).

This leads to the conclusion that a breakaway European league could be opposed by UEFA but that it must be careful in its choice of tactics. Banning players who compete in a rival league by the 'official' federation would be the most legally dubious tactic as this would almost certainly run counter to the players' freedom to move under Article 48. Expelling clubs from their national leagues would also be legally dangerous. This is clearly anti-competitive and the defence could only be a 'sporting' defence that leagues have total freedom to include or exclude clubs in the 'interests of the game'. Another tactic could be to have clubs sign loyalty contracts, although agreeing not to participate in part of the market could be considered anti-competitive.[23]

SPORTING FEDERATIONS AS REGULATORS

Sporting federations can still clash with European law if they trespass on the economic interests of clubs. At one level of analysis, it may be possible to argue that clubs within a federation have agreed to jurisdiction being exercised over them. Nevertheless, one example of a successful challenge to UEFA's general powers of regulation is the issue of cross-ownership of football clubs. ENIC, a public company listed on the London Stock Exchange, controls three European football teams. Two of these teams (AEK Athens and Slavia Prague) qualified for European competition in the UEFA Cup in 1998/99. UEFA responded to this situation by announcing that football clubs with the same owners would not be allowed to play in the same competition. ENIC claimed that this was a breach of European law as the effect of the ruling was anti-competitive. UEFA replied that without such a rule, the clubs could be drawn to play each other thereby creating a danger that genuine sporting competition would be compromised. The parties subsequently agreed to take their case to voluntary arbitration before the Court of Arbitration for Sport (CAS).[24] The Court ruled that it was unlawful for UEFA to introduce a new rule without warning so stressing the need for sporting federations to observe procedural fairness in making their decisions. Whilst this meant that the CAS had to make no direct finding on the substance of the decision by UEFA, they nevertheless took the view that such rules did have a purely sporting objective (namely to prevent clubs with the same owner playing each other), and as such should be outside the scope of Article 85. However, there is also an issue of 'proportionality'. The fact that economic loss could be suffered by the rule's implementation means that the width of the rule should be no greater than needed to achieve the sporting purpose. It would perhaps have been feasible for UEFA to construct a solution which allowed both clubs to play in the competition, but not be drawn to play each other. Such a solution would, perhaps, have been fairer than the hasty blanket prohibition.

BROADCASTING RIGHTS

The popularity of football on television has made the right to broadcast a game, or series of games, a valuable commodity. Television rights are a major source of income for football today and the whole financial structure of European football is now dependent on their sale and exploitation.

The right to broadcast a game belongs, in principle, to the home club under most national systems of law.[25] The reason appears to be that most clubs are the owners of their grounds and can control access. This right of ownership means that broadcasters require permission to mount their facilities from the home club. Effectively, this is what is being sold when a company buys the right to broadcast a game.

However, most football leagues in Europe, including the Premier League, have insisted on the collective selling of broadcasting rights. This is achieved by making it a rule of membership of the league that the club assigns their broadcasting rights to the league. The purpose behind this arrangement is to achieve some form of equality and redistribution of the broadcasting revenues. Left to the free market, it is assumed that games involving the top clubs would be more popular and thus more valuable.[26] Collective selling allows both greater financial equality between clubs and a method of ensuring that all clubs get reasonable television coverage.

Collective selling of broadcasting rights is, arguably, anti-competitive in principle. Most deals restrict the total output of games on television. Individual clubs are restrained from selling their own products on the open market. The price paid per game is artificially inflated, which prejudices potential buyers of the broadcasting rights and also the ultimate consumer, the paying viewer. All these factors suggest that the Commission will, in the future, scrutinize broadcasting deals carefully.

The Commission considered the original television deal between BSkyB and the football authorities in 1989–93 and took the view that it may have been objectionable were it not for the fact that BSkyB was a new entrant into the broadcasters' market and needed the economic security of a long deal to establish itself. The chief objection to this agreement was the granting of exclusive rights to BSkyB (apart from the offer of delayed highlights to the BBC). Exclusive rights to a single buyer are, in principle, anti-competitive but sports broadcasters can only charge for channels or programmes of football if they have a unique product. The European Court of Justice has ruled that exclusive licences of performing rights are not automatically an infringement of Article 85, and similar principles could apply to sports rights. However, they still need to be considered on their merits. The current economic view seems to be that exclusivity carries a premium in the sports broadcasting market. The football authorities and clubs can get more by selling exclusive rights. A counter-argument might be that the absence of live football on free-to-air channels does not help to expand the market for viewers or fans.

The other anti-competitive element in broadcasting deals might be their length. The Premier League's contract with BSkyB has typically run for four years. Many regulatory authorities including the European Commission have taken the view that exclusive deals should not last more than one year. BSkyB's initial argument to the Commission that, as a new entrant, it needed a foothold in the market is no longer operative. Indeed, in 1999 the Monopolies and Mergers Commission concluded that BSkyB was the dominant player in the premium sports broadcasting market.[27] Broadcasters thus appear vulnerable to regulatory action and declarations of illegality if they continue to negotiate long-term deals. The football authorities may argue that long contracts allow them to make plans on the basis of financial security but annual auctions and a more transparent process of bidding with proper tenders might be required by the European Commission.

CONCLUSION

The above survey shows that European law is beginning to have a major impact on football. The whole regulatory structure of governance within European football is coming under close scrutiny. Even so, there are a number of issues that have not been covered in this survey.[28] For example, the Commission is still pursuing and has already fined the French organizing committee of the last World Cup tournament over its allocation of tickets. The committee reserved 60 per cent of all tickets for French citizens. It was successfully argued that this system discriminated against other European citizens. In order to avoid similar illegality, the ticketing arrangements for Euro 2000 in Belgium and the Netherlands have been organized so that tickets are freely available to all fans across Europe without any preferential treatment for people in the two host countries.[29]

The rapid commercialization of football at the end of the twentieth century has meant that the game's administrators have had to realize that, like any other international business, they are subject to European law. This was the overriding inference from *Bosman*. But the European Commission, in its zeal to apply the law, has also had to recognize the uniqueness of sport as a business and modify its free market economic model accordingly. A direct confrontation between European football and the European Commission has, for the moment, been avoided and the emerging guidelines which will lead us into the twenty-first century are relatively consensual. Sport's cultural importance means that its unique features are being recognized. UEFA needs to operate within the legal rules for it is running a business but, at the same time, the European Commission must learn that whilst football may be a business, it is a funny old business.

NOTES

1. *Union Royale Belge des Sociétés de Football Association ASBL* v. *Bosman* (case C-415/93) [1996] All E R (EC) 189 ECJ.
2. The Treaty of Rome Articles have been renumbered but here I have used the original numbering. Article 48 is now Article 39 and Articles 85 and 86 are now 81 and 82 respectively.
3. Article 85 prohibits restrictive agreements between enterprises including football clubs and federations. Article 86 deals with the 'abuse of a dominant position'. UEFA, arguably, occupies such a position as the sole governing body of professional football within the European Union.

4. It formally notified UEFA on 19 January 1996 that its regulations infringed Article 85 (*Bosman case – background*; European Commission).

5. Declaration to the Amsterdam Treaty 1997. The text is summarized in *The Development and Prospects for Community Action in the Field of Sport* (European Commission Staff Working Paper, DG X, Brussels, 29 September 1998).

6. Ibid. p.4.

7. First European Conference on Sport 1999. Discussion papers on *The Fight against Doping, the European Model of Sport, Relations between Sport and Television* (European Commission, DGX, Brussels, April 1999). An earlier consultation document offers an excellent analysis; *The European Model of Sport: Consultation Document of DG X* (Brussels, 1998).

8. UEFA has applied for exemption from the European competition laws for its central marketing of the television and sponsorship rights to the Champions' League, partly on the grounds that some of the revenue pool is used to support amateur and youth football (case No IV/ 37.398; OJ 99/23).

9. European law does not apply to purely domestic issues. This would not prevent transfer fees being illegal under English law as an unlawful restraint of trade.

10. *Bosman* allowed an apparent exception for clubs to claim compensation for training and developing young players. This has been seized upon by the football authorities to allow 'compensation' fees when players under 24 leave their first club. See also FIFA's Statutes: Regulations Governing the Status and Transfer of Football Players, Article 14(1).

11. See also *Tibor Balog* v. *Royal Charleroi Sporting Club* (case C-246/98; 1998/OJ/C278).

12. FIFA has since decreed that *Bosman* rules apply to all international transfers, subject to 'compensation' for young players.

13. Article 47 in the revised numbering.

14. European Report No. 2280, Europe Information Service.

15. Wimbledon's claim to move is based on Article 52 as an infringement of their freedom to set up business wherever they wish. But the obstacles being put in their path are based on the national football federations' claim to exercise exclusive jurisdiction over the operation of professional football in their countries; these claims are anti-competitive under Articles 85 and 86.

16. A similar case, but decided solely under domestic law, was the attempt by the Welsh FA to force some Welsh clubs to leave the non-league pyramid in England and compete in the newly formed Welsh League. The clubs refused and were barred from playing in Wales. This was held to be an illegal restraint of trade. See *Newport AFC* v. *F.A. of Wales* [1995] 2 All E R 87.

17. *Deliège* v. *ASGC Ligue Francophone de Judo* (case C-51/96 joined with C-191/97; Advocate-General's opinion, 18 May 1999). National quotas can be a constituent element of sporting organization and thus outside the scope of European law. The European Court of Justice has yet to hear the case but they rarely depart from the view taken by the Advocate-General, who is appointed to give an expert preliminary opinion.

18. *Dona* v. *Mantero* [1976] ECR 1333 (case 13/76) ECJ.

19. European Commission Press Release IP/ 99/133 (24 February 1999).

20. *Lethonen* v. *ASBL Fédération de Basketball* (case C-176/96; Advocate-General's opinion, 22 June 1999).

21. Case No IV/37 398: 1999/OJ/C99/23.

22. Whether this is the case in European football seems less obvious. There is little direct evidence that overall attendances are related to the degree of sporting 'centralization'. Some European leagues, such as the Spanish leagues, appear well supported despite the effective duopoly of Barcelona and Real Madrid. See also S. Szymanski and T. Kuyers, *Winners and Losers: The Business Strategy of Football* (London: Viking, 1999), pp.258–63.

23. This was tried in Australian Rugby League where two rival organizations had competing leagues. The practice was held to be illegal under the Australian restrictive practices legislation. See *News Ltd* v. *Australian Rugby Football League* (1996) 139 ALR 193.

24. The Court of Arbitration for Sport was established by the International Olympic Committee to resolve sporting disputes without going to the courts. It is staffed by legally trained arbitrators, and is based in Lausanne. Many sporting federations now make it a condition of membership, or entry by sportspeople into competitions, that they agree to submit disputes to the CAS and not to the courts. The IOC required all competitions in the 1996 Atlanta Games to do so in order to avoid litigation in the American courts. Its awards are treated as legally binding on the respective parties. For a detailed description, see N.K. Raber, 'Dispute Resolution in Olympic Sport: The Court of Arbitration for Sport', *Seton Hall Journal of Sport Law*, 8 (1998), 75.

25. This has not been directly tested in English law, although the outcome of the case at present before the Restrictive Practices Court concerning the legality under domestic law of current television deal between BSkyB and the Premier League should clarify the issue. In Germany it was held in 1997 that broadcasting rights belonged to the club.
26. See the Monopolies and Mergers Commission's assessment in its report on the proposed take-over of Manchester United by BSkyB that games involving Manchester United, Liverpool or Arsenal produced a television audience 20 per cent greater than other games. *MMC Report on the proposed merger between BSkyB and Manchester United* (Cm 4305) paras. 4.112 and 4.113.
27. Ibid.
28. The recent consultation document of the European Commission, supra note 7, adds other aspects of sport, such as doping and the impact of sport on the environment, as areas in which Community action may be desirable to supplement or reinforce domestic legal measures.
29. 'Fans win better deal on tickets', *Independent*, 21 January 1999, 30.

PART 2
Football Politics

4

FIFA and the Men Who Made It

ALAN TOMLINSON

La Fédération Internationale de Football Association (FIFA) is the governing body of world football. Its greatest asset is the World Cup, which has become one of the biggest media spectacles and profitable cultural events in the world. The World Cup finals in France in 1998 was the biggest and longest ever, amplifying a trend that since Italia '90 has established the competition as a lucrative mega-event of global interest, increasingly valued by politicians intent on nation-building.[1] After the success of the Euro '96 event, the English FA, spurred on by the Labour government elected in 1997, has, through the England 2006 World Cup bid, sought a place at the centre of world football lobbying and politics. This is in a blatant attempt to attract the vote of FIFA executive committee members, 24 of whom cast the votes that decide where the 2006 World Cup finals will take place. The English FA, and the British government, sought to re-establish an English presence in the corridors of world football.[2] Why had the English influence waned? What interests had FIFA represented for almost all of the twentieth century? One way of answering this is to look at the men who have dominated FIFA's leadership.

From its foundation in 1904 FIFA has had eight presidents:

Robert Guérin	France	1904–6
Daniel Woolfall	England	1906–18
Jules Rimet	France	1921–54
Rodolfe Seeldrayers	Belgium	1954–55
Arthur Drewry	England	1956–61
Sir Stanley Rous	England	1961–74
Dr João Havelange	Brazil	1974–98
Joseph 'Sepp' Blatter	Switzerland	1998–

Daniel Woolfall's years at the helm were blighted by the Great War. Seeldrayers, a veteran football diplomat, was, like Rimet a lawyer, but also a classic all-round sportsman of the old school tradition. He was founder member of a prominent football club, a hockey international, national champion in the 110 metre hurdles, had been president of both the Belgian Olympic Committee and the Belgian Football Association, and throughout his life espoused the virtues of British athleticism.[3] He was very much a figure in the Rimet mould.

Arthur Drewry was close to Stanley Rous, who, though general secretary at the English FA at the time, was the power behind Drewry's throne. Drewry was a faithful football administrator, president of the (English) Football League from 1949 to 1954, a fish-processing businessman from Lincolnshire, who had been chairman of the FA's International Selection Committee between 1944 and 1949.[4] In November 1945 he was with Rous in Switzerland, negotiating Britain's re-entry into FIFA, and was appointed vice-president of FIFA by Rimet. After service in the Middle East during the First World War, Drewry had married the daughter of the chairman of Grimsby Town Football Club, and begun work in his father-in-law's fishing business. He became chairman of the Grimsby club in turn, and increasingly involved in the administration of the English game, and its international dimensions, through both the League and the FA. He left the League to become chairman of the FA in 1955, to Rous' general secretary, just before succeeding Seeldrayers as FIFA president, by now in his mid-60s. He died, after a year-long illness, in March 1961. Before assuming the FIFA presidency, Drewry was therefore along with Rous one of the two top figureheads in the administration of the English game. Rous was closer to the top man at FIFA than anyone else.

Between them, three men have dominated FIFA's history, holding the presidency for 70 of the organization's first 94 years. These were Europeans Rimet and Rous, and Brazilian Havelange. The profiles, style and impact of these three football bureaucrats, and Havelange's successor Blatter, provide the main focus of this essay.

FIFA's first two presidents established the foundations for the French and English domination of FIFA for its first 70 years. Guérin was an engineer and newspaper editor who did all he could to bring the English and the British into FIFA at the beginning. He had suggested the formation of an international federation to the secretary of the English FA, Frederick Wall, an approach that was clearly rebuffed. Wall's response was in the classical mould of the phlegmatic English upper class: 'The Council of the Football Association cannot see the advantages of such a Federation, but on all such matters upon which joint action was desirable they would be prepared to confer.'[5]

He met Wall twice in 1903 to discuss his planned federation, but receiving no encouragement he went ahead alone. He recalled, in the 1920s: 'Tiring of the struggle and recognizing that the Englishmen, true to tradition, wanted to wait and watch, I undertook to invite the delegates from various nations myself.' So seven nations attended FIFA's first meeting in Paris: Belgium, Denmark, France, the Netherlands, Spain, Sweden and Switzerland. The roots of the organization were central European. But it was a novice organization, and three of the founders – Sweden, France and Spain – did not yet have autonomous football associations.

Once FIFA was formed, the FA considered it wise to become involved. A special FA committee invited Continental nations to a conference on the eve of the 1905 England–Scotland match in London. The outcome of this meeting was that the British associations accepted FIFA's general objectives and expressed willingness to co-operate. However, Guérin's early optimism proved short-lived, and he resigned after his efforts to organize a first international competition came to nothing. The English were by now ready to step in and offer leadership. Daniel Woolfall had met other nations in Switzerland in 1905, and his summary of the FA's position is crisp and to the point: '... it is important to the FA and other European Associations that a properly constituted Federation should be established and the Football Association should use its influence to regulate football on the Continent as a pure sport and give all Continental Associations the full benefit of the many years experience of the FA'.

So the British, and particularly the English, joined in when it was clear that they could be at the helm. It was now time for the dependable Englishman to take over and Woolfall was elected FIFA president. He was a civil servant from Blackburn, and had been an integral part of Blackburn Rovers' domination of the English Cup in the 1880s. He believed in footballing excellence, but was rooted in amateur values. Membership of FIFA expanded from seven to 24 by 1914, by now including some non-European members – South Africa joined in 1909–10, Argentina and Chile in 1912, the United States in 1913. But it was Great Britain that continued to take top honours in the unofficial world championship, the Olympic Games, in 1908 and 1912. It was after the Great War that FIFA became more truly international, with Rimet as president.[6]

RIMET – FRENCH FAVOURS

Rimet was a self-made professional and religious do-gooder who dominated the growth of international football. Like so many senior sports administrators Rimet was trained in law. Although, as an older man, the thoroughly bourgeois Rimet became an established figure among Parisian polite society, he came from humble origins. Rimet was born in 1873, into a modest family in rural France, and from an early age helped his father in the family's grocer's shop. He was a conscientious and able schoolboy. From the age of 11, he was raised in Paris where his father had moved in search of work. He lived in the heart of the city, learning to survive and play football on the street and to work ambitiously at school and at church. The young Rimet worked his way towards a full legal qualification, and was active in encouraging football among the poorer children of the city. He was a philanthropist for whom sport was a means of building good character.

Rimet was Christian and a patriot. His love of God and nation united in his passion for football. He believed in the universality of the church and saw in football the chance to create a world-wide 'football family' welded to Christian principles. Like his countryman, founder of the modern Olympics Baron Pierre de Coubertin, Rimet believed that sport could be a force for good – bringing people and nations together, promoting physical and moral progress, providing healthy pleasure and fun, and promoting friendship between races. For meritocratic reasons he promoted full-time professionalism. During the Second

World War his opposition to the nationalization of the game implemented by the Vichy regime saw him marginalized and he resigned from his position in charge of French football.

Despite his desire for FIFA to encourage a global football family, Rimet found it difficult to overcome an innate European imperiousness. Rimet did not believe that the administration of world football should be based upon geographical or regional groupings, and the development of continental confederations and the empowerment of football confederations in Africa and in Asia was resisted. Rimet's consistent goal was to preserve FIFA as a unit, and he argued that 'decentralization will destroy FIFA, only direct membership will retain FIFA as one family'. The Rimet philosophy was reaffirmed in his opening address to the FIFA Congress in Rio in 1950, in which he listed four 'finest human qualities' which football should impart. These were discipline, guided towards the achievement of a common goal; loyalty to the spirit of the game; moderation in competition and sporting rivalry; and solidarity in clubs and games. He proposed that such idealistic qualities be transferred from the game to everyday life. With one heart and one will, he preached, the world football family showed a 'perfect unity that holds us together, the spiritual community to which we all adhere …'.[7]

At the first World Cup in Uruguay in 1930 only four of the 15 competing teams were from Europe. Rimet had worked hard to establish the World Cup, and in many ways Uruguay was the obvious choice. Uruguay had shattered the world football establishment by winning the Olympic football championship in 1924 and 1928. These were the most dramatic achievements of the emerging football superpowers of South America. Football was also well established in Brazil and Argentina, where the game had been growing for half a century. It thrived initially in the ranks of nomadic British diplomats, planters and engineers who took their football togs and the Football Association rule book wherever they went. The colonials' love of the game soon spread among the local, poorer classes. But however much it spread, Rimet saw no case for the devolution of the game's administration.

The South American confederation – CONMEBOL – records its founding date as 1916, long before any other continental confederation. In its early days FIFA was so Eurocentric that no need was seen for any separate European organization. Rimet's concept of the world football family was deeply rooted in an entrenched colonialism but his successors would need to be aware of the dynamics of a post-colonial world if the football family was to hold together in the second half of the century. It was a bourgeois Englishman who inherited this challenge.

ROUS – AN ENGLISHMAN ABROAD

Although Stanley Rous did not become FIFA president until 1961, he had been an influential force in the world game since 1945. He was secretary of the English

Football Association from 1934 to 1961, and even though England was not a member of FIFA, he retained relations with the world body.[8] Walter Winterbottom, England's first manager, says that 'in our own country he took us out of being an insular Association Football League and got us back into world football and this was tremendous'. Winterbottom also praised Rous's exceptional charm and diplomatic skills.[9]

After service in Africa during the First World War, Rous studied at St. Luke's College, Exeter, and then taught at Watford Grammar School. He was not born into the establishment but through football he became an establishment figure. For him, teaching and football were acts of public service. Rous played football at college, then in the Army during the Great War. Though he may have been good enough to play professional football, Rous's commitment to amateur ideals denied him the chance. Instead, he became a referee of international repute.

This is where he made his first impact on world football. His rewriting of the rules of the game was immensely influential. In administration, he went on to modernize the English game, establishing a more efficient bureaucratic base, introducing teaching schemes for all levels of the game – coaching, playing, refereeing. But this mission was about more than just football. Britain was in crisis after the Second World War, losing an Empire and looking for a role. Educating football players as coaches, practitioners as educators, was one way of restoring British prominence in the world game.

The FA had left FIFA in 1928 and Rous believed that it should be reintegrated into the world football family. In a paper which he presented to the Football Association, first drafted in May 1943, he claimed that the activities of the FA's War Emergency Committee had boosted football's international profile by fostering relations with government departments and by establishing links with influential people through co-operation with the armed forces. 'The unparalleled opportunities which the war years have given the Association of being of service to countries other than our own,' he wrote, 'has laid an excellent foundation for post-war international development.'[10]

Rous, recognizing that Britain's political empire was about to shrink dramatically, saw in football a chance to retain some influence over world culture. Yet despite this commitment to modernizaton and expansion, as early as the 1962 World Cup in Chile, in the first years of his presidency, he mourned the loss of the 1930s when international tours were 'free and easy affairs'. A modernizer compared to Rimet, Rous remained nevertheless trapped in an anachronistic set of values. 'We used to look upon it as a sport, as a recreation,' he said in a 1985 BBC interview, 'we had little regard of points and league position and cup competitions. We used to play friendly matches mostly. There was always such a sporting attitude and the winners always clapped the others off the field and so on. That's all changed of course,' he concluded on a regretful note.

From the old world of the English middle class, but negotiating the volatile world of post-colonialism, Rous's life and philosophy were a bundle of contradictions. Rous could be both innovative and traditional, adventurous yet crabbily cautious; modern yet steeped in traditional values. With World Cup finals looking increasingly lucrative, and emerging Third World nations wanting more representation in the world game, Rous appeared ever more old-worldly. The contradictions surrounding Rous were to be cleverly exploited by Havelange.[11] Even within Europe, he was viewed as too English as his home country strolled to its home-based World Cup victory in 1966. An English FIFA president, Drewry, had been in place when Rous secured the 1966 World Cup finals, and one Swiss commentator saw this, and the culminating clinching of the cup, as far too cosy and collusive. In a fascinating document called 'Thoughts on the 1966 World Championship', within FIFA's technical study of the event, the coach to the Swiss national team, Dr A. Foni, argued that top Latin American and European teams were favoured in their respective continents, meeting the weakest teams in opening games, having more rest than their distant cousins. In Chile, for instance, European teams had only 48 hours of rest between games, the Latin Americans recovering and preparing for a day more. Foni had some genuine complaints:

> Four years later the story was repeated in England, naturally with the necessary changes being made and, let me add, with a subtlety that worked still more … in favour of the host country.
>
> I mean simply that England won its victory with the last two games, but also that the premises for this victory were created well in advance: selection of a definite ground, longer breaks between games, decisions by referees that were slightly but very clearly favourable. It is very likely that English football, no doubt one of the best in the world, did not need these little 'nudges', but it is a fact that they were given, they were not refused.[12]

To raise the 'moral and the athletic level of the World Cup', Foni proposed a more representative participation. The 1996 finals had offered just one place for a team from Africa and Asia, promoting a boycott by those confederations and a wild-card entry from North Korea. 'The Jules Rimet Cup will have attained its aim only when the five continents are effectively represented – football probably being the most universal of all sports,' prophesied Foni. Rous's response, in immaculate longhand, was 'disappointed – unfair, shows himself partisan, attacks referees officials organisers, is *bitter* … inaccurate, uninformed'. But there was an objectivity to Foni's analysis – after all, England played all its games at Wembley – and a widespread concern throughout FIFA, that Rous was unwilling to recognize.

When he stood for re-election as FIFA president, claiming that he wanted 'just a couple of years to push through some important schemes', Rous had either a confidence that was misplaced, or he miscalculated the institutional politics of FIFA. Ten years on Rous put his defeat down to the limitless ambitions of his rival: 'I know what activity was being practised by my successor, the appeals that he'd made to countries.'

Rous's recollections have some truth in them, for Havelange did run a ruthless and aggressive campaign, but football administrators in the Third World believed that Rous viewed them and their problems through the eyes of the British imperialist. In the years leading up to the 1974 elections Rous could have sought to challenge and change these perceptions, but he chose not to do so.

HAVELANGE – BRAZIL STRIKES BACK

Brazilian Dr João Havelange can lay valid claim to have done most to shape the destiny of the world's most popular sport. Havelange has a physical presence and power that he was never slow to use in his presidential role in FIFA. 'Havelange had such an aura about him,' comments vice-president David Will, 'people were actually physically scared of him, were frightened of him, in a one-to-one situation. He's devastating. His control of himself is amazing.'

Havelange recalls with relish how he made his way in the world.[13] Son of a Belgian industrialist and arms trader, Jean-Marie Faustin Godefroid Havelange was born on 8 May 1916 in Rio de Janeiro. He went to his father's arms company as a youngster and learned the rudiments of business administration. His father died when he was 18, and he went to work and studied part-time: 'I wasn't earning very much, but I was learning something for life.' After working as an employee for six years, he went to the company boss and told him that he was resigning and never wanted to work for another boss in his life: 'I have never had another boss in my life, except maybe my wife,' he boasted. He branched out on his own, building a business empire in the transport and financial industries of a modernizing Brazil.

Young Havelange was an athlete of some distinction. He had played junior football with Fluminense, the amateur sporting club for Brazil's élite. To belong to this club it was necessary to belong to a family of means – which meant being white. When a famous mixed race player, Carlos Alberto, sought to pass himself off as white by powdering his face in the locker rooms, they called it the 'face-powder club'. Professionalism would later bring more opportunities for non-whites and also herald the end for mediocre upper-class footballers like Havelange. Not good enough to play alongside the talented professionals, he redirected his energies to swimming. From the mid-1930s to the early 1950s Havelange competed at the top, élite levels of his two chosen performance sports, representing Brazil in the Olympics in Berlin in 1936 in swimming, and in Helsinki in 1952 in the water polo team. He said that 'water polo served to discharge my aggressiveness and all my occasional ill humour' – it is a common boast of his that he swims every morning of his life.

Havelange's memories of the 1936 Hitler Olympics are extraordinary. 'The first thing I remember is that the organisation of the transport was perfect, and the equipment and the facilities for 25,000 people were very well arranged.' He remembers the convivial hospitality provided by the Nazis and the seven visits some athlete guests made to hear the 700 musicians playing in the Berlin Philharmonic. 'From the start it was a pleasure to be in Berlin,' Havelange recalled, and like many others he received the travel and privileges that Hitler's and Goebbels's friends in the Olympic movement laid on. Trains could be booked at a 75 per cent discount, and the 20-year-old Havelange saw 25 different cities. The young Havelange appears to have greatly enjoyed his sojourn in Hitler's Germany.

Returned from 1930s Germany, Havelange spent the years of his peak sports performances building up business and social contacts in São Paulo. Brazil declared war against Germany and Italy on 22 August 1942. Brazil had a quiet war. It joined the defence of the South Atlantic against Axis submarines and also sent an expeditionary force to Italy in 1944, which conducted itself courageously in several bloody engagements. Back home, the young entrepreneur sensed some real business openings in the transport industry. With the State in temporary control of the economy and a black market thriving, it was a busy and productive war for a young businessman on the make. The city government requisitioned the transport system, creating a municipal company. This was not to Havelange's liking, nor in line with his individualist market philosophy, but he was not slow to spot a business opportunity around the corner. In his own words, the post-war years were for him ones of opportunity for fighting government interference in the market. 'Since I did not want to be a public servant, I and some friends founded the Viação Cometa in 1947.'

By the mid-1950s Havelange had established a power base in national business networks. His time with the steel-making company Belgo-Mineira helped him learn how to oil the wheels of bureaucracy. Senior partners realized that if they wanted to speed their imported buses through customs, young João was their man. Havelange was a minority shareholder, but was chosen as director-president of Viação Cometa.

Contacts in the sports world were big-business contacts too. During his São Paulo years, Havelange had swum and played water polo at the Espéria rowing club, cultivating and consolidating friendships with some of the country's leading industrialists. From his mid-20s onwards he was displaying the qualities of the wheeler-dealer fixer that would serve him well for the following half century. No other world sports figure had combined sports and business networking and interests so closely, so early in the century of modern and global sport.

In Havelange's view, just being a Brazilian made him the man for FIFA's top job. 'It was an advantage for me when I became president of FIFA,' he says, 'that since a small child I have lived together with all the different races and understood their mentalities. It is nothing new for me to be in FIFA's multi-racial environment … In São Paulo and Rio there are streets with Arabs living on one side and Jews on the other side and they live in the same street in perfect harmony.'

Havelange points out that Brazil is the eighth largest industrial power in the world, that São Paulo is a city like those of Germany. Yet Northern Brazil is less developed, a little like Africa. Havelange claims that Brazil is both a mid-point and microcosm of the world: a leader of the non-aligned nations with First, Second and Third World features. With this self-image Havelange cleverly positions himself as representative of the advanced world, as much as of the Third World – but with an empathy for the whole of the world.

Trading on his achievements in the swimming pool and associated networks and contacts, in the late 1950s Havelange brought his business and administrative skills into Brazilian sport. His base in the Brazilian Sports Federation (the CBD) gave him authority over the country's major sports, including football. 'I brought with me the entrepreneurial skills, the business skills from my own company to the federation,' he says. 'There were just [sports] coaches, but I brought in specialist doctors, administrators for the federation to give it a wider basis. This is what made the difference and why we won the World Cup in 1958, 1962 and 1970.' Havelange recognized the potential football had to promote Brazil's international image, and his own global profile in both sport and business.

He used his experience of restructuring football in Brazil, with an expanded national and regional league and cup set-up underpinned by commercial intervention, as a model for the expansion of the world game when he seized FIFA's reins of power from Englishman, Sir Stanley Rous, in 1974.[14] Once at the FIFA helm, Havelange set about taking control of world football from its established North European, Anglo-Saxon stronghold. To do this he would have to fulfil the commitments he had made to the developing world – especially Africa, and Asia – during his election campaign. There were eight of these: the increase in the number of World Cup final teams, from 16 to 24; the creation of a junior, under-20 World Championship; the construction of a new FIFA headquarters; the provision of materials to needy national associations; help in stadium development and improvement; more courses for professionals; medical and technical help; and the introduction of an inter-continental club championship. Rous was no match for this manifesto, and Havelange won the presidency on the second ballot.

When Havelange took over at FIFA, it was a modest operation with few personnel and negligible finances, it had less than 100 members and operated a single tournament, a 16-nation World Cup final. After a quarter a century, when Havelange stepped down, on the eve of the first ever 32-nation senior competition, according to his own estimates FIFA had more than $4 billion in its coffers, and as a global industry he reckoned football to be worth in the region of $250 billion annually, way in excess of General Motors' $170 billion. This huge expansion, including the addition of a series of world championships for youth and women, was achieved in partnership with transnational media partners and global business interests including the giants Coca-Cola, Adidas and McDonald's. Towards the end of his 24 years in power, Havelange listed the 11 competitions that FIFA now stages, and summarized his achievements:

For all of these 11 competitions, FIFA bears the cost of travelling, board, accommodation and local transport.

Allow me to inform you that the principle for the evolution of industry lies in improvement and this also applies to football. Since I have been President of FIFA, which is now 22 years, we have organised courses for technical matters, refereeing courses, sports medicine courses as well as administration courses in every continent on a permanent basis, for the benefit of approximately 40,000 people. This is the reason for the global expansion of the game.

Apart from that, the FIFA administration service may be considered perfect. The economic and financial situation due to the development which has taken place has been envied. Under the economic aspect, I would mention the buildings which have been constructed and acquired in favour of the continuity of football development. On the financial side we are, together with our sponsors, attaining such conditions which will permit us to reach all our aims. [Letter to Professor Tomlinson, dated Zurich, 29 October 1996]

Not much false modesty here! A mere six weeks or so later, Havelange was to announce that he would not stand again, so fuelling speculation on his succession, and giving his successor, Joseph 'Sepp' Blatter, plenty of time in which to plot his strategy. Havelange bowed out from the presidency with a sense of mission accomplished.

Havelange, with the help of his close ally and confidant, the late Horst Dassler of Adidas, had been the first to recognize the full commercial potential of sport in the global market, and to open the game to the influences of new media and new markets.[15] Havelange was also a consummate political operator who ruled FIFA in autocratic style. Henry Kissinger, having acted as spokesman for the USA's failed bid to host the 1986 World Cup, experienced Havelange's managerial style. 'It made me feel nostalgic for the Middle-East,' he said. British sports minister, Tony Banks, declared in 1998 that compared with Westminster, the politics of FIFA in the Havelange era were 'positively Byzantine'.

Former FIFA media director, Guido Tognoni, said that on a clear and sunny day 'Havelange could make you believe that the sky was red when it was really blue.' People wonder at Havelange's almost supernatural powers of strength and concentration. 'Havelange was a master of managing meetings,' Tognoni recalled, 'he was also a master of giving people the feeling that they are important without giving power away. He was just a master of power. He was always fully informed about everything, whereas the members, they were not professionals, they had to eat what was served.' After a reflective pause, Tognoni concluded that Havelange 'had the power to do everything that he wanted'.

In his early pronouncements on the race to host the 1998 Finals, the FIFA president had not indicated that France was the favoured host. In late 1988 –

within five months of receiving his Nobel Peace Prize nomination from the Swiss Football Association – he praised Switzerland for its good transport network, telecommunications systems, hotel provision and stable currency. Havelange told the Swiss that they were 'able to organise an outstanding World Cup as in 1954', and that while the stadiums would require extensions and renovation, 'the financial strength of the country' meant that this would present no problem. But it was France that gained the Finals, and Havelange himself a Légion d'honneur along the way to the decision.

Like many other sports leaders, Havelange has claimed to be promoting world peace through sport. He claimed to have done much through football to bring China fully into world economic and political networks. He declared high hopes that the co-hosting arrangement between Japan and South Korea for World Cup 2002 would have a positive impact on international relations even though – close as he was to Japanese interests – he had been bitterly opposed to the principle of co-hosting.

One of his final ambitions was to organize an international 'friendly' between Israel and the fledgling Palestinian state in New York, the seat of the United Nations, to show, in his words 'that football can succeed where politicians cannot'. This was initiated by US Vice-President Al Gore, who approached Havelange during the 1994 World Cup finals in the United States. Havelange recalls that Gore was 'very upset' when the suggestion was not received with great enthusiasm, the FIFA boss initially saying, 'No, we are a sport, we are not politics in that sense.' Magnanimously, in his own telling, Havelange reconsidered and through the liaison of Prince Faisal of Saudi communicated with the Saudi King, Fahed, who 'offered to give the Palestine Football Federation 100 million dollars to get them going. Now things have moved on and Palestine is a more clearly defined political entity.'

Havelange, within a year, was seeking to arrange this game for the end of 1997. Palestine was accepted as a full FIFA member at the June 1998 Congress. It was a defining moment when the Palestine delegate carried its flag around the Equinox stadium, welcomed along with a few other nations as the newest members of the FIFA family. There were few doubts as to where its vote would go in the election for the FIFA presidency later in the day.

Havelange claims that FIFA is truly democratic, with each member country having one vote. But the secret ballot, one member one vote system gives him absolute control. Vanuatu has the same voting rights in a FIFA congress election as Germany, the Faroe Islands the same voting weight as Brazil. For years this has worried more powerful football nations, as voting outcomes and decisions can be assured from the accumulated commitment of tiny constituencies. Majorities necessary to change the rules, procedures or statutes of FIFA are exceedingly difficult to mobilize or muster.

In the 1970s, if world football was to become truly global, Havelange was FIFA's man, fulfilling his 1974 election promises and making football a truly world game. The Brazilian himself is not slow to claim credit for they way he, personally, remodelled FIFA to this end, claiming as he does the credit for making the perfect organization.

FIFA claims to be non-commercial as well as democratic. Under Swiss law it has non-commercial, almost charitable status – despite its $4 billion reserves – and escapes the usual company reporting requirements. A FIFA document in 1984 claimed that Havelange was a 'football magnate who combined the qualities of far-sightedness and openness, an entrepreneur in body and soul' who 'in no time transformed an administration-oriented institution into a dynamic enterprise brimming with new ideas and the will to see them through, so that now the administration is managed in the form of a modern firm'.[16] Guido Tognoni, though, said that 'people say that he was leading FIFA like an industry – but he was leading FIFA like a private enterprise, like a proprietor'. 'As if he owned it?' I asked. 'Yes, exactly,' said Tognoni.

As late as the end of the 1990s, deals on the scale of the television rights for the World Cup finals of 2006 were completed without reference to FIFA's executive committee. UK associations' representative David Will recalls, 'It's depressing. I think we just have to keep chipping away at this. The first task is to have the committees properly chosen, and not to have committees packed with pay-offs. We don't know how the [2006 television] deal was made. Per Omdal and I have seen the contracts, but we asked that the contracts be laid before the Executive Committee for final approval, and instead we were told at the Executive Committee that the contracts were signed that day.'

Havelange has ridden a torrent of allegations concerning missing funds in the accounts of the Brazilian sports federation, involvement in arms deals and other murky business practices, whilst keeping his football empire together on the basis of the concept of the family. This concept has had as its binding theme the idea of the family inherited from Rimet, but reinvented in the Havelange era towards world markets and huge profits.

Even as he planned for his retirement in 1998, Havelange worked ceaselessly behind the scenes to ensure that the regime he had developed at FIFA House would continue through the election of his hand-picked protégé, Joseph 'Sepp' Blatter.

Havelange believes that he has done no wrong. Responding to criticism of his visit to Nigeria as dissident Ken Saro Wiwa was about to be executed, Havelange uttered a stunningly revealing personal philosophy: 'I don't want to make any comparisons with the Pope, but he is also criticised from time to time, and his reply is silence. I too am sometimes criticised, so explanations about such matters are superfluous.' HEAD up his ass

FIFA'S FUTURE – BLATTER TAKES CHARGE

Sepp Blatter emerged victorious in the battle for the FIFA presidency in June 1998.[17] He had secured sufficient support from African and European countries to fracture the Europe–Africa alliance behind UEFA president Lennart Johansson. Blatter's campaign was masterfully organized, with the support of a Swiss commercial partner and a private jet provided by Qatar. Blatter prospered on the back of his long-standing working partnership with Havelange, and all of the infrastructure of FIFA that had aided his bid long before he formally entered the race. The circumstances in which so many nations supported Blatter are shrouded in controversy,[18] but his campaigning strategy was so effective that he came out of the first ballot with 111 votes to Johansson's 80. The devastated Swede soon realized that there was little point in proceeding to a second ballot.

Havelange, with heavy irony, allied to consummate diplomatic skill, praised the European president as 'sportsman, gentleman, leader and friend', whose 'qualities and values' would help the football family enter the next century. Blatter hailed his defeated rival as 'a great personality, fair and realistic' and pledged 'to unite football' and establish 'continuity in the good sense'. 'I am a servant of football,' beamed Blatter. 'I shall play, live and breathe football,' he said. 'I am deeply, deeply touched, deeply, and offer a message of friendship, openness, understanding, a message of solidarity.'

Blatter had learned well under Havelange's tutelage, and he understood football politics in Africa. While Johansson busied himself working on the hierarchy of the African confederation, Blatter, often accompanied by Havelange, met the representatives of some of the continent's remotest and poorest countries, making personal contact with those who would be marking the ballot cards in Paris in June. It was a strategy that worked for Havelange in 1974 and it was about to work for Blatter in 1998.

Blatter was steeped in the world of international sports politics. He had business and administration experience as an organizer of the 1972 and 1976 Olympic Games, and had been general secretary of the Swiss ice-hockey federation. As Director of Sports Timing and Public Relations at Longines SA, he was noticed by Adidas boss Horst Dassler. Dassler alerted Havelange to Blatter's qualities, and Havelange brought him in to FIFA, where he worked on the implementation of Havelange's programme, and the funding needed from early commercial partners such as Coca-Cola and Adidas itself. Blatter rose quickly through FIFA's hierarchy, becoming general secretary in 1981, and even marrying the former general secretary's daughter.

At the launch of his presidential campaign Blatter, like many of those before him, claimed that football stands for basic education, shapes character and combative spirit, and fosters respect and discipline. It can make a valuable contribution to health, he added. And it is theatre, entertainment, art. 'But, first and foremost,' he told his audience, 'it is an endless source of passion and excitement. It stirs the emotions and can move its enthusiasts to tears of joy or frustration like no other game and it is for everybody.'

In a veiled reference to the European base of Johansson's campaign Blatter stressed the 'universality' of the sport, and was nominated by several national associations, initially by Jamaica and the United States. Others included countries from the Gulf and South America.

As the date of FIFA's first contested presidential election for almost a quarter of a century drew closer, Johansson's Euro-African alliance was looking increasingly fragile. Evidence of Blatter's confidence emerged when he emphatically rejected Johansson's offer that he could continue as general secretary should he fail to become president. Here was serious evidence of the Swiss's confidence.

At the Equinox congress hall in June 1998, as freelance heavies and government agents patrolled the razor-wired fences, the FIFA family anointed Blatter as its new president. With a public fanfare, England had jumped ship from Johannson at the last minute; having backed a winner, Alec McGivan, England's 2006 campaign manager, looked smug.[19]

In his last presidential address Havelange said that he took his leave with indelible memories of 'Sepp Blatter at my side for 23 years. I leave, with a clear conscience, the governing body of the world's, the planet's most popular sport.' With his protégé in charge, Havelange would be close to the action for the foreseeable future.

In the Equinox hall the post-mortem on the result was under way. Questions were still swirling. Mihir Bose of *The Daily Telegraph* asked Blatter, 'Was your campaign corrupt? Is FIFA not clean?' Blatter's face tightened, his smile subsided. 'The accounts were cleared in congress,' he snarled, 'no questions were asked then.' Show me my accusers, demanded Blatter. 'It might become uncomfortable for anyone whose name you mention.' The day after Blatter's victory, Kenya's *Daily Nation* reported how grateful the Kenyan football federation was to former president Havelange for promising to pay team travel costs to an obscure regional tournament in Rwanda. Chairman of the federation, Peter Kenneth, said in Paris, 'It has been a gruelling battle but in the final analysis we are proud to have been associated with the winning candidate.' 'You've got the FIFA you want, you want this FIFA of corruption, that's what you've got. Get on with it,' said one executive committee member to another. The pompous and acidic response said it all. 'Sure it's all about money. Your side didn't spend enough money.'

Once in power new president Blatter moved swiftly to neutralize his enemies. In his first Exco (Executive Committee) meeting he dropped a controversial proposal to create a special bureau – an inner circle empowered to take decisions outside of the executive committee 'to cope with FIFA's increasing volume of work'. Johansson and his supporters would never have stood for this. Cleverly, Blatter withdrew his proposal at the last minute, proposing instead to double the number of full Exco meetings. Members would have to jet in to world capitals twice as often now, for the continuing (FIFA's motto) 'good of the game'.

In his second meeting Blatter reshuffled the FIFA committees, giving his supporters key positions, but also making sure that potential opponents were kept inside the FIFA family. David Will was rewarded for his open commitment to Johansson by being removed from the chairs of the prestigious referees and legal committees, and handed the grand-sounding – but lower profile – national associations' committee. Blatter also proposed that for the first time Exco members should be paid in addition to already generous expenses. He suggested $50,000 a year. There were no objections from committee members.

*money
money
money*

The English FA had turned its back on the European alliance, and publicly backed Blatter for the presidency, and had also tried to mobilize Wales and Northern Ireland in an attempt to discredit Scot David Will, and so get the FA president, Keith Wiseman, onto the FIFA committee that would be voting for the World Cup finals 2006. This had involved a projected gift to the Welsh FA of more than three million pounds.[20] Trying to enter the corridors of power of world football, the English managed to look both arrogant and naïve, premised as their actions were on behind-the-scenes deal-making with FIFA men whose words of support often had proved worthless to football lobbyists world-wide throughout the previous two decades.

Blatter provided FIFA with continuity, but within his first year showed that he lacked the presidential gravitas of his Brazilian mentor. His suggestions that the World Cup be held every two years, and his vigorous promotion of a World Club championship, would be controversial issues. He accepted the invitation to become the International Olympic Committee's (IOC) 108th member, in the wake of its expulsion of exposed corrupt members, and its drive to clean up its act following bribery and voting scandals. But most revealing was his lack of authority over the FIFA Congress. In Los Angeles, in June 1999, the Asian delegation walked out in protest at not getting an extra place in the 2002 finals, to be co-hosted by South Korea and Japan.

CONCLUSION

In the earlier days of FIFA, figures such as Rimet and Rous led world football almost as volunteers, as idealist missionaries, with backgrounds in education and public service. Their successors were from far different backgrounds, in business, economics and marketing. Whilst a politics of football has driven FIFA dynamics throughout its history, the motives of the men who made FIFA have differed as the power base switched from France and England to Brazil and non-aligned Switzerland. While FIFA men exalted their work 'for the good of the game' in glitzy surroundings cushioned by modern communications technology, they would be gleefully rubbing their hands knowing that FIFA was now one of the most high profile and lucrative businesses in the global consumer and cultural industry. In whatever directions FIFA might steer the game in the years and decades ahead remains to be seen. Processes of rapid technological change, commercial development and cultural globalization seem set to transform football. Whatever the response of the FIFA men who run the game might be, it seems certain that – as has been the case for nearly a century – this will be determined, in part at least, by geo-political machinations and Machiavellian practices at the heart of the organization.

NOTES

I am grateful to personnel at and within FIFA for provision of materials and expression of views, to Rose Marie Breitenstein for access to her collection of Sir Stanley Rous's papers, to the (English) FA for access to their records and archives, and to Professor John Sugden for detailed editorial responses to some drafts of material included in this essay. Parts of this study draw upon collaborative work with Professor Sugden, which is included in the book *Great Balls of Fire: How Big Money is Hijacking World Football* (Edinburgh: Mainstream Publishing, 1999). Thank you too to the organizers of the University of Leicester's 'Football 2000' symposium in September 1998, for their invitation to speak and their patience in awaiting delivery of this piece.

1. For overviews of FIFA's emerging importance throughout the twentieth century and global power struggles around football see: A. Tomlinson, 'Going Global: The FIFA Story', in A. Tomlinson and G. Whannel (eds.), *Off the Ball: The Football World Cup* (London: Pluto Press, 1986); A. Tomlinson, 'FIFA and the World Cup: The Expanding Football Family', in J. Sugden and A. Tomlinson (eds.), *Hosts and Champions: Soccer Cultures, National Identities and the USA World Cup* (Aldershot: Ashgate/Arena, 1994), pp.13–33, and J. Sugden and A. Tomlinson, *FIFA and the Contest for World Football – Who Rules the Peoples' Game?* (Cambridge: Polity Press, 1998).
2. See J. Sugden and A. Tomlinson, 'FIFA's World Cup Wars', in *New Statesman*, 1 May 1998, 38–9 and J. Sugden and A. Tomlinson, *Great Balls of Fire: How Big Money is Hijacking World Football* (Edinburgh: Mainstream Publishing, 1999).
3. See H. Guldemont and B. Deps, *100 Ans de football en Belgique* (Brussels: Union Royale Belge des Sociétés de Football Association, 1995).
4. See S. Inglis, *League Football and the Men Who Made It* (London: Willow Books/Collins, 1988) and A. Tomlinson, *The Game's Up: Essays in the Cultural Analysis of Sport, Leisure and Popular Culture* (Aldershot: Ashgate/Arena, 1999), p.155.
5. See A. Tomlinson 'The Game's Up', p.100; I draw upon this piece for the detail on FIFA's earliest years.
6. The following discussion of Rimet draws upon two main sources: J.-Y. Guillain, *La Coupe du Monde de Football – L'Oeuvre de Jules Rimet* (Paris: Editions Amphora, 1998) and S. Rous, *Football Worlds – A Lifetime in Sport* (London: Faber and Faber, 1978). It uses material, too, that is also reported in Sugden and Tomlinson 'Great Balls'.
7. See Rous. 'Football Worlds', 131.
8. See P. Beck, 'Going to War, Peaceful Coexistence or Virtual Membership?: British Football and FIFA, 1928–46', *International Journal of the History of Sport*, 17,1 (March 2000).
9. Winterbottom was talking in a BBC radio tribute to Rous; and in a personal interview with the author, 24 November 1996.
10. S. Rous, 'Post-war development – a memorandum prepared by the War Emergency Committee for the Consideration of the Council', May 1943; and 'Post-war development – an Interim Report', October 1944. Both these papers are in the minute books of the Football Association's Council.
11. See J. Sugden and A. Tomlinson, *FIFA and the Contest*; J. Sugden and A. Tomlinson, 'Global Power Struggles in World Football: FIFA and UEFA 1954–1974, and their Legacy', *International Journal of the History of Sport*, 14, 2 (1997), 1–25.
12. This annotated document is in the Sir Stanley Rous papers kept by Rose Marie Breitenstein, a copy of which is in the Rous papers in the Sports Cultures Archive for Investigative Research (SCAIR), Sport and Leisure Cultures, Chelsea School Research Centre, University of Brighton.
13. This discussion of Havelange draws upon: J. Sugden and A. Tomlinson, *FIFA and the Contest; Great Balls*; D. Yallop, *How They Stole the Game* (London: Poetic Publishing, 1999); E.J. Farah (ed.), *Young Havelange: FIFA in the Third Millennium* (São Paulo: J.S. Propaganda Ltd, 1996); and an interview by the author with Havelange, in Cairo, September 1997.
14. See J. Sugden, A. Tomlinson and P. Darby, 'FIFA versus UEFA in the Struggle for the Control of

World Football', in A. Brown (ed.), *Fanatics! Power, Identity and Fandom in Football* (London: Routledge, 1998), pp.11–31.

15. See J. Sugden and A. Tomlinson, 'FIFA and the Marketing of World Football', in G. Lines, I. McDonald and U. Merkel (eds.), *The Production and Consumption of Sport Cultures: Leisure, Culture and Commerce* (Eastbourne: LSA Publications, 1998), pp.55–73.

16. And this was reiterated in FIFA, *90 Years of FIFA, Souvenir Edition* (Zurich: FIFA, 1994), p.6: 'Havelange transformed an administration-oriented institution into a dynamic enterprise brimming with new ideas and the will to see them through.' A decade more of new ideas, still the same wording and tribute.

17. The discussion of Blatter is based upon my personal observation of proceedings during the FIFA Congress in Paris, on 8 June 1998, and of Blatter at various hotels, stadiums and functions throughout that tournament; as well as continued monitoring of his style and impact during his first year of presidential office.

18. See Yallop, *How They Stole*; and J. Sugden and A. Tomlinson, *Great Balls*.

19. On England's bidding see also: J. Sugden and A. Tomlinson, 'War of the Worlds', in *When Saturday Comes*, 143 (January 1999), 28–9; J. Sugden and A. Tomlinson, 'Out of Their League', in *When Saturday Comes*, 144 (March 1999), 22–3. On the public relations elements of the offer to Wales, see A. Tomlinson, 'Executive Distress', *When Saturday Comes*, 146 (April 1999), 18–19.

20. At the end of 1998 controversy surrounding this 'gift' led to the departure of Graham Kelly, General Secretary, and Keith Wiseman, President, from their post and position at the English FA.

5

The Administration of Football in the Twenty-First Century

PAT DAY

I joined the (English) Football Association (FA) in July 1965 as a Junior Secretary and over the next 33 years, as my career in football administration progressed, I was able to witness at first hand the development of football not only in England but throughout the world. In the last half of the twentieth century we have seen dramatic changes in the organization and participation of football at domestic and international level. Areas of change have included the elimination of the maximum wage, the growing role of television companies, the development of marketing and commercial opportunities and the increased importance placed on both club and national team participation in international competitions. These changes form the context in which football administrators will operate in the twenty-first century.

In July 1965 the Football Association was just 12 months away from hosting the 1966 World Cup finals, involving 16 national teams. At that time the Association, as the governing body, had overall responsibility for the control of the game throughout England. The professional game, involving 92 clubs in four divisions, was managed by the Football League, and the League came under the jurisdiction of the Association. At the turn of the new century, the Football Association is again bidding to host a World Cup final tournament, but this time the event will involve 32 national teams and have a budget of over £9 million solely devoted to the bid to host the tournament. Meanwhile, what was the Football League has split and the top 20 clubs now form the FA Premier League. The remaining 72 clubs form the three divisions of the Football League. However, the principle of fluid club movement across the whole game – of promotion and relegation – continues, enabling clubs such as Wimbledon, a strong amateur club in the late 1950s and early 1960s, to achieve promotion to the most senior league in the country.

All levels of the professional game, however, have had to face up to the problems created due to the poor safety standards within its stadiums and the hooligan element who have chosen to follow football, both at home and abroad, seriously damaging the reputation of genuine English football supporters. The two disasters in May 1985 – the fire at Bradford City's Valley Parade ground and the hooliganism at Heysel Stadium – and the Hillsborough stadium disaster of

April 1989 – when Liverpool supporters at the Lepping's Lane End were crushed shortly after the start of the FA Cup semi-final tie between Liverpool and Nottingham Forest – resulted in the deaths of many innocent football supporters. These events necessitated all those connected with the game to work closely with government and other relevant authorities both to provide safer stadiums for football supporters and also to rid the game of those followers whose sole purpose was to create violence both within the stadiums and in their environs.

In the late twentieth century the reputation of English football was damaged immeasurably by hooliganism, both at home and abroad. As a result of close co-operation between football authorities, government and other authorities, great improvements have been achieved domestically to ensure that genuine supporters are able to follow their chosen team in a safe and secure environment. However, many will argue that the problem has not been solved, but only controlled and it will be necessary for the responsible parties to continue in their efforts to rid the game of this mindless minority as we move beyond the year 2000.

However, as a result of the hooliganism problems in the '70s and early '80s, culminating in the aforementioned Heysel Stadium disaster in 1985 (when Liverpool FC were competing in the final of the European Champion Clubs' Cup competition), we saw English clubs barred from international competition for five years. It was indeed fortunate that a similar ban was not placed on the national team and, in an effort to ensure that such a ban was not imposed, when England qualified for the World Cup finals in Italy in 1990 the Football Association established the England Travel Club (now called the England Members' Club). This club was designed to ensure that only genuine and responsible English football supporters were able to purchase tickets for England's matches and over the last ten years the organization has gone from strength to strength. Followers of the national team now see it as the correct vehicle through which they can support the side.

More recently the England Members' Club has established national and regional liaison groups as a means of promoting the interests of its members. Through these liaison groups, the Football Association has the opportunity to work closely with a cross-section of supporters throughout the country and to develop objectives for the benefit of the game as a whole. For many years football supporters have argued that they were an essential part of the game and yet did not have a voice. There are now two main supporters' organizations, the National Federation of Football Supporters Clubs and the Football Supporters' Association; the latter founded in the aftermath of the Heysel disaster. These bodies now meet senior representatives of the various football authorities on a regular basis and there is no doubt that through these meetings and through liaison with bodies such as the England Members' Club the supporter now has a clear channel through which to express his or her views and to influence the overall organization of the game. From an administrator's point of view, it would be inconceivable that their role should diminish as we enter the new century.

However, despite the problems that beset the game in the last half of the twentieth century, football remains our national sport and retains an extraordinarily high profile within our society. I do not believe anybody could have forecast the changes that have occurred within the game in the past 50 years and it would be a brave person indeed who was prepared to forecast where the game would be in the next 20 years, let alone by the middle or even towards the end of the twenty-first century. But, having assessed and learned from the events over the last 50 years, there are certain measures which those responsible for the control of the game in this country will undoubtedly follow in order to safeguard the interests of football at all levels – from the performance of the national team to the ongoing development of the game at grass roots – to ensure not only that where talent exists it has an opportunity to flourish, but also that all those with an interest to participate at their chosen level are able to do so.

Co-operation and liaison between football authorities and the government has increased considerably in recent years, in large part as a necessary response to the hooligan problem. There is no doubt that this co-operation must be in the interests of all those who care about the game. We have seen the impact that the performance of our national team has upon our society; from winning the World Cup in 1966 to reaching the semi-final stages of both the 1990 World Cup finals in Italy and the European Championships (hosted by England) in 1996. However, the interest and participation in our national game are not reflected in the successes we might expect our national team to achieve on the field. Time and again in recent years other countries have achieved comparatively greater success when the total population and the number of participants in football within their own country is considerably less than that of England. This shortfall remains a particularly strong concern for football administrators.

To address this, under the leadership of the Football Association's Technical Director (at the time of writing, Howard Wilkinson), those responsible for the development of football skills in this country have recognized the importance of having a strong coaching infrastructure. Such an infrastructure ensures that, from a very early age, participants have the opportunity to develop their talent and enhance their skills. One of the major developments in this area is the establishment of football academies at various clubs throughout the country and it will be interesting to assess the results of these academies in the first quarter of the next century.

Yet it will also be important to ensure that a proper balance is maintained between the promotion of the game at the domestic and the international level. With the success of the FA Premier League, there is increasing pressure on the governing body to limit its demands on players for the national team. With the changes in the format of the UEFA Champions League in the 1999/2000 season and, with them, the dramatic increase in revenue for participating clubs, there is likely to be further pressure on governing bodies of football throughout Europe in relation to the standing of their own domestic competitions. Perhaps the first sign of this was the decision of Manchester United FC not to participate in the FA Cup – or more correctly, the FA Challenge Cup competition – in the 1999/2000 season. This decision has been the subject of considerable comment – from all parts of the game, the media and from many political figures. Whatever the pros and cons, there is no doubt that this decision reflects the increasing demands being placed on top domestic clubs to excel at the international level. These demands have, in part, led to an influx of overseas players bolstering the squads of our senior clubs in recent years. This raises concerns for those charged with protecting the interests of the game in this country; more specifically, concerns over the number of opportunities for young and developing players. At the same time though, considerable emphasis must be placed on the success of the national team and, therefore, there is an ongoing need for a country's top players to be available for international fixtures. It has been suggested that one compromise to this club–country dilemma might be that a club's players should not be required for 'friendly' international matches. However, it would be unreasonable to expect a national coach to have his players available only for competitive fixtures; when, for instance, would the coach be able to experiment with new players, systems or tactics? What is essential, therefore, is that the correct balance is achieved between club and national fixtures and this might be one of the greatest challenges facing the administrators of the game in the twenty-first century.

The major domestic and international fixtures in England have, since 1923, been played at Wembley Stadium and there is no doubt that it is the dream of every top player throughout the world to play on its 'hallowed turf'. The ground is commonly known as the 'Venue of Legends' and it has witnessed some truly memorable events in its lifetime including the 1948 Olympic Games, the 1966 World Cup final and, more recently, the final of the 1996 European Championships. For some years its owners had endeavoured to improve the facilities of the stadium to keep pace with modern stadiums by gradual refurbishment including, for instance, the conversion of Wembley into a covered, all-seater stadium. However, it has been apparent for some time that a continuous refurbishment plan would not bring Wembley up to the standard of the purpose-built football stadiums that have been developed throughout the world in the last decade. With the launch of the National Lottery in November 1994 substantial funds have been generated with much being directed into sport. With this has come the opportunity for football and other authorities to debate not just the possibility of a new national stadium but also where it should be located. After lengthy debate, numerous meetings and the input of hundreds of experts from various fields, it was finally decided that the home of the national stadium should remain at Wembley. Moreover, in order to provide a stadium which would be considered not just a first-class venue but the best in the world for many years to come, it would be necessary to knock down the current stadium and build in its place a world-class replacement. There have been many twists and turns throughout the process, during which the current stadium and its site have been purchased by a subsidiary company of the Football Association, with the assistance of National Lottery funding. There are many obstacles still to be overcome but we look forward to the dream becoming reality. Early in the new millennium Wembley will once again be able to boast the best football stadium in the world.

The development of this new national stadium is, of course, an essential element of the Football Association's bid to host the World Cup in 2006. The 1990s have seen a great improvement in English football stadiums, assisted initially by grants from the Football Trust but also more recently by National Lottery funding. As we move into the next century many clubs are planning to develop their current stadiums or to relocate to a new site, with the aim of improving their facilities and increasing their capacities, but also in a bid to provide their supporters with a 'home' of which they may be proud. Few people would argue with the fact that England is able to provide some of the best football stadiums in the world. With the new national stadium finally becoming a reality, it provides the England bid with further compelling arguments in the campaign to host the World Cup finals in 2006. As the campaign moves into the final stages England has every reason to be hopeful that it will succeed but, whatever the outcome, it can take comfort from the fact that those responsible have run an excellent campaign, always focusing on positive issues. What a tremendous achievement it will be if, before the first year of the new millennium is passed, England is awarded the 2006 Final tournament.

Hosting such tournaments is, of course, a great honour but they do bring with them their own administrative problems. With the passing of each European Championship or World Cup final in the last half of the twentieth century, so we have witnessed an ever-increasing expectancy on the part of participants, supporters and commercial partners. For both tournaments the number of participants have doubled and, with the increase in revenue generated through commercial partners, so the demands of those partners have also increased. Not surprisingly, the participants expect the highest standards, not just as far as stadiums are concerned, but also for training facilities, accommodation and internal transport. At the same time, with the improved facilities that football supporters are becoming accustomed to throughout the world, they attend these tournaments in the expectation of receiving a high quality service. When England was awarded the 1996 European Championships in May 1992 it was on the basis that it would involve eight teams. Shortly afterwards it was decided to double the number of countries competing in the tournament. The Football Association readily accepted this challenge and, under the leadership of the Tournament Director, Glen Kirton, it is generally accepted that the Association hosted the most successful European Championships to date.

But perhaps the organizational issue which has received most publicity in recent years is the ticket allocation process. Whilst this is the case for major sports events in general, it is an issue which has been particularly prominent in recent football World Cups and European Championships. Ticketing is perhaps the least glamorous element in the organization of these tournaments, but it is essential that it is given careful attention in the early planning in order to ensure that the general public get to see the matches that they want to see, that the presence of ticket touts is minimized, and that matches are played in stadiums which are full. By avoiding such chaos and confusion the organizers can prevent detrimental publicity in the weeks immediately before and during the tournament. In its planning for Euro '96, the Football Association, in consultation with Union of European Football Associations (UEFA), developed a new ticketing strategy which enabled it not only to market tickets some two and a half years before the tournament began but also at the same time to develop a strategy to enable the genuine supporters of the home and visiting sides to follow their teams, not just in the group stage but throughout the knock-out matches up to and including the final. Any new system will not be perfect but the Football Association was pleased to see that in the planning for Euro 2000, UEFA and the host countries of that tournament (Belgium and Holland) have retained and developed much of the ticketing strategy that was used in 1996. It was unfortunate that the organizers of France '98 did not operate a similar ticketing strategy for their tournament, but it must be hoped that in future there will be closer co-operation between host associations of these and similar tournaments to ensure that experiences are shared in order to develop and improve systems for future use.

Finally, perhaps one of the most interesting developments we will see in the first part of the twenty-first century is the development of women's football in England. The organization of women's football in England came under the jurisdiction of the Football Association in 1969, but it was only in the early 1990s, with the formation of the Women's Football Alliance and direct representation on the Football Association's Council, that the Association took direct responsibility for the promotion of girls' and women's football throughout the country. Since that time, and following the recruitment of full-time staff with specific responsibility for the development of girls' and women's football, we have seen that part of the game flourish. However, there is still a long way to go before we catch up with our colleagues in a number of other countries (in particular America, China and many Scandinavian nations). I have no doubt that all those directly involved with the promotion and development of the game will welcome this challenge in a part of the sport that has been sadly neglected for too many years.

As mentioned earlier in this essay, the last two or three years of the twentieth century saw a much closer co-operation between football authorities and Government. Indeed, the support of the Government is an essential element in our World Cup 2006 bid. However, this co-operation also results from a general recognition of the important role that football plays in our society today. The fact that it is our national sport is perhaps not surprising. It provides the opportunity for those in our community both to participate at their chosen level and to follow their local and national teams in various competitions for virtually 11 months of the year. It was essential that every effort was made to combat the hooliganism problem which dogged the game in the latter part of the century. As a result of the improvements in safety and security that have been achieved in and around stadiums, we have witnessed an increasing number of females and families developing an interest in football and supporting their chosen team. There are many challenges awaiting football in the twenty-first century including:

- the need for our national team to achieve a consistent level of excellence whilst ensuring that the grass roots of the game continue to flourish;

- the provision for a fair distribution of the money that is generated from the game, so that football prospers at all levels and that an unbridgeable gulf does not develop;

- and ensuring that those responsible for commercial and marketing strategies continue to work in the interests of the sport.

Those charged with the management of our national game face many challenges in the new century and have a heavy responsibility to ensure that football in this country goes from strength to strength for the benefit of future generations.

6

Democracy and Fandom: Developing a Supporters' Trust at Northampton Town FC

BRIAN LOMAX

The relationship between the football industry, football clubs and supporters is complex. Although the contemporary football industry has become big business, and many clubs are placing marketing activities at the top of their agendas,[1] it is too simplistic to view fans in terms of merely being 'customers' of the game. Their commitment normally extends to investing a degree of time, energy and loyalty, as well as money, into the club they support. The essence of the 'customer' relationship – that a person makes a rational choice in the market place by selecting a product that he or she considers the best value for money – is largely absent from the relationship between the fan and the club he or she supports. Most football supporters 'choose' their club at a young age, and then stick to this choice, however irrational it may seem at face value. Even if the team is struggling, and the 'product' could be seen to be substandard, many supporters continue to invest in their chosen club. These fans view their club differently from how they may regard other leisure services or retail outlets, and feel a type of emotional bond that does not exist in these other spheres. Yet this bond, powerful as it is, can leave supporters open to exploitation by football clubs, which may overcharge for replica team kits or tickets, for example.

In order to prevent this kind of exploitation, and to give supporters a genuine voice and a sense of empowerment, a number of fan groups have appeared since the mid-1980s.[2] The national Football Supporters' Association gained a high profile during this time, and successfully campaigned on a number of issues, including the prevention of the identity card scheme for supporters, an idea proposed in the late 1980s by the then Prime Minister Margaret Thatcher. Other fans' groups have also appeared, including a plethora of independent supporters' associations, and those campaigning on single issues, such as opposing racism.[3] Yet fans have very rarely achieved tangible power *within* a football club, and particularly in the boardroom. The first club successfully to integrate a supporter onto the club's board of directors was the one I support, Northampton Town, and this essay will outline the history and benefits of this development. Through forming a Supporters' Trust, fans at the club have managed to obtain a seat on the board of directors, and the Trust would strongly recommend that every football club should have elected supporter representation on the board. Not only is it morally right, it also works; but in order to be effective the process of electing a fan must be truly democratic and involve a degree of accountability, and I shall discuss these points in more detail at the end of this piece.

Within the context of supporter empowerment, I wish specifically to address the first three items of the Football Task Force's 'Terms of Reference': anti-racism, access for disabled supporters and greater supporter involvement in the running of clubs. At least in the case of Northampton Town, these three issues are organically linked and interconnected. In order to establish this case, a brief introductory explanation of the origins and role of the Northampton Town Supporters' Trust is necessary.

NORTHAMPTON TOWN SUPPORTERS' TRUST: A BRIEF HISTORY

Northampton Town Supporters' Trust was formed in January 1992, as a result of a large public meeting attended by over 600 fans. This meeting was called by a group of ordinary supporters, including Rob Marshall, editor of the fanzine *What a Load of Cobblers*, and myself, in response to a financial crisis at the club and a series of misleading statements issued by the then chairman. The club was reluctant to send representatives to the meeting, but relented at the last minute, and the situation disclosed by them was a debt approaching £1.6 million, representing more than two years' turnover for the club. As the Trust subsequently discovered, the rot had set in some time before, and unpaid bills stretched back several years, to the time of the previous régime at the club. The crisis, however, had been precipitated by the club's failure to pay the previous two months' players' wages, which amounted to about £64,000. The Professional Footballers' Association had had to cover this, and so it too had now become a creditor of the club.

The Trust was set up with two objectives: first, to raise money to save the club (but not for the then current régime), and to be accountable to the supporters for the expenditure of that money; and second, to seek effective involvement and representation for supporters in the running of the club in order to ensure that such a crisis situation would never occur again. In this latter respect, the Trust marked itself out as being distinct from normal supporters' clubs, in that from its inception it has had an inescapably political dimension. By doing this, the Trust was a forerunner of a variety of independent supporters' associations and other similar bodies, who have sought to change the way that their clubs are run and how they relate to their fans.[4] The Trust has also had a representative of Northampton Borough Council on its executive committee since its inception.

The Trust's initial strategy was a dual approach: campaigning for change and fundraising in public, whilst negotiating in private with the club's creditors, former directors, the Football League and the Professional Footballers'

Association. In this way the Trust was able to establish its credentials within the first three months to play its part in the running of the club.

The Trust's publicity campaign met with almost universal support from the public and the media. Fundraising efforts began spontaneously in pubs, clubs and workplaces, and dozens of individual donations ranging from £1 to £1,000 were received. A bucket collection at the first home match after the Trust was formed yielded £3,500, over £1 per head of the gate. This particular occasion became immortalized locally by the chairman's attempts to evict the collectors from the ground in front of television cameras. In the eyes of supporters, this only added to the legitimacy of the Trust and its members, and the bucket collections continued successfully for the rest of the season.

The private negotiations were aimed at bringing a winding-up petition against the club in court. Strange though it may seem that loyal supporters might take such drastic action, the advice we received was that this was the only way to wrest control from the chairman. The Trust could not, of course, bring the petition itself, because it was not a creditor of the club, so we had to persuade others to take this course. The company that eventually did so was Abbeyfield Press Limited, the club's programme producers, who were owed over £11,000. Abbeyfield was owned by Tim Vernon, himself a lifelong supporter, and his partner. Despite pressure from various quarters, they stood firm and went ahead with the action.

When the petition was brought, the chairman was granted an eight-week adjournment on the basis of preparing a 'rescue plan' for the club. This was worrying because it would have taken until the end of the season when, with fixtures completed, the Football League would have had much less incentive to help keep the club going. For a brief period it appeared that the club's only future lay in the route already taken by Aldershot Football Club, which found that after the old company folded in 1992 and a new one formed, the team itself had to resume playing five divisions lower in the league 'pyramid'. Northampton Town's only 'assets' in these circumstances would have been the £13,000 thus far raised by the Trust, and the right to continue playing at the old County Ground. This ground no longer even met Southern League Premier Division standards.

The chairman's 'rescue plan' collapsed within days and shortly afterwards he called in administrators to run the club. On his own admission, he thought that by doing this he would obtain a year's breathing space, and then return to run a club free of debt. Barry Ward, the administrator, took a different view. He first had to obtain an Order of Administration from the High Court and in order to do so had to convince the Court that the company was capable of returning to solvency and normal trading within a reasonable period of time. His two main pieces of evidence were the continued interest of former directors, and the volume of public support as evidenced by the formation and rapid growth of the Trust. The Trust, meanwhile, was continuing its public work through fundraising, bucket collections and open meetings.

On obtaining the Order of Administration, Ward's first action was to cancel the contracts of the three management staff and nine players. This led to much sorrow and heart-searching among supporters, but they fundamentally knew some sort of action of this kind was necessary to bring costs under control. The process of political education had already begun.

The same morning Ward held a meeting at his offices in Birmingham to which former directors and Trust officers were invited. The chairman and his wife were already present when the four of us arrived. Barry told us all that he was forming a local board to run the club on his behalf, of which he would be chairman. He then invited us to decide whether the current chairman and his wife – by then the sole directors – would continue in post, and left us to discuss the matter. We took the opportunity to vote them out, and at that point they left with good grace. The meeting then resumed and it was agreed that the new board would consist of four former directors and two representatives of the Trust. We insisted that they be elected. On 10 April 1992 Phil Frost and I became the first two elected supporters' directors on the board of an English League club.

When the club came out of administration and returned to normal trading in 1994, this was reduced to one but that place is guaranteed by Northampton Borough Council until at least the year 2019 as a condition of the club's lease and licence to occupy its new stadium at Sixfields, Northampton, which was completed in 1994. The Borough Council also has a non-executive seat on the board for the same duration.

This stadium, built and owned by Northampton Borough Council with the aid of a £1 million grant from the Football Trust, is a perfect symbol of the partnership between the local authority, the football club and the Trust. It is also state-of-the-art in its safety provisions and its facilities for disabled spectators. It is truly a community stadium. The Leader of the Council has recently said that he regards the Trust member on the board of directors as representing not only the supporters but the community as a whole. Councillors have also frequently stated that the stadium would never have been built were it not for the Supporters' Trust and the democratic guarantee it provided. If the Trust had not existed it would have been politically unacceptable to provide a football ground from public funds for an unreformed club recently guilty of gross mismanagement.

In financial terms, the Trust has paid over £102,000 into Northampton Town FC in the last seven years, with funds still in hand, and it own 30,592 shares in the club, over seven per cent of the total issued. The sum invested bears good comparison with that of any individual director over the same period.

We have advised or assisted in the formation of several Trusts at other clubs, with similar objectives, including Kettering Town, Middlesbrough, Plymouth Argyle and AFC Bournemouth. These trusts have enjoyed varying degrees of success, the most notable being AFC Bournemouth, to which I will refer later. We have also advised groups who wish to form similar trusts at Dundee United, Manchester City, Partick Thistle, Lincoln City and Chester City among others.

I now turn to the Task Force Terms of Reference, with the assertion that certain key developments at the football club have stemmed entirely from the Trust's representation on the board and the three-way partnership with the Council described above.

THE ELIMINATION OF RACISM

In November 1995 a working party was set up at Northampton Town to organize the relaunch of the 'Let's Kick Racism Out Of Football' campaign at local level. I was asked to chair this working party, which now has representatives from the Supporters' Trust, the football club, Northampton Borough Council, Baxter and Platt Ltd (the Sixfields Stadium Management Company), the Commission for Racial Equality, Northampton Racial Equality Council, Northamptonshire Police, the Scarman Centre at the University of Leicester, Middlesex University, the British Asian Association, Northamptonshire County Council, the Kick It Out campaign, Northampton Town Football in the Community, and Nationwide Building Society. After successfully achieving the initial objective of bringing the aims and message of the campaign to the supporters' attention, at the home match against Darlington in February 1996, we decided that this one-off gesture was insufficient, and therefore set ourselves the task of drafting an equal opportunities policy for the football club. The working party examined various examples, and chose to base the policy upon that used by the charity of which I am chief executive, but adapted to meet the particular needs and circumstances of a football club. It was adopted unanimously by the board of directors in October 1996, and then in public on the pitch at our home match against Chester in January 1997, in the presence of Members of Parliament and other distinguished guests.

Thus Northampton Town became the first League football club formally to have adopted an equal opportunities policy. Since then, the club has been contacted by others who wish to do the same, many of whom have been referred to the club by the Football League or the Football Association. The policy has already had a number of positive outcomes in terms of anti-racist education of supporters, who will now habitually report and identify offenders within the crowd. The board has approved a banning policy for those established as guilty of racist words or behaviour.

This match was designated the Walter Tull Memorial Match, in honour of the club's first black player. Walter was only the second black professional footballer in history.[5] He joined Northampton Town from Tottenham Hotspur in 1911, and played over 100 games for the Cobblers, scoring nine goals from midfield. In 1914 he was among the initial army volunteers at the outbreak of the First World War, and two years later became the first black officer to receive a commission in the British Army. He was killed in action in 1918 on the Somme, only weeks before the Armistice, and has no known grave.[6] In partnership with the Borough

Council, the working party has now established a Walter Tull Memorial Garden at Sixfields, where the ashes of those supporters who request it may be interred. This was officially dedicated in July 1999.

Northampton Town 'Football in the Community', of which I was also chair, recently launched a highly successful initiative to establish regular 'Football Fun Days' for the Bangladeshi youth in the town, in collaboration with the local Mosque and Muslim Community Centre. It is believed that this is another 'first' for Northampton Town, reaching out to a community who for various reasons have had little contact with local football, although they love the game.

IMPROVING DISABLED ACCESS

Northampton Town have been pioneers in addressing the issue of playing opportunities for people with disabilities. The 'Football in the Community Scheme' has taken the lead in organizing league football on a national level for players with learning disabilities, so much so that when the England learning disabilities team won the European Cup in Belgium in 1996 (beating Germany 4–2), eight of the squad and the team manager were from Northampton Town. The club has also been in the forefront of establishing the first Duke of Edinburgh's Award Centre with specific emphasis on disabled candidates, at Sixfields in 1997. In 1998 the club hosted two of the quarter-finals of the World Cup for players with learning disabilities.

In terms of spectator facilities, in 1997 Northampton Town won the Football League Award and the overall McDonald's Award (England, Scotland and Wales) for the best disabled spectator facilities in British football. Sixfields is the only football ground in the country to allocate over one per cent of its entire capacity to disabled spectators and, at the time of writing, is the only ground with dedicated disabled areas on all four sides, thus giving the maximum choice of where and with whom disabled fans wish to watch the match. Whilst the major credit for this must go to Northampton Borough Council, who built the stadium, the award was not only for physical facilities but for customer services. The Supporters' Trust, too, has played its part. Since its inception in 1992, it has generated several thousands of pounds for the better provision of facilities for disabled fans through an annual fundraising event, this money most recently being used for the purchase of Sennheisser Units to relay a match commentary within the stadium to supporters with sight problems.

SUPPORTER INVOLVEMENT IN THE RUNNING OF CLUBS

Northampton Town Supporters' Trust organizes regular monthly open forums for all supporters, whether Trust members or not. Speakers have included the chairman and directors of the football club, the manager, the secretary, members of the playing staff, the local police and the stadium management company. At all meetings the elected director is present and available to answer any questions about the running of the club. Many policies have been changed and/or improved as a result of discussions at these meetings, including, for example, the thorny issue of ticket pricing.

The elected director is subject to annual re-election by single transferable vote, and must therefore remain active and sensitive to the views of the membership if he or she is to retain the position. After seven years, the Trust's membership now stands at a record level, as do attendances at its meetings which average over 100.

In the time since the Trust joined the board of directors, average attendances have risen from 2,000 to over 6,000. This growth in support is, of course, related to the team's success and the new stadium, but it is interesting to note that the gates had already risen to over 3,500 before the club went to Sixfields in October 1994, and while the team was still near the bottom of Division Three. The increase is, in my view, partly because supporters now know they are stakeholders and not just turnstile fodder. Price increases for tickets have been accepted because they have been properly explained and justified, and not just imposed 'from above'. There is a feeling of everyone being on the same side in a common enterprise, rather than the supporters developing an 'us and them' mentality in their relationship with the club. That is not to say that there are not disagreements and tensions – there are – but there is a forum for resolving them and arriving at acceptable solutions. The club's historic debt has now been paid off in its entirety, the last payment of £50,000 having been made in August 1998.

The involvement of supporters at director level has therefore produced commercial as well as social advantages for the football club. The chief benefits, I believe, have been felt in the areas identified above: anti-racism, equal opportunities and disability, on which the voice of the Trust has been specific and radical. In these areas it is delivering the policies and services of the local authority in a very high-profile context, and thus is a truly equal partner with them. The club is also succeeding where other boards of directors, who often do not prioritize issues such as racism or disability, fail to act.

Historically, it has usually taken a crisis such as potential insolvency before directors have turned to supporters for help and participation. There is no good reason why this should be so, given the number of successful outcomes we have witnessed from fan involvement at Northampton which were unrelated to the club's financial position. Northampton Town is living proof that supporters' democracy, and close attention to social issues, do not preclude success on the pitch: two Wembley play-offs in successive seasons and promotion tell their own story! Although the club was unfortunately relegated back to Division Three in 1998/99, the infrastructure now in place will ensure that the organization will continue to be run competently and solvently, giving every chance of a recovery of the progress made in playing fortunes in recent seasons.

CONCLUSIONS

Over the last seven years, and particularly recently, I have been contacted by officials and/or supporters of nearly 20 clubs, who either wish to form a Trust similar to our own, or to achieve democratic supporter representation on their board of directors, or both. As a result of detailed discussions with all these people, I believe that in order to be effective on any lasting basis, a scheme for supporter representation on the board must have five hallmarks.

First, the scheme should ensure that any supporter elected to the board enjoys full *executive* powers, rather than merely non-voting or purely observer status, as has been tried elsewhere. The directorship must be registered as such at Companies House, and carry with it the entitlement to full access to all board meetings in their entirety, and to all written and financial information available to the other directors. Symbolic or bogus experiments like the one by Francis Lee at Manchester City expose the limitations of anything less.

Second, the scheme must be truly *democratic*, ensuring one person one vote, not one pound one vote. A bond scheme such as was launched at Charlton Athletic entitling subscribers to a vote for each unit purchased, to elect a director, is not democratic, and in fact merely enshrines the concept that money speaks louder than supporters in football.

Third, and following on from the above point, it must be *affordable* for all supporters. If a subscription is the basis of the electorate, it must not be set at a level which is beyond the purse of any supporter, despite the temptation to use subscriptions as a quick fundraiser. The Supporters' Trust at Northampton has subscription levels at £5 per year for adults, £2 per year for 'concessions' (old and young), and £25 for life. These rates have not been increased since our formation. An otherwise splendid scheme at Lincoln City, 'Impetus', was marred only by the subscription level which has been set at £50.

Fourth, the scheme must be *entrenched*, so that it cannot be set aside at the whim of the board if the representative says or does something the other directors do not like, or fails to come up with a sum of money requested. As previously stated, the Trust at Northampton is fortunate to have its position guaranteed in the stadium lease until 2019 at least. Similar opportunities arise wherever clubs become involved in partnerships with their local authority, whether over the stadium or some other financial contract or arrangement. The sad example of Kettering Town, where the Trust representative was cast aside by the new owners following a short period of administration, illustrates the importance of this point.

Last, the scheme must be *independent*, meaning that the representative, and the Trust where applicable, retain the right to criticize the club and the board on behalf of supporters when all other avenues have failed. This, it appears to me, is the snag with the otherwise highly successful example of AFC Bournemouth, where a Trust, initiated by key supporters but comprising a coalition of local interests, acquired the football club three years ago. When the honeymoon period ends, as inevitably one day it will, whom will the supporters criticize? Themselves? And who will be in a position to represent them in doing so? Also, I am not aware of any democratic structures having been put in place there during the last three years to enable supporters to decide who they want to represent them in future.

Lastly, we at Northampton have been greatly encouraged by the endorsement we have received from the Football Task Force in all the reports which they have published so far, most notably the third, 'Investing in the Community'.[7] This report gives approval to the twin principles of democratic supporters' trusts, and of elected supporter representation on boards of directors. It even proposes a funding mechanism via the Football Trust to enable these principles to be established in clubs generally. I hope this proves to be a prelude to a period when full supporter involvement is the rule rather than the exception.[8]

NOTES

1. See Barrie Pierpoint's contribution to this volume for an insight into the marketing philosophies of Leicester City.
2. For analyses of the relationship between clubs and supporters, see, for example, S. Redhead, *Post-Fandom and the Millennial Blues: The Transformation of Soccer Culture* (London: Routledge, 1997); R. Taylor, *Football and its Fans: Supporters and Their Relations with the Game, 1885–1985* (Leicester: Leicester University Press, 1992); A. Brown (ed.), *Fanatics! Power, Identity and Fandom in Football* (London: Routledge, 1998).
3. An examination of the efficacy of antiracist fan groups can be found in J. Garland and M. Rowe 'Field of Dreams: An Assessment of Antiracism in British Football', *Journal of Ethnic and Migration Studies*, 25, 2 (1999), 335–44.
4. For an account of another fans' group that successfully changed the direction of their club, see S. North and P. Hodson, *Build a Bonfire: How Football Fans United to Save Brighton and Hove Albion* (Edinburgh: Mainstream, 1997).
5. P. Vasili, *The First Black Footballer: Arthur Wharton 1865–1930* (London and Portland, OR: Frank Cass, 1998).
6. P. Vasili, 'Walter Daniel Tull, 1888–1918: Soldier, Footballer, Black', *Race and Class*, 38, 2 (1996), 51–69.
7. Football Task Force, *Investing in the Community* (London: Football Task Force, 1998).
8. In his speech at the Labour Party conference in September 1999, Chris Smith, Secretary of State for Culture, Media and Sport, called for fans to become more involved in their football clubs through the setting up of trusts similar to the one described in this piece. Since this article was written, Chris Smith has announced the formation of Supporters Direct, the Supporters' Trusts initiative described in the last paragraph, with Brian Lomax as its Chairman. Supporters Direct was launched by Chris Smith at Birkbeck College, London University, on 27 January 2000, as a constituent part of the new Football Foundation, successor to the Football Trust.

PART 3
Football and its Communities

7

The Changing Face of Football: Stadiums and Communities

JOHN BALE

Football is regarded as a 'representational' sport. Professional football clubs represent places large and small – villages, towns, cities and nations. Football communities exist in a number of forms. A community of fans is a social network of interacting individuals but it is not necessary for such a community to be concentrated in a defined territory such as a city. The development of television, international transportation and the Internet has meant that today and in the future fandom can and will exist as a community without propinquity. Football possesses its own community of followers but the sport also imposes itself on broader communities, upon which it has various impacts. This essay will not deal with national or global football communities but will focus on the urban scale where the notion of 'community' can be conceptualized in two forms. The first is the urban community in which the club is located, after which it is invariably named, and which the club can be said to 'represent'. The second is the smaller community within which the club is sited. This second community is made up of the people and businesses lying in proximity to the football stadium. I will explore the relationship between club and community by first making some general observations about such a relationship and secondly by focusing on changes that have taken place since the Taylor Report. The implications of such changes are clearly relevant to the map of British football in the twenty-first century.

Though 'community' is a central theme in this study, it is almost impossible to deal with club–community relations without focusing on the changing geographical and social role of the football stadium. The stadium has always exemplified a facility that generates both positive and negative effects. These impact on both the broader urban community and the local community situated around stadiums. Drawing on ideas from welfare geography it becomes clear that location and distance are crucial variables in understanding the different effects that football may have on local and regional communities. This is an important point to bear in mind in what follows.

SOCCER AND THE CITY

The presence of a professional football club of league status can create both benefits and disbenefits to the urban area that it nominally represents. The football club does (re)present the city. It publicizes it in a way that no other cultural entity can. Almost all clubs in England are named after places (exceptions include Port Vale) and consequently they are announced each week of the football season as their performances are broadcast to the nation and beyond. This free advertising has often led city managers to welcome the elevation of their local football club to Football League status. Benefits also come from revenues generated by the club – directly and indirectly – and the 'psychic income' generated by the success – or even the presence – of the club on the well being of (at least some of) the population. Some studies have alluded to the increased work rate of the urban workforce following the success of the local team.[1] Some retail outlets, notably pubs, benefit considerably from the presence of a soccer match nearby. The psychological benefits to be derived from football have led the stadium to be seen by some as a source of topophilia – a love of place.[2] Those who regularly frequent their 'home ground' articulate such a feeling. For example, talking about Easter Road, the home ground of Hibernian FC in Edinburgh, a supporter stated: 'that piece of land is wrapped into my Saturday you know, in the sense that it is consistent with how I conduct Saturday, where I go before the game, who I meet up with, what time I leave'.[3] Moving to a new ground would 'be like losing someone in the family' noted another fan,[4] typifying the strength of feeling that can be attached to a football ground as a place, an emotional tie which can take the stadium beyond a simple functional space for the production of football matches. The stadium is also a source of 'geographical memories'. A study by E. Hague and J. Mercer revealed that the Scottish football club Raith Rovers served as 'a reference that triggers wider memories of friends, relatives and people living in the urban space that is Kirkaldy'.[5] This modestly sized town, through its football team, is provided with a focal point for local pride and awareness and a source of dynamic geographical memories.[6] Football fans living in the city that the club represents benefit financially solely by not having to travel out of their town to see a match. However, virtually no studies have been done in the United Kingdom to assess the local economic multiplier effects of football clubs, that is the local income generated by a football club resulting from football-induced expenditure that would not otherwise have been spent locally. This stands in contrast to the experience in the United States where several studies have examined the urban income effects of sports teams in the course of a season.[7]

This is not to say that football fails to create problems for the overall urban community. Policing around grounds imposes costs on the local taxpayer and especially on the substantial number of urban residents with no interest in football. Football-induced nuisances such as traffic congestion, crowding and hooliganism can be felt at considerable distances from the ground but especially by those living in proximity to it. So while the presence of a football club creates potential benefits across the urban area, it often creates nuisances for those in a relatively small part of it. Members of this latter community are linked together through their nearness to the stadium. The centrality of place in the consumption of football nuisances is summarized by the distinction between urban residents who may benefit from their *accessibility* to a football stadium and others who suffer from their *proximity* to it.

The implication of all this is that for many the football stadium is seen as a 'noxious facility' – something to be avoided so that its negative spill-over effects are not consumed in one's own back yard. Within the urban area, this has led to a number of planning conflicts concerning exactly where new football grounds should be located. In this context, rather than cementing the urban community in support of 'our team', the promised (or threatened) development of a new football stadium in a particular part of the town can serve to fracture the overall community into NIMBY-inspired groups of local activists. Opposition to the location of football grounds in particular parts of the city has always been a problem but has become of particular significance as a post-Hillsborough example of single-issue politics.

The Taylor Report argued for a new generation of football stadiums that would be surveilled, safe and sanitized.[8] At the same time the growing marketization of football contributed to a new generation of facilities which were more than football stadiums – 'tradiums' was one description used for those public-private spaces that linked leisure with spending. Improved catering and integrated conference and banqueting facilities, museums, hotels and merchandising typified the contents of such multi-functional spaces. Additionally, stadium space would, ideally, be used for sports other than football and for entertainment other than sports. Rugby, rock concerts, religious revivals and a whole range of other activities were seen as providing sources of revenue for the post-Taylor world of British football and all these developments clearly had implications for the communities within which the stadiums were located.

Such developments created different 'ways of seeing' the football ground (indeed the application of the word 'stadium' as opposed to 'ground' could be argued to imply an up-grading of the game's image). Consider the case of the proposal some years ago to provide a new home for Bristol Rovers in the suburb of Mangotsfield in the neighbouring borough of Kingswood. The football club tried to promote its case for a location in a suburban area by evoking the benefits that the stadium would bring to the greater Bristol community. It presented itself in its promotional material as 'the family club', of 'caring for the community', of creating 'a closer tie with local schools', of using stadium facilities for 'Bingo and Tea Dances'. In a detailed environmental assessment of the proposed site, it concluded that a new stadium would not create any deleterious environmental effects. It promoted the stadium as a facility for the entire Bristol community, not merely for residents in the immediate locality. However, the residents who opposed the stadium in Kingswood also invoked the notion of 'community'. Here the quality of life of the *local* community was seen to be at stake. A football stadium signified violence, parking problems, noise, litter, floodlighting, hooliganism and a negative impact on house prices. It became a case of the *Rovers Stadium Support Committee* v. *The Kingswood Borough Action Committee*. For the people of Kingswood, a football stadium promised them more football than they would freely choose. They would be forced to bear the costs of the production of a football match; they would be providing a 'free ride' for those living outside the borough who wanted to watch Rovers' games; they would be unwilling consumers of football's 'negative externalities'. The planning proposal to build the stadium was rejected.

A similar situation has been well documented for the proposed relocation of Portsmouth FC from its old inner-urban Fratton Park to a new facility in the leafy suburbs of Framlington and Drayton.[9] In a public consultation about the relocation, 63 per cent of those in the city as a whole who opposed the planning application came from Framlington and Drayton.[10] Their reasons for objecting to a football stadium were the perceived increase in traffic generation, associated retail developments which would harm the business of local shops, and the loss of amenity. Objectors' comments included: 'Framlington and Drayton are very quiet areas and there are a lot of old people living here. They are all very distressed at the thought of all this noise and pollution not to mention hordes of hooligans bringing carnage and fear into the community.'[11] Those supporting the new site saw it from the city perspective. The stadium was seen as 'putting Portsmouth on the map' and 'an asset to the city of Portsmouth'. One respondent said that 'the council should view this matter on a larger scale and with regard to the benefits of the community as a whole'.[12]

These examples illustrate the 'place' of community in the football relocation debate. It can be both invoked and researched at different levels of scale. It is now appropriate to see how stadiums old and new have impacted on the local communities living within 'the shadow of the stadium' and how this impact, which is likely to be characteristic of developments in the twenty-first century, has changed in the post-Taylor generation of UK football stadiums.

IN THE SHADOW OF THE STADIUM

The examples of Bristol Rovers and Portsmouth cited above illustrate a typical public reaction to the thought of living in proximity to a football stadium. It reveals the stadium as a facility to be avoided, a facility to be kept away from one's own back yard. In American terms, the conflicts resulting from the contested terrain of proposed stadiums are examples of (appropriately) 'turf politics'. But the residents of Kingswood and Framlington seem to have had a typically exaggerated image of the environmental reality of living in proximity to a football ground. In the late 1980s, at a time when football hooliganism was providing the sport with a negative image, a survey of a random sample of 100 people revealed that about 95 per cent thought that if they lived within 500 metres of a football stadium they would experience nuisances on average match days. In addition, 45 per cent thought they would be 'serious nuisances'.[13] Even living two kilometres from the stadium, 25 per cent believed the stadium would be a nuisance. This highly mediated perception contrasted considerably from the experiences of 4,597 people who actually did live around football grounds. For instance, only 55 per cent of those living within 500 metres of a stadium said that they experienced nuisances on match days while only about 17 per cent described these as 'serious nuisances'. This, however, is a highly generalized picture and the survey revealed considerable variations in the consumption of nuisances around grounds in different divisions and in different parts of the country. Hence, at Crystal Palace where, at the time, games were being played every week as a result of ground sharing between two clubs, around 80 per cent of the population living within 500 metres of the ground claimed to experience football nuisances. On the other hand, in the cases of clubs like Crewe Alexandra and Hartlepool United the nuisance effect was minimal. The extent to which negative effects of football are perceived as a nuisance does of course, depend on whether or not one is a fan. It has been argued, for example, that 'if all local residents were fans, the number perceiving football nuisances would be halved'.[14]

Another popular feeling during the 1980s, and one reflected in the responses of the people of Framlington and Kingswood in the following decade, was that hooliganism was the major problem associated with British football. This 'moral panic' was largely media-led and for most local residents football fan violence was not perceived as a problem. The late 1980s survey noted above revealed that only ten per cent of those living in proximity to league grounds perceived hooliganism as a nuisance.[15] This is not to say that hooligan incidents, when they occur, are anything but unpleasant and I do not ignore the fact that the areas around, and indeed inside, some stadiums could be 'landscapes of fear',[16] but more people living near stadiums rated car parking and traffic congestion as a problem (18 and 22 per cent respectively). As early as 1971 it was estimated that a crowd of 60,000 people would generate 10,800 cars parked within a mile of the stadium.[17]

The picture painted above is based largely on data and information from the 1980s. How has the situation changed following the publication of the Taylor Report? Since 1989 the relationship between football and its communities has assumed a number of new dimensions. I will deal with four of these. First, there has been the rapid growth in the number of relocated clubs. Secondly, a number of clubs have expanded and redeveloped their grounds in situ, recognizing that the all-seat recommendations of the Taylor Report necessitated ground enlargement. Thirdly, what could be seen as a postmodern turn in the football landscape has been the growing multi-functionalism of football stadiums – their use for other sports and other revenue-generating activities. The stadium has become more than a football ground.[18] Fourthly, the football industry has witnessed the emergence of a growing 'voice' for stadium communities. This has been orchestrated, not so much by the traditional supporters' clubs and fanzine movement, but by local groups – usually made up of non-fans who are often anti-football. In many cases these have become members of the nationally organized Federation of Stadium Communities. Each of these developments can be reviewed in turn.

INTO THE TWENTY-FIRST CENTURY

During the last decade a number of football clubs have relocated. From a geographical perspective it is noteworthy that, despite the mooted move of Wimbledon to Dublin, all existing relocations have been over relatively short distances – often under two kilometres from the club's previous site. In some cases, such as Fulham and Charlton, fan resistance has proved crucial in preventing club relocation. These examples imply that there exists a certain territorial imperative as far as both clubs and fans are concerned. Though fan resistance to long-distance moves is a significant factor in deterring such relocations, the balance between the voice of fans and the strictures of the British planning system is not easy to disentangle. Ultimately relocation is dependent on the planning process and applications for stadium developments on greenfield sites have frequently been rejected. There is a feeling, however, that the dislocation of the club from the place bearing its name is anathema to fans and something clubs have tended to avoid, reflecting a local sense of sentiment, place pride or topophilia. All this remains at odds with the logic of a fully marketized industry in modernity. What are basically intra-urban relocations contrast dramatically with intra- (even inter-) national moves that occur in North America. Furthermore UK football clubs have rarely adopted the economic logic of ground-sharing. The potential to achieve such economies of scale, widely achieved in France, Italy and Spain, remain aberrations for the typical British football club. The thought of clubs like Liverpool and Everton sharing the same suburban stadium has been mooted but not realized. The conspicuous lack of interest of both Sheffield clubs in sharing (or even using) the Don Valley Stadium which was built for the 1991 World Student Games reflects British sentiment for the football ground rather than for the multi-sport 'facility'. Charlton Athletic's successful campaign to return to 'The Valley' after ground sharing at Crystal Palace (17 miles away) graphically exemplifies this local conservatism.[19] In the early 1990s the fans of Edinburgh club, Heart of Midlothian, successfully protested against the move of their club from Tynecastle park to an area east of Edinburgh, strongly regarded as Hibernian country.[20] More recently, it has been demonstrated that Brighton and Hove Albion – or at least their fans – need to be close to Brighton. After two years' ground sharing with Gillingham in north Kent, the Sussex club moved 'home' and pledged itself to a Brighton location.

In some cases of stadium relocation it is implicit that the nuisances, previously consumed by residents in older, often inner-city sites, will be 'internalized' by the stadium's proximity to compatible land uses – namely open space, warehousing, leisure or manufacturing industry. In several cases these planned locations have been on reclaimed industrial sites, such as the cases of Walsall, Stoke City and Middlesbrough. Planners are well disposed towards these brownfield locations, because they contribute to urban regeneration. However, it is far from clear that negative spill-overs have been fully eliminated by such moves. At the present time the full impact of new, relocated stadiums on local residents has not been researched but what limited evidence exists suggests that urban nuisances have not been fully eliminated. The most detailed study undertaken to date has been into the relocation of St. Johnstone FC in Perth which in 1990 moved from its former inner-urban Muirton Park to the new, suburban McDiarmaid Park. A welfare-geographic study compared the nuisances (as perceived by local residents) that were generated by the old stadium with those of the new.[21] In both cases car parking and traffic congestion were the main nuisances, hooliganism being relatively unimportant. However, the proportion of residents who perceived football nuisances around the new ground was smaller than that recorded for residents who had lived around the old ground. On the other hand, the nuisance effect of the new ground was experienced over a wider geographical area than that of the old, inner-city site. At Stoke City's new stadium problems continue to centre on traffic congestion, parking and danger to crowds taking hazardous short-cuts via dual carriageways and even railway tracks. New stadium developments cannot totally distance themselves from the negative perception of residents if the broader urban infrastructure is lacking. The ability of existing road systems to absorb traffic generated by a new stadium constitutes widespread concern among urban residents. It is anticipated, for example, that a new stadium such as that proposed for inner-urban Southampton, would generate 10,000 additional vehicles on match days.

The refurbishment of existing grounds to meet the all-seat requirements of government legislation, is a second strategy that has been widely adopted in the post-Hillsborough period. This has created new problems in certain communities where the increased height of the stands has resulted in reduced sunlight and increased shadows. A dramatic example is that of Arsenal where a long-running feud has resulted in articulate, middle-class local residents leading a vigorous programme of resistance against the club. There is no reason why the all-seat stadium should reduce traffic congestion and pollution around grounds. Given the actual and planned increased frequency of use at many of the nation's football grounds, it could be argued that car traffic has increased. This is certainly likely to be the case should we witness the construction of peri-urban stadiums. The growth of the number of games played per season and the increased number of mid-week matches also provide a cause for concern to residents in *fin de siècle* soccer. In the Arsenal case, the response of the Islington Society and the

Highbury Community Association can be gauged by the following comment: 'the demolition of homes for a non-essential, private business, though deeply abhorrent to many, is only the tip of the iceberg as far as environmental impact is concerned'.[22] Activists point to other clubs such as Leeds United who plan to hold 180 events per year at Elland Road, to Newcastle United which, at the time of writing, were applying for a seven-day-a-week licence in their gigantic inner-city St. James's Park, and Chelsea, where planning permission was being sought to obtain a nightclub licence.

It would be wrong to assume that it is not only the in situ developments associated with internationally known clubs that cause local problems. During the demolition and subsequent reconstruction of the East Stand at unfashionable Darlington FC local residents' lives suffered long disruption. On completion of the project a new pub and entertainment facility, integrated into the ground, generated a doubling of the traffic flow in what had previously been a quiet cul-de-sac.[23]

A considerable increase has already occurred in the intensity of the use to which stadiums are put. This has included both their use for sports other than football and, as noted above, their use for non-sporting activities. Banqueting and conference facilities and retail outlets represent gains to the club as pressures have increased to finance improved facilities. They have been major earners in the revenue generation of clubs like Manchester United. The proposal for a new 40,000 seat stadium for Leicester City included three non-food retail warehouses, a hotel, a restaurant/casino, and two fast-food restaurants. The growing multi-functionality of stadiums creates problems as well as gains. The recent ground-sharing scheme between Bristol Rovers and Bristol Rugby Club at the latter's Memorial Ground has created added problems for residents in the Bristol area of Bishopston. These included the usual traffic and parking problems as well as anti-social behaviour by fans. It is worth noting that a report into the situation at Bishopston referred to the football club being less sensitive to community issues than the rugby club.[24] However, it is not possible to generalize the extent of such inter-sport variations in such attitudes.

The increased use of stadiums for non-sporting activities such as rock concerts and religious gatherings tends to produce a lower level of nuisance than on days when soccer is played. This is not to say, however, that the impact of late night musical performances in stadiums surrounded by residences should be underestimated. A study of the comparative effects of football and rock concerts is exemplified by research into such effects at Portman Road, home of Ipswich Town FC. A survey undertaken in the mid-1990s revealed that the noise nuisance ('unwanted sound'), generally not rated as particularly significant in surveys of football effects, was the major source of nuisance for rock concerts for those living closest to the stadium.[25] However, a study of football and non-football uses of the Kenilworth Road ground, Luton, typified the finding that non-football activities (including other sports events) were perceived by local residents as less of a nuisance than football-induced effects.[26] The intensification of stadium use can be seen as a welcome sign of a growing involvement of football clubs in the community (see the essays by Perkins and Watson in this collection). The potential for club-education links has been developed in some cases. Links with local schools have been facilitated through the provision of stadium-based classrooms. At the same time, however, it seems possible that some local people can be offended by some stadium-based initiatives, naively assumed by the football club to be innocuous (a particular example being an incongruous sex-trade fair at Stoke City's new Britannia Stadium).

The visual and architectural merit of the new generation of stadiums, new or refurbished, varies considerably. At one extreme some stadiums have been almost indistinguishable from DIY superstores; rectangular metallic boxes, anonymous in style and, in the words of Edward Relph, 'placeless'.[27] In other cases imaginative and innovative design features have been incorporated in stadium construction. The new stadiums at Middlesbrough, Huddersfield and Bolton might be cited as examples.

A further significant development during the 1990s has been the growth of the Federation of Stadium Communities (FSC). Its regular newsletter, *The Shadow*, publicizes the nature of its activities.[28] Established in Sheffield after the Hillsborough disaster but now with its headquarters in Stoke, the Federation grew out of the actions of local activists in Sheffield and Birmingham who sought not only to counter the activities of football clubs, but also seek to build bridges between them. The FSC seeks to serve clubs and communities. It would see Sheffield United's attempts to develop links with the local community, during the redevelopment of its Bramall Lane stadium, as a model of club–community links. By giving preference in job opportunities to those living in the local area of Sharrow and by providing facilities for local groups within the overall stadium complex, a genuine and successful partnership between club and community has been established.[29]

The FSC offers services such as the undertaking of surveys for local residents, seeking the views of the community on the most acceptable sites for stadium development. It convenes meetings where options can be debated within the community. It prepares reports for clubs and councils and provides information and advice. The FSC claims to aid the establishment of frameworks and timetables for proper consultation and participation in the planning process. It also fulfils training for community representatives and offers advocacy and representational skills where appropriate. The FSC has grown significantly in the last decade and can now be regarded as a significant player in drawing up the map of football in twenty-first century Britain.

CONCLUSION

Great strides have been made in changing the map of British football since the publication of the Taylor Report. It is difficult to deny that stadiums are now safer places than they were previously. Improvements in safety may have resulted from increased surveillance as much as the move to all-seat facilities (see the essay by Garland and Rowe in this collection). Yet this piece has suggested that the problems of British football have not yet been fully solved. The new generation of stadiums, while regarded as improvements on their antecedents, have not yet been fully isolated from the anti-social outcomes of the impacts that they generate. As a result, the image of the stadium is one that is not necessarily benign. Such problems cannot be resolved without adequate infrastructure in the urban area as a whole. The sort of spectating experience that will occur in what, at worst, could be dystopian, sanitized 'leisure zones' remains to be seen. One thing seems clear, however: the role of communities, however defined, but often in conflict, will be central in the emerging cartography of the national sport in the twenty-first century.

NOTES

1. E. Derrick and J. McRory, 'Cup in Hand: Sunderland's Self-Image after the Cup', Working Paper 8 (Centre for Urban and Regional Studies, Birmingham University, 1973).
2. Yi-Fu Tuan, *Topophilia* (Englewood Cliffs: Prentice Hall, 1974).
3. D. Mackay, 'A Sense of Place: The "Meaning" of Easter Road' (unpublished MA dissertation, Department of Geography, University of Edinburgh, 1995), 25.
4. Ibid., 35.
5. E. Hague and J. Mercer, 'Geographical Memory and Urban Identity in Scotland: Raith Rovers FC and Kirkaldy', *Geography*, 83 (1998), 105–16.
6. Ibid., 114.
7. J. Bale, *Sport, Space and the City* (London: Routledge, 1993).
8. Lord Justice Taylor (Chairman), *The Hillsborough Stadium Disaster: Final Report* (London: HMSO, 1989).
9. A. Burnett, 'Community, Local Politics and Football', in J. Bale (ed.), *Community, Landscape and Identity: Horizons in a Geography of Sport* (Keele: Department of Geography, Occasional Paper, 20, Keele University, 1994), pp.19–32.
10. In contrast, of 76 individual letters of support for the development of a new stadium in an inner-city area of Southampton, 39 were from people living outside the city. This again illustrates the significance of geographical scale in the exploration of stadium politics. See Federation of Stadium Communities, Southampton St. Mary's: An Appraisal (Southampton: St. Mary's/Northam Stadium Working Group, 1999).
11. Burnett, 'Community, Local Politics and Football', p.27.
12. Ibid., p.26.
13. J. Bale, 'In the Shadow of the Stadium: Football Grounds as Urban Nuisances', *Geography*, 75 (1990), 325–34.
14. Ibid., 328.
15. Ibid., 327.
16. Yi-Fu Tuan, *Landscapes of Fear* (Oxford: Blackwell, 1979).
17. M. Grayson, 'Travel Generated by a Football Stadium' (unpublished master's dissertation, University of London, 1971).
18. J. Bale, *Landscapes of Modern Sport* (Leicester: Leicester University Press, 1994).
19. R. Everitt, *Battle for the Valley* (London: Voice of the Valley, 1994); see also Bale, *Sport, Space and the City*.

20. H. Hognestad, 'The Jambo Experience: Identity, meaning and social practice among supporters of Heart of Midlothian Football Club' (unpublished Cand. Polit. Dissertation, Department of Anthropology, University of Oslo, 1995), 162.
21. C. Mason and A. Moncrieff, 'The Effect of Relocation on the Externality Fields of Football Stadia: The Case of St. Johnstone FC', *Scottish Geographical Magazine*, 109 (1993), 96–105.
22. A. Carmichael, 'Arsenal Update', *Islington Society Newsletter* (1998).
23. T. Marshall, 'A Tale of Access and Excess', *The Shadow*, 10 (1999), 8.
24. Federation of Stadium Communities, 'Bishopston, Bristol: The Impact of Ground-Sharing on a Local Neighbourhood' (Report, 1, 1998).
25. J. Chase and M. Healey, 'The Spatial Externality Effects of Football Matches and Rock Concerts', *Applied Geography*, 15 (1995), 18–34.
26. C. Mason and R. Robins, 'The Spatial Externality Fields of Football and Non-Football at Kenilworth Road, Luton', *Applied Geography*, 11 (1991), 251–66.
27. E. Relph, *Place and Placelessness* (London: Pion, 1976).
28. The Federation of Stadium Communities has its headquarters at The Lodge, Burslem Park, Moorland Road, Burslem, Stoke-on-Trent, ST6 1EA.
29. See 'The Sharrow Partnership', *The Shadow*, 10 (1999), 9.

8

Exploring Future Relationships between Football Clubs and Local Government

SEAN PERKINS

The extraordinary growth in support and particularly in *income* at top professional football clubs in England and Wales during the 1990s has tended to focus recent public attention on the sport both on a relatively small number of financially buoyant clubs, and on the burgeoning new 'external' sources of income now increasingly available to a still select band of larger clubs. One small sign of the ways and the extent to which public discussion about football has changed in the past decade is that in the troubled 1980s most conferences and public debates about football were about hooliganism and public policy. Today they are, instead, about *capital*. Most of these forums on football and business spend much of their time talking about FA Premier League football, income from television, corporate sponsors, the potentially lucrative public flotations of a handful of clubs, and increasingly, too, about the prospects of takeovers of top clubs by major media players. The recent attempted BSkyB purchase of Manchester United and the interest shown in other top football clubs by Carlton, Granada and other media players suggest that a completely new set of ownership structures may soon be on the horizon for the English game.

As a handful of top English football clubs have continued to diversify and accumulate across a range of financial activities, in some cases incorporating new sporting interests, in others extensive merchandising operations, services and new businesses, many clubs lower down the professional hierarchy have been the subject of the sort of media coverage which has routinely focused on their likely financial ruin. Even clubs some way distant from the game's basement – Portsmouth, Crystal Palace, Oxford United to name but three – have been reported to have severely, possibly terminally, overstepped their fiscal limits. However, amidst this regular litany of clubs 'on the brink' there are also examples of seemingly 'unfashionable' football clubs turning around their fortunes as a result, for example, of successful and innovative *community* involvement. Northampton Town and Bournemouth are probably the best known recent cases of successful so-called 'community' football clubs which had previously been facing oblivion in their earlier guises as clubs based on the more traditional market model. At AFC Bournemouth, a trust fund was established by supporters in order to save the club from extinction in 1996/97. Ultimately, the group of supporters was able to take control of the club and ensure survival. The Northampton Town Supporters' Trust, which owns a block of shares in the club and has a representative on the board of directors, has worked constructively with the club and local authority to establish the first equal opportunities policy at any league club in Britain. Lomax's contribution to this collection provides further insight into the former's experience in the period following their 'crisis'. This arrangement has also ensured the provision of excellent facilities for disabled fans at the club's ground, Sixfields. However, many other professional and semi-professional clubs also benefit, in a rather less acclaimed way, from strong local ties involving fans, public bodies and other forms of community action and partnership.

The reality is that most smaller clubs can and do work most effectively as part of a partnership which involves the use of private and public expertise and resources. In fact, as one or two examples show, even larger football clubs might better hold on to local links via connections with the public sector at a time of growing market-led global pressures. Furthermore, clubs interact on a regular basis with local government through the granting of licences, safety certificates, and via policing and traffic management, and so forth. However, this routine resourcing and support of football clubs by local government is often ignored in current debates about the game.

Research undertaken by the Sir Norman Chester Centre for Football Research sheds new light on the relationships between local government and football clubs.[1] Over 300 local authority leisure departments were surveyed via a postal questionnaire, and several case examples were examined in depth. This essay will outline briefly the kinds of partnership which exist in England and Wales, the barriers and pathways to project development, and the future prospects for local authority and football club relations.

FOOTBALLING ACTIVITIES IN THE COMMUNITY

Where football clubs have adopted innovative and effective anti-racist campaigns, where better access to football and football clubs for the disadvantaged has been successfully negotiated, and where opportunities for females to play football have been best promoted and sustained, it has often been as a direct consequence of partnership work between a perceptive and supportive local authority and a club in need of skilled guidance and direction. Significantly, issues such as those concerning questions of 'race', education and football development can also encourage the club and local authority to think rather more deeply about the scope and nature of their relationship in the widest sense.

Many football clubs, particularly the larger professional clubs, are now in a position to offer the sorts of facilities for use by local communities unimaginable even a decade ago. The publication of the final Taylor Report in 1990 led to a major restructuring of the football stadiums in the United Kingdom (Lord Justice

Taylor (Chairman), *The Hillsborough Stadium Disaster: Final Report* (London: HMSO)). Many of the new and redeveloped grounds now offer facilities for community use, and a radically different emphasis with regards to the stadium site, with many open for six or seven nights a week for business, social and community events. Consequently, over four out of ten (42 per cent) of our local authority respondents reported involvement in partnerships around the use of club facilities 'for the community' in recent years.

However, only 22 per cent of our respondents said that stadium developments had actually improved local relations. This seems a low figure considering the extent of football stadium modernization over the last decade. At some smaller clubs, new developments had actually worsened relations between the local council and club; is this because of discord about planning? Or, perhaps there has been disagreement about the uses to which new spaces might be put? A new stadium development, therefore, may not always be a blessing in terms of making a positive change to local partnerships, especially if the local club is a smaller one struggling with financial pressures.

In areas such as education and training for local students, young players and staff, positive local authority partnerships are growing ever more important for top football clubs. Government-initiated national programmes of learning through football (such as 'Playing for Success'), with football clubs as sites for classrooms, or Study Centres, have reinvigorated aspects of the 'civic' functions of stadium spaces, especially perhaps in relation to otherwise 'difficult' male students. Such programmes also provide useful opportunities for football clubs to familiarize potential young fans with the club and to illustrate the role of the club as an important civic site and institution.

Holiday coaching schemes are now widespread – almost all clubs and local authorities run them. So, too, do some private companies. There is clearly a major input here from local authorities, but unless a partnership can be arranged, competition from football clubs and private schemes can lead to duplication and insufficient delivery:

> The city manage a highly successful football development programme (financially supported by the club) which in some cases (holiday courses/schools courses) competes with the club's own football in the community scheme. There is duplication, competition for good staff, scrapping for children etc. The present set-up is too fragmented and unsustainable in the long term.[2]

Coaching in schools is a priority area for football club involvement according to our research, and just over half of our sample is actively involved in this area.

A number of local partnerships now operate across the country which seek to involve ethnic minority communities in the local football club.[3] Notable schemes like the Charlton Athletic Race Equality Partnership; the Sheffield United Football Unites Racism Divides Project, the Leicester City Foxes Against Racism partnership, and Leicester Asian Sports Initiative are all good examples of effective local projects. However, it would appear from our survey that clubs on the whole could do much more, both in their work with communities and in promoting anti-racist initiatives around football. According to our survey, the majority of clubs are not active in promoting anti-racist initiatives in partnership with the local authority, and this is certainly an area where the expertise of local government and 'race' equality councils can be employed to great effect in partnership with the football club.

Women's and girls' football appears to be the area in which most local authorities want to expand their work. The rise of new female centres of excellence, and the priority given to female football by Sport England means that it is now firmly on the agenda for most of our respondent local authorities, if not their local clubs. The training of coaches was also identified as an area in need of improvement, and a sphere where effective delivery could be improved via greater co-ordination between club and local government.

It is no coincidence that in a survey of facilities for disabled football fans conducted in 1997 by the Sir Norman Chester Centre for Football Research, two of the clearest examples of good practice were at stadiums either wholly, or part-owned by local authorities.[4] At Huddersfield's McAlpine and Northampton's Sixfields Stadiums, excellence in design was achieved through local authority access officers working in partnership with architects and user groups. General local authority input is also important in trying to ensure that clubs act on their responsibilities to the disabled.[5] However, in the eyes of our local authority respondents most clubs are still inactive in this area.

In many ways the most appropriate point of contact between club and local authority is through the club's Football in the Community Scheme.[6] The club is keen to make contact with local people, especially the young, in order, potentially, to recruit supporters and to be seen to be contributing something 'in the community'. The local council has an interest in encouraging participation in sport and in ensuring that the 'brand' of the local club is put to best use in its work with the young and 'disadvantaged' groups. Bringing together the local knowledge and expertise (equity issues, access, and so on) as well as the contacts (local community groups, ethnic minorities) and resources (leisure spaces, for example) of the local authority, and the pulling power and appeal of the local football club and its players would seem to be something of a priority here.

BARRIERS AND PATHWAYS TO IMPROVED RELATIONSHIPS

Unfortunately, the good examples outlined briefly above are relatively few, with most clubs and local authorities failing to see the benefits of such links. So what are the crucial elements in establishing such relations, and what are the barriers that prevent partnerships being formed?

There is considerable evidence from the surveys that *personalities* can be critical in forming productive local links:

> There is a current shared interest in exploring the feasibility of developing a new stadium. A change in personnel at the club has resulted in a more positive attitude to the football in the community project.

> [Relations are] improving due to a change of management at the club and new partnership initiatives between local authority and club, mainly surrounding anti-racism and education.

At the same time, of course, there remained individuals whose very presence in the local networks was seen to create what might seem to be near insurmountable problems. The smaller the club one deals with the more powerful particular individuals can become. Several respondents pointed specifically to individuals who were hampering local prospects of improved relations.

A particular individual upsets and angers too many people who are only too willing to help if given the right approach.

> The club is now in a lower league, therefore [there is] a need for partnerships. It cannot exist in isolation now. The new chairman is a businessman, who is more used to partnerships and deals.

However, at some clubs, having one particular individual who is open and proactive in pursuing good relations is obviously a good thing. When such a key individual moves on, things can change, and the good work that has gone on before may collapse: 'The new chairman of the football club has improved relations, but this reliance on one person is a barrier.' An election, of course, can also lead to positive partners on the local authority side moving on. Clearly, structures which are relatively independent of particular individuals or parties need to be established to ensure the longer-term success and smooth running of local partnerships. However, this can be difficult at some smaller clubs where instability is virtually routine.

Although the attitude of new club staff was a breakthrough in some places, the clash of occupational and working cultures between football club and local authority can also create serious tensions that then serve only to worsen relationships. Several of our respondents mentioned what they took to be the highly 'business-oriented' and profit-driven stance of the club being at odds with the wish of the authority to 'deliver' to the local community.

Some clubs in the survey criticized their local authority from the opposite perspective to that expressed above, arguing that the authorities are too bureaucratic, and even unbusiness-like. The feeling among several of our respondents was that football clubs can be very insular and detached organizations with regard to working collaboratively with the local authority – until, perhaps, the club needed co-operation and support locally. Here, there was a strong feeling that some club chairmen saw the proper role of the local authority as simply to pump money into ailing football outfits; that clubs had a right to local public money. This is clearly a difficult area. In today's competitive climate, most clubs are certainly becoming much more 'business-like' in their attitudes but, as we have seen, this can also make them more efficient and better organized for work with outside bodies. Attempts by clubs to open up new markets or to appeal to 'family' spectators can also have beneficial effects in terms of access and 'equity' issues along the lines of gender and 'race', if not in terms of opening up opportunities for those who are economically disadvantaged. These are areas where negotiation and a recognition of where interests are actually *shared* can be positively mobilized in local partnerships.

Finance, of course, is one of the main barriers to good partnerships. The threat to the very existence of some clubs in the lower divisions may also harm the relationship with the local authority. Here, the desperate and single focus on survival can lead to the ignoring of the relationship between the club and its local partner agencies.

> Increased finances have raised the development aspirations of the club, sometimes resulting in conflict with the local authority, from a planning/control point of view. Relegation and subsequent reduced income have similarly caused conflict/tension with the club being forced to release other assets, e.g. redevelopment of club owned land for uses which may not be supported by the local authority.

> Clubs have major commercial pressures at this level and tend to be inward looking. They need adequate resources if they are to make any meaningful contribution to their local communities.

But when fortunes change, then attitudes can also shift:

> The promotion at the end of last season to the second division has created a new wave of popular support for the club and hence attracted councillor interest and support.

Resources are a concern for most clubs outside the élite, and for local councils. There is also the issue of the motives and role of clubs in the community. It was very clear that a number of our respondents were more than suspicious of the motivations of some clubs in this area and also very wary that partnerships which might be struck with them might potentially open up local authorities themselves to criticisms about delivery of service and policy. Could clubs be *trusted* to maintain a reliable and authentic community focus, given all the other pressures they face? There is certainly room for doubt, according to some of our local authority respondents:

> The community scheme is very commercial and tends to work in areas where they will make money and find it difficult to offer their biggest asset

(the players) to act as a promotional tool for our activities even though we have written agreements for them to provide this.

The funding of development initiatives is an issue. The club see themselves as a business and is therefore reluctant to assist with the finance of schemes. The club is perceived as having a hidden agenda when involved in community activity i.e. the production of young players (development) for the club.

I believe there is a real opportunity for delivering worthwhile activities to members of the community, if the 'conscience' of the club is used to full effect. However, this is being lost due to the club's view of the community as a means of raising money. The problem is that community activity is not seen as a marketing tool for the club's business plan.

Planning is clearly the first point of 'new' contact for many clubs with their local authorities. This can work positively as the catalyst for developing wider, continuing relationships:

The club has tended to ignore the Borough Council but recent ground improvements require our consent. For the council's part the club's increased prestige and success have led to our recognizing the club's value and led to a genuine attempt to improve relations.

There is now a partnership relating to the proposed redevelopment of the ground, and partnership relating to the proposed 'Asians in football' initiative and the existing football in the community scheme.

However, relations can also often worsen as a result of disagreement over planning issues. Clearly, where clubs are ambitious – or desperate – and where local authorities have a wider set of responsibilities and constituencies to serve, planning matters can often cause real problems even where relations between the club and local administration have traditionally been good: 'Planning was a concern when the club wished to move sites. This they finally achieved on appeal. Non-planning links have always been good, e.g. leisure links.' At a time when stadium facilities and location is a real sign of the ambition and long-term prospects of clubs (and for some a lifeline for the future), it is not surprising that 35 of our local authority respondents stated that planning issues specifically were creating significant barriers to forging good relations: 'The club requires planning permission for various initiatives: youth academy, new stadium (or altered old one) plus first team facility for training. Negotiations are delicate and politically volatile on all these issues, which makes for strained relationships at officer level.'

Positive relationships, therefore, can fail to be established with some clubs (and in some local areas) due to long-standing enmities or simple hostility to the principle of such partnerships; or else a lack of awareness on one or both sides of the mutual benefits of such a link; or because of conflicts over planning proposals; or because of a lack of communication between club and local authority, which may reflect the pursuit of very different private and public agendas; finally, inevitably, finance is also a major stumbling block in forging good relations between football clubs and public bodies of this kind.

Despite some of the frustrations highlighted above, most local authorities clearly place a great deal of importance on maintaining good relations with the local football club. Six out of ten of our respondent authorities said that they wanted to extend links with their local clubs. Such plans to extend or improve links come under several different classifications, the most common being centred around football development and coaching activities. The club community scheme, use of the stadium and other club facilities, and planned Centres of Excellence or Football Academies also provide best scope for extending or improving links according to many of our respondents:

> As the Sports Development Officer I tried to assist the clubs by getting them to write a development plan and improve links with the local youth football club.

> Develop stronger links between local authority managed football development programme and the [Premier League club's] youth Academy.

> The council is currently developing a football in the community project with local schools in a disadvantaged area. Links with the [First Division] football club would be a positive step and good for the kids.

> There were previous tensions over a planning issue. The club is now more open, as it is actively seeking support for a lottery bid for a 'Centre of Excellence' at a local college.

Given that 82 per cent of our respondents felt that their local clubs were either 'quite open' or 'very open' to extending or improving local authority links, the scope for productive change seems considerable. To this end, pathways to better relations would appear to be through partnerships around single issues; improved communication and co-ordination; the identification of resources, and the attitude and willingness of key individuals.

THE FUTURE OF FOOTBALL CLUB/LOCAL GOVERNMENT RELATIONS

The local football club is often the most readily recognized institution within any town or city. These days football clubs are important in *place marketing* on a national and international level. Success for a local club, either in terms of the major prizes at home and in Europe, or for smaller clubs in the shape of an heroic Cup run, can bring considerable economic and social benefits to an area; at the very least such sporting progress can often make local people feel much stronger and more positive about their local ties and associations. In the minds and the newspaper pages of the nation it can also, almost literally in terms of smaller clubs, put 'forgotten' towns back on the map of public debate and recognition. In these times when sport and talk about sport – especially football – has seeped into almost all kinds of popular culture and is now a regular feature of *political* debate, and as identity formation becomes more closely associated with leisure and consumption rather than with work, football clubs are likely to become more important for local people as time goes on. Our local authority respondents did, indeed, feel that their local football club would *increase* in its importance for local people, a fact which, obviously one might suppose, increases the need for public bodies to try to forge successful partnerships with clubs in the future. Of course, as larger clubs become increasingly national, even global in their scope, it may be that smaller clubs become invested with even stronger local significance to counter the likely growth of 'distance' between larger clubs and those people who support them.

At least half of our respondents considered that their local football club is at least becoming more interested in working on projects with the local authority. Some clubs are now opening up to links with outside agencies as common goals become more apparent, as new administrators move into the sport, as planning becomes a major issue in some places, and as the ambitions of some clubs take them into other areas of service and business. Finally, some clubs, as modern businesses do seem to be more concerned these days about issues of *access* and *equity*, even if in some cases this is mainly from the point of view of their commercial and marketing ambitions and public image rather than some notion of collective public 'good'. Problems remain at the lower levels of the Football League where the interest of some clubs in partnerships seems to be diminishing as financial problems grow. Perhaps new models of development are necessary here for some smaller clubs along the lines that we have already seen work successfully at clubs such as Bournemouth and Northampton Town.

In fact, 85 per cent of all local authority respondents who have local FA Premier League club connections feel generally *optimistic* about the future; a reflection, certainly, of the current popularity of top-flight football, of some of the changes in club approaches to external contacts, of the new marketing emphases at top football clubs and of the successful establishment of several new partnerships at this level. The last named also depends, of course, on the imagination and the energy of the *public* sector. There is less optimism lower down the football hierarchy, but perhaps that is to be expected, and even here around six in every ten authorities feel confident and optimistic about future relations. Of course, it is perhaps here that new approaches to running and financing football clubs are most needed and where, potentially at least, new partnerships, properly thought through and well resourced, might work best. For this to occur, clubs – and local authorities – will have to rethink radically the traditional place of the smaller football club in local networks and the real *priorities* of clubs at this level. More work – and some deep thinking – certainly needs to be done at these levels before some smaller clubs, perhaps forever, slip quietly under the water.

To summarize, local authorities are optimistic about the future of relations with their local football clubs for *four* main practical reasons:

1. The recent establishment in some places of regular meetings of working groups/liaison committees/partnerships around individual projects/single issues such as football development, grant applications (including Lottery funding), anti-racist projects and use of stadium and other facilities.

2. The recognition of the *mutual benefits* of partnership, with the club recognizing the value of good local authority links and the latter being more responsive to the attractions offered by having a positive relationship with the club.

3. Good existing links with, and/or proposals for, the expansion of the existing club Football in the Community scheme.

4. The availability or prospects of new stadium or training facility developments at the club, and the rise of centres of excellence and football academies.

Local authorities are *pessimistic* about the future of relations with local football clubs when they view clubs as, simply, economically driven, with no real interest in playing a responsible and responsive role in 'community' affairs or in collaboratively extending participation in the sport locally:

> The club doesn't want to be involved in our own scheme. They want to make money: almost a hit and run set up until numbers drop then they don't come back for a while!

> The club seems to have had their money and stadium and have left us alone. Communication has ceased in terms of 'sport' development.

Clearly, there are barriers to overcome in the future, but with the dissemination of best practice, and an understanding of the problems involved, then wider progress can be made.

CONCLUSION

The link between football clubs and local authorities is likely to increase in significance in the post-millennium period. For the major 'global' clubs it will be a means of anchoring themselves to their immediate community as they seek to expand their support in overseas markets. For smaller professional clubs, whose very survival is, at best, uncertain, effective local partnerships will contribute to ensuring their day-to-day existence.

There are several good examples of effective multi-agency partnerships which have tackled issues around education, community involvement,[7] sports development, racism, drug abuse[8] and other social concerns. There is general recognition that the club brand, allied to the wider expertise of the local authority can often bring about greater awareness in such schemes. This 'value added' approach is vital in terms of assessing what each partner gets out of local links. The club brand is also recognized as a possible means of opening gateways to alternative sources of funding for local initiatives, and increasing public awareness and interest.

It is clear that, in many instances, clubs and their local partners are still slowly learning what each other is best at, and that some 'experimentation' is bound to take place initially before partners fully 'hit it off'. As the first active contact with a club is often as a result of a contentious planning issue, it is obviously best to try to establish contact and a good working relationship before this occurs in order to try and overcome any difficulties around critical issues such as planning. A specific single concern, such as a football development or anti-racist project is often the reason why good relations can develop, and it appears that partnerships around FA Academies and Centres of Excellence are indeed kick-starting hitherto dormant relationships.

At present, the good relations reported with clubs is often with the Football in the Community scheme alone, and is not necessarily strong with senior club personnel. Watson's contribution to this volume offers further reflection on the marginalization of Football in the Community schemes within clubs. Such executive level contact is important and should be encouraged, and evidence suggests that partnerships are likely to be stronger and more enduring when both the club and the local authority recognize the value of links at all levels and not just through the community scheme.

Inevitably, limited resources are a stumbling block to good relations, especially for authorities trying to work with smaller clubs. Good projects can be established, which appear to deliver in the short term, but because they lack longer-term support they can often generate local demands which cannot then be fulfilled. At the same time, some clubs, even larger ones, can look on the local authority as its 'servant', there only to help to secure the long-term future of the club or to pump money or other resources into *club* initiatives. Proper and successful partnerships are based, instead, on a clear understanding of the proper role and responsibilities of the respective partners and the *limits* to their involvement in joint initiatives. Convincing smaller clubs to contribute, socially, when times are good, so that they might be looked upon more favourably in more 'difficult' times, is probably important here, as clubs want to be left alone, with few public responsibilities or duties, to be run as private businesses when times are good; when times are bad they claim to be an indispensable part of the local social fabric.

Undoubtedly, the current attraction and appeal of football provides scope for enormous development on social and cultural fronts. What football and football clubs can be 'used for' almost has no bounds these days given the huge public interest in the sport. However, partners often fail to see the real potential of such links, and clubs and local authorities often need convincing about what might actually be possible by seeing or hearing about something actually working positively in a similar location in another part of the country. This greater *national* or *regional* communication and co-ordination seems an important omission from current programmes.

NOTES

1. S. Perkins and J. Williams, *Local Authorities and Football Club Partnerships: Some Research on New Developments* (Leicester: Sir Norman Chester Centre for Football Research, University of Leicester, forthcoming).
2. All quotes in this essay are taken from Perkins and Williams. Respondents are all local authority officers, from leisure departments, who work regularly with football clubs.
3. Kick It Out, *Annual Report 1997/98* (London: Kick It Out, 1998).
4. J. Williams and S. Perkins, *Leaving the Trackside: Facilities for Disabled Fans at British Football Stadia, post-Hillsborough* (London: The Football Trust, 1997).
5. Football Task Force, *Improving Facilities for Disabled Supporters* (London: Football Task Force, 1998a).
6. J. Williams and R. Taylor, *The National Football in the Community Programme: A Research Report* (Leicester: Sir Norman Chester Centre for Football Research, University of Leicester, 1994); N. Watson, 'Football in the Community: "What's the Score?"' (unpublished dissertation, University of North London, 1998) and N. Watson, 'Football in the Community: "What's the Score?"' in this collection.
7. Football Task Force, *The Community Role of Football Clubs* (London: Football Task Force, 1998b).
8. T. Crabbe, *Going for Goals!! An Evaluation of the Tower Hamlets Drug Challenge Fund Project* (Goldsmiths College, London: Centre for Urban and Community Research, 1998).

9

Football in the Community:
'What's the Score?'

NEIL WATSON

'Football in the Community' schemes have been a feature of the vast majority of professional football clubs since the early 1990s. Originally suggested as an interventionist measure in order to combat the effects of football hooliganism as far back as 1975, their recent growth and development has been extraordinary. It now seems that many community schemes are mature and sophisticated organizations developing sport from grass roots to excellence, tackling serious social issues and working in partnership with both the private and public sectors.

However, very little research has been done examining the type of work such schemes undertake, for what reason and for whose benefit.[1] It should also be remembered that many were initiated in the mid-1980s when the football industry was experiencing one of its worst periods, with falling attendances, widespread incidents of disorder in and around grounds, and the Heysel and Bradford disasters of 1985. That these programmes have proliferated and, in many cases, expanded since that period, is something in itself that is worthy of investigation.

The following is a short extract from a research project which attempted to focus on the changing role of the Footballers' Further Education and Vocational Training Society (FFEVTS),[2] and assessed the aims and priorities of individual 'Football in the Community' schemes and how their work is funded. The project also looked at the position of schemes within football clubs and how they attempt to reconcile the different agendas with which they are often confronted.

METHODOLOGICAL APPROACH

The central concern of the research was to collect data in relation to the development of community programmes in professional football in a new era of the game, where individual projects appear to have been reshaped and redesigned to meet the needs of football clubs of various size, status and ambition. The methods deployed to collect this data were specifically tailored to the particular context in which 'Football in the Community' schemes operate. The research methods were built around a triangulated approach[3] which utilized a multi-dimensional, qualitative and quantitative strategy, utilizing two key approaches:

short, structured questionnaires and detailed semi-structured interviews. The data collected from the questionnaires and interviews were further supplemented by participant observation and informal discussion with 'Football in the Community' officers, and I also drew upon my own experiences as Director of the Leyton Orient Community Sports Programme.

Given the reliance on a limited number of qualitative interviews to reveal significant amounts of data it was important that the quality of the interviews was maximized. In this context, establishing a good rapport with interviewees was a vital element of the interviewing process. C. Glesne and A. Peshkin state: 'Rapport is tantamount to trust, and trust is the foundation for acquiring the fullest, most accurate disclosure a respondent is able to make.'[4] After ten years of experience of working with a 'Football in the Community' scheme, I have a good understanding of the culture and language of 'Football in the Community' officers and the particular environments in which they work, as well as having established a high level of rapport with many officers working in other schemes.

M. Hammersley and P. Atkinson emphasize the importance of reflexive interviewing in a qualitative approach to research.[5] They argue that the interviewer must be able to respond flexibly to the interviewee as an individual, subjective being. However, such interviews cannot be completely free-flowing and the interviewer needs to have a clear idea of what particular issues or topics are to be focused on. Accordingly, following a pilot phase, a detailed interview schedule was drafted so that interviews could be directed in a logical order.

The semi-structured interviews concentrated on key issues which included: the difference between 'big' and 'small' club 'Football in the Community' schemes; the main aims and objectives of such programmes; their biggest obstacles and challenges; changes in the focus of work of community schemes; the management structure and power relations within clubs in which such programmes operate; the relationship between football clubs, community schemes, local authorities and the public sector; and related funding issues.[6]

Theoretical concerns relating to questionnaire design[7] were taken into account in terms of style, format and length. H.W. Smith argues that the wording of individual questions is a significant issue in survey research, and suggests that there must be a 'shared vocabulary' between researcher and respondent.[8] Accordingly, the questionnaire was compiled using uncomplicated sentence structures and vernacular language and terminology. A pilot survey was conducted in January 1998 and also one trial interview. Following this pilot several minor amendments to the questionnaire and interview schedule were made. The main final questionnaire was then distributed in February 1998 with the final returns coming back in April 1998. Detailed semi-structured interviews were then conducted during May and June 1998.

The questionnaires were distributed by post via the FFEVTS to each of the professional football club and semi-professional 'Football in the Community' schemes in England. The size of the sample group was informed by what was realistic within the time and resource limitations, the experience of other research studies and the size of the overall sample. In this particular study, a questionnaire was distributed to each of the 85 Football in the Community schemes and five follow-up 'case studies' were conducted involving detailed semi-structured interviews with community officers at the selected schemes. In selecting individuals for the follow-up case studies and detailed interviews I sought out community programmes which met a series of contrasting criteria relating to the size of the club, control and management of the scheme, the scope of activities undertaken and regional location. The following range of schemes was selected:

– Scheme A: at a relatively 'big', but unsuccessful Division One club in the north of England, with its community programme under FFEVTS control with part local authority funding and representation on the management committee.

– Scheme B: at a mid-ranking, successful Premiership club in London with football club-controlled community scheme not reporting to a separate management committee.

– Scheme C: at a low status, but fairly successful Division Three club on the east coast of England with its community programme existing as an independent organization with part local authority funding but no representation on the management committee.

– Scheme D: at a reasonably 'big', financially insecure Division Three club in the south of England with its community scheme under the control of the football club with part local authority funding and representation on the management committee and funding from the football club.

– Scheme E: at a relatively small, fairly successful Premiership club in London with its community programme reporting to a management committee with funding from the football club and the private sector. Community officers are employed directly by the football club and income raised through football and community activities is paid back to the club.

Additional interviews were conducted with the National Scheme Manager of the FFEVTS and one of the five regional directors from the same organization.

Of the 85 Football in the Community schemes sent a questionnaire 81 responded, representing a response rate of 95 per cent. Eleven of the respondents to the structured questionnaire indicated that they would not be prepared to participate in a more detailed follow-up interview. All of the 'Football in the Community' officers and FFEVTS administrators who were formally requested to participate in a follow-up interview agreed to do so. These in-depth interviews were conducted at a time convenient to the respondents and took place in the working environments occupied by the interviewees.[9] Interviews were taped with the respondents' consent and then transcribed.

DISCUSSION

Although it is difficult to draw concrete conclusions from the research undertaken, due to the limited number of case studies carried out, some informed comment can be made. Firstly, the role of the FFEVTS has changed over the last 12 years from a 'hands on' management style to one of less direct involvement, as football clubs have taken more responsibility for their own schemes. This became inevitable as the majority of schemes grew and developed and football club officials began to recognize, in some cases, the benefits that could be accrued from the work of such programmes.

There is no evidence that any significant number of football clubs initially embraced the concept of 'football in the community': indeed it seems that some were fairly sceptical about what they could achieve. As the FFEVTS National Scheme Manager recalled:

> When I started, 12 years ago, one of the six pilot scheme clubs would hardly let me through the door. When I did get in he [the club secretary] gave me five minutes to describe what the scheme was going to do for his club. I remember him saying: 'If this involves one more piece of paper crossing my desk I will stop it.'[10]

This is not to say that all clubs adopted this position, as some have remained fairly consistent in their endorsement of schemes and often have provided excellent support. However, the long-term approach that the FFEVTS adopted in initiating and developing schemes that football clubs eventually began to embrace should be commended and acknowledged. It seems that the FFEVTS has allowed events to run their 'natural course' on a club-by-club basis, neither passing responsibility to the clubs before they were ready to accept it or attempting to adopt principled stands when football clubs took decisions about their schemes which would not normally receive their approval. Instead, the FFEVTS regarded its role as being to advise, support and arbitrate where necessary, and yet understand that it is the football club which will ultimately determine the direction of its own scheme.

The majority of schemes now report to a management forum which is primarily composed of representatives from only the football club and the FFEVTS, suggesting that these two organizations are the key players (see Figure 9.1). Others have representation from local authorities, sponsors or the police, for example, but it is unlikely that any of these will be in a position to determine the policy of the scheme. In addition, schemes are generally based at football clubs which ensure that the regular line of communication is between the senior community officer and a named official at the club.

Generally speaking, there does appear to be a *laissez-faire* attitude towards schemes from the clubs at which they are based. From the case studies carried out, all community officers expressed the same kind of answer when asked about

FIGURE 9.1

REPRESENTATION OF BODIES ON THE MANAGEMENT COMMITTEE AT
INDIVIDUAL CLUB SCHEMES

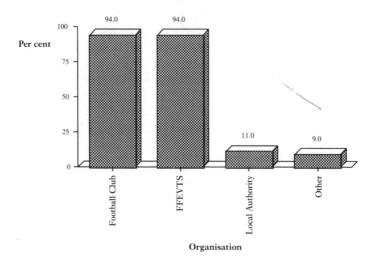

the type of influence exerted by their clubs. They believed the club was happy with the work they were doing and content to let the schemes decide on the type of projects they wished to pursue in order to achieve their aims. It was apparent that community officers understood the priorities of the football club and that Football in the Community programmes were unlikely to be near the top. However, that is not to say that community officers did not understand their worth at those times when the football club was dealing with the local authority over planning permission, for example, and seemed to understand the kinds of events and activities that were of interest to the directors and senior staff at the football club, and in turn realized the importance of the media coverage such activities generated.

There have been examples, though not many, of football clubs which feel that it is in their best interests to leave the national programme and run an 'independent' community scheme. This situation, it seems, has been created as a result of both the FFEVTS and the football club being unable to agree on the role of the community programme, and often in these cases the football club seems to see the scheme only as an opportunity to generate income, an approach the FFEVTS advises against. However, it should be noted that the FFEVTS does not ask clubs to withdraw from the national programme, as this decision is ultimately the prerogative of the football club.

This research project was primarily concerned with the differences between schemes based at 'big' and 'small' clubs, and from the data generated it seems that 'big' club schemes are now likely to employ more permanent staff and generate more income than those at 'small' clubs. There is a definite correlation between the size of the scheme and the size and status of the club. The majority of big schemes, those that employ more than five full-time members of staff or generated more than £250,000 per annum are now found in the Premiership (see Figure 9.2). Schemes based at football clubs playing in the bottom division of the Football League were more likely to have a single worker generating between £10–20,000 per annum.

FIGURE 9.2

CORRELATION BETWEEN THE STATUS OF THE CLUB AND THE TURNOVER PER ANNUM OF THE COMMUNITY SCHEME

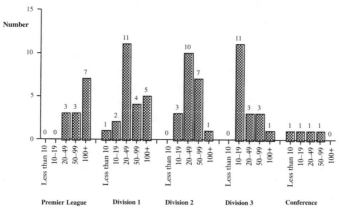

Status of Club and Annual Turnover (£s thousands)

Overall, those clubs in the higher divisions were more likely to fund their own community schemes. More than half of those based in the Premiership (53 per cent) made funding available to the programmes, slightly less than half in Football League Division One (44 per cent), a handful in Division Two (15 per cent) and none in Division Three. In addition, it is likely that schemes based at 'big' football clubs would be able to attract funding purely because of the name and stature of the club. Again, there is a similar correlation between commercial money being attracted to the scheme and the size of the club where the scheme is based. Although there is no indication about the amount of money provided by commercial sponsors, it should be safe to assume that the larger sponsorships are more likely to be associated with the 'big' clubs.

Interestingly, local authorities and educational trusts are more likely to fund the work of schemes based at clubs in Divisions One and Two, and only a very small minority in either the Premiership (five per cent) or Football League Division Three (nine per cent) attract funding from either. Over half in Divisions One and Two receive local authority income (53 per cent) and around one-third (30 per cent) from trusts. Again, although no information of the amounts of money is available, it does suggest that the majority of Premiership-based schemes operate through football club and commercial funding while those lower down rely more on local authorities and educational trusts. This could be partly due to necessity rather than choice for smaller clubs as they have attempted to stabilize and grow more gradually.

Although it is outside the scope of this study, it may be interesting to find out how these partnerships between clubs and local authorities and educational trusts have been created, and what the expectations of the partners are. Those that have been created between football clubs and local authorities are particularly interesting as both are concerned to some degree with providing access to sport for young people. Whether 'small' football clubs and local authorities are more likely to make better partners than 'big' football clubs and local authorities is worth further research.

The aims and priority areas of Football in the Community schemes are not particularly different depending on the size of the football club where the scheme was based. Results from the survey indicated that there was a general consensus throughout programmes at all clubs about what their aims were. It was generally agreed that community schemes should be about involving young people in football activities (82 per cent thought this important or very important), creating links between the club and its local populace (78 per cent) and providing a good public image for the club (68 per cent). Only a small number responded that scheme was there to recruit young players for the football club's youth development programme (20 per cent) or to provide sponsorship opportunities for the football club (18 per cent). However, this is not to say that community officers did not recognize that an active programme would have potential benefits in both these areas, it was just that neither was deemed sufficient a justification for operating the scheme.

Those running both Premiership-based schemes in the case study seemed certain about what was deemed important by their clubs. One community officer reported that his club thought it was more important for the scheme to be a football development programme which would ultimately produce talent for the club. Although this was not directly conveyed by the club, the perception existed that the officer's role would eventually be linked to the club's new football academy. In the other case, the scheme was expected to contribute to increasing the attendance at home matches through an active and large football development programme targeted at children and young people. The club had acknowledged that the programme had been successful at this yet was keen to stress that targets were not given and that this process was being allowed to take its natural course.

Those involved in the schemes based at both the 'small' clubs analysed were mainly concerned with developing and sustaining links between the club and the community, primarily through football coaching courses or through a balance of coaching courses and 'social issue' and education projects (it should be noted that the club undertaking the latter projects was one of those rare cases of a big scheme based at a 'small' club). Both clubs, however, recognized their role in involving children with the club's activities and the need to promote the club within the locale of the stadium.

The case study of the scheme based at the high status club currently playing outside the Premiership was very different from the others. This programme had successfully managed to forge a close working relationship with the local authority and its work was a balance of football coaching courses and educational projects. It employed a dedicated education officer whose role involved developing links with schools and using football as a vehicle to support academic work. The officer saw the name of the football club as being critical to this process but admitted the programme was perceived as being outside the club, as evidenced by the Senior Community Officer: 'Over the years the community scheme has been seen as an add-on to the club rather than part of the club ... I think most clubs are hard up for cash and they tend to prioritise, and to be fair "Football in the Community" schemes are not top of the list.'[11]

Those running the schemes are also agreed on the types of project that they undertake as a priority. Football coaching courses aimed at children and young people are regarded as the core business (88 per cent thought this was their top priority), and in a sense this work meets the important aims of creating tangible links between the club and the community and helps increase the clubs' standing within their local communities, since they are seen as putting something back without necessarily taking much in return.

To understand why some schemes continue to run only as a football development programme while others have decided to diversify is more difficult. The community officer in one case study suggested that the scheme would continue as a football development programme for the foreseeable future and another admitted that education projects took precedence. Therefore, the decision to diversify schemes could be explained simply by the stance taken by individual senior community officers, although this may provide only part of the answer. The path that schemes take could also be explained by other factors including funding opportunities, the influence of local authorities, football club perceptions about the programme or evidence of good practice elsewhere provided by the FFEVTS.

It may be that schemes at 'big' clubs have a more prescribed role in that they fulfil a particular function of the football club and that those at 'small' clubs adopt a more holistic approach to their work, attempting continually to create a positive profile for the club within its catchment area. Whatever the case, it seems that not many clubs are setting targets for their schemes to achieve. Even in those cases where the club funds the programme and there is an understanding about what that money is for, community officers did not feel under any great pressure to deliver. It seems to be the case that, for whatever reason, Football in the Community schemes are at very different stages of their evolution and it now seems likely that they will become less rather than more similar over the next few years.

There is certainly little difference between 'big' and 'small' club schemes about their aims and priorities as they remain similar to those outlined by the FFEVTS. This suggests that their initial stamp on schemes and continued support is paying off. It seems that the majority of Football in the Community schemes which continue to attract huge numbers of participants from differing backgrounds in a range of diverse projects are satisfying the demands and expectations of both the club where they are based and the communities in which they operate. A consequence of a large and successful football development programme might be improved access and opportunity for all, better young players for the football club and stronger links between the club and its local communities. The next stage in their development will be crucial: for some schemes may be more of the same, while for others it could be something very different.

CONCLUSION AND RECOMMENDATIONS

What then may be the future of Football in the Community schemes? It would seem that in the majority of cases over the last 12 years schemes have grown steadily and are now firmly established in as much as they are part of the structure of football clubs. It would seem that there is evidence to suggest that most exist for the same purpose, but that those based at 'big' clubs are more likely to generate more income and employ more staff than those based at 'small' clubs. The questions that now need to be addressed are whether schemes will change in terms of their operation and aims, and specifically how they are funded and by whom, what types of influence they will be subjected to and what will be the role of the FFEVTS.

The National Scheme Manager mentioned that community schemes are 'one of football's best kept secrets'.[12] It would seem that they are precisely this because of clubs' ambivalence towards them during their initiation and development phase. It is unlikely that they would be fulfilling the functions they currently do if football clubs had taken any real interest in them. Now that they are established it may be safe to assume that football club directors and staff will be reviewing their role within the whole organization. For some, including the two Premiership case study schemes, this process has already begun.

Football in the Community schemes may soon have to make important choices if they are going to continue to develop and increase their level of influence. For some, this decision may have to be made quickly or they run the risk of having it made for them. However, before outlining what this may involve it might be worth examining the future contribution of the FFEVTS.

There may be an assumption that as football clubs rediscover and redirect their own community schemes, the level of influence of the FFEVTS will begin to decline. However, as has been mentioned above, community schemes are attractive and important to football clubs, communities and the public and private sectors precisely because of the template produced by the FFEVTS. If its influence was to decline a situation could be created whereby there was a narrowing of interests and a limited number of beneficiaries. If this were to happen, the role of the FFEVTS would be one of 'firefighting', arbitrating between club-based schemes over who does what and where. The result would be a community programme governed by its lowest common denominator – money. Those who have the ability to pay, or who consider the activities provided by schemes as important to the club and therefore worth funding would be the winners, and those who could not or did not would be the losers. In essence, those within local communities for whom schemes were ultimately designed, the socially disadvantaged or those with low levels of sports participation, would be discriminated against. How then does the FFEVTS continue to ensure that both football clubs and their communities remain satisfied with their community programmes?

It would be unrealistic to appeal to individual football clubs in an attempt to have them to put either the 'good of the game' or disadvantaged sections of the community before their own interests. It is in the nature of clubs to put themselves first, for they perceive this as the difference between winning and losing. The immediate battle that the FFEVTS must fight if it is to win the war involves the positioning of community schemes at the football clubs where they are based.

The overriding objective in the development of community schemes should be to retain and develop all that is successful about their programmes and yet, at the same time, meet the different agendas of football clubs and the public and private sectors. For schemes based at 'big' football clubs this could involve a moving towards the centre of operations. The Football Association Blueprint may provide the first real opportunity for some football clubs to utilize fully the skills and network of contacts of their community schemes.[13] In order to fulfil the criteria laid down by the Football Association Blueprint, football clubs are required to provide liaison and services for a minimum of 100 junior schools, 10 secondary schools and 50 junior football clubs.[14] It is suggested that this role could be taken by the Football in the Community schemes which have been performing this task for the last ten years or so. The football development programmes initiated by such schemes could form the basis for the academies' work and, in turn, the opportunities presented by the academy link could provide a useful marketing and sports development tool for the community schemes.

Only two things need to be avoided if football clubs are to orientate their community schemes in this fashion. First, the community development work undertaken should not be affected in any adverse way; football clubs could achieve this by making a specific financial contribution for this work or persuading commercial sponsors to do so. Second, football development work should not damage community development initiatives being carried out by 'smaller' clubs. This would entail 'big' football club schemes having clear aims and honest agendas when working with children in schools, for example. It seems somewhat duplicitous for clubs to pressure community officers to discover emerging talent under the guise of curriculum coaching programmes, when they have been sold to educators as 'sport for all' sessions.

Community programmes based at 'small' clubs may have to move towards a position of independence and away from the main body of the football club. At present schemes exist in a 'no mans land', somewhere between the club and those organizations who serve the needs of the community. Their sustainability will be ensured only when those organizations which benefit understand the schemes' value. Although it may appear a draconian move, shifting the balance of power away from those at the football club may be the long-term answer.

As those schemes undertaken at the case-study 'small' clubs demonstrated, their programmes are primarily football and community development initiatives aimed at young people and other disadvantaged social groups. That the football club benefits because of an improved image and increased interest from the local community is merely a consequence, albeit an intended one. Therefore, these community schemes are fulfilling an important public sector role, and, because of the numbers involved and profile of the participants, also attract the commercial sector. Although a limited number of community programmes have representation from both sectors on management forums (7 per cent) and others have funding from either or both (20 per cent), their influence on schemes is kept to a minimum.

It may be in the interest of these schemes to decrease the level of football club influence and increase the involvement of those other sectors which would then take 'ownership' of the programmes. What is not being suggested here is representation on a management forum of those who stand to benefit, but rather the opposite: that those who have the skills and levels of influence to make a real difference are at the disposal of the community scheme. In this way, community schemes are able to sell their organizational and community development skills to those who wish to buy them. This will include the football club which may want to finance a grass roots football development programme in the same way that it funds a youth development programme; a local authority or public sector organization for a community development initiative which uses football as the vehicle to effect social change or a commercial sector organization which may simply want access to a target market. It will only be with a management forum or board of trustees with expertise in each of these fields that will ensure that the community scheme makes the best decision.

The parallel for these types of community schemes may be the 'Action Sport' programmes of the early 1980s which appeared to be at a similar phase of development when funding was withdrawn and their future handed over to local authorities.[15] What is now apparent is that local authorities did not want sole control, but if they had remained 'partnership' projects they might have stood the test of time. If community schemes continue to attempt to do 'community' work as a department of a 'small' football club rather than as an independent organization then they are relying on the public sector to continually fund without influence or the support of a 'socially aware' football club.

The logical conclusion of a move in this direction would be Football in the Community programmes becoming charitable organizations with independent trustees, neither from the football clubs or from those public sector bodies who fund their work. In turn, this would allow schemes to access new money from charitable trusts and through commercial donations and ultimately it may even provide the kind of base from where 'small' club-based schemes could grow, develop and become more influential.

It is clear that at the time of writing it is a pivotal period for all Football in the Community schemes and for the communities they purport to serve. It now seems that programmes based at different sized clubs will become much less similar during the next phase of their development. This is to be expected and reflects what is happening in the wider context. However, what must be avoided is a situation whereby communities living around football grounds are further disadvantaged because their football club either cannot or will not contribute to the quality of their life. This is a difficult challenge, but one the football clubs and authorities must rise to if they are to continue to build on the first 20 years of Football in the Community schemes.

NOTES

1. For an assessment of the development of football community programmes in the early 1990s, see J. Williams with R. Taylor, *The National Football and the Community Programme: a Research Report* (Leicester: Sir Norman Chester Centre, 1994).
2. The Footballer's Further Education & Vocational Training Society (FFEVTS) was set up in 1979 to administer the national Community Programme in Professional Football. It is the umbrella organization for Football in the Community schemes.
3. See N.K. Denzin, *The Research Act in Sociology* (London: Butterworths, 1970) and N.K. Denzin, *Sociological Methods: A Sourcebook*, 2nd ed. (New York: McGraw-Hill, 1978).
4. C. Glesne and A. Peshkin, *Becoming Qualitative Researchers: An Introduction* (New York: Longman, 1992), p.79.
5. M. Hammersley and P. Atkinson, *Ethnography: Principles in Practice* (London: Routledge, 1989).
6. N. Gilbert, *Researching Social Life* (London: Sage, 1993). D.A. de Vaus, *Surveys in Social Research*, 3rd ed. (London: Allen & Unwin, 1991).
7. P. McNeill, *Research Methods* (London: Routledge, 1992).
8. H.W. Smith, *Strategies of Social Research: The Sociological Imagination* (Englewood Cliffs, New Jersey: Prentice Hall, 1975).
9. For an account of conducting interviews in differing environments, see R. Jenkins, 'Bringing It All Back Home: an Anthropologist in Belfast', in C. Bell and H. Roberts (eds.), *Social Researching: Politics, Problems, Practice* (London: Routledge & Kegan Paul, 1984), pp.147– 64.
10. Interview conducted with the FFEVTS National Scheme Manager, May 1998.
11. Interview conducted with the Senior Community Officer, May 1998.
12. Interview conducted with the FFEVTS National Scheme Manager, May 1998.
13. The Football Association Technical Department, *Football Education for Young Players, A Charter for Quality* (London: Football Association 1997).
14. Ibid., 4.8.2.
15. 'Action Sport' pilot schemes, funded by the Sports Council, were initiated in 1982 and their common features were target group work, an emphasis on drawing non-participants into activity through the use of Sports Leaders and the development of activities in non-purpose-built sports spaces.

PART 4
Football Crowds and Policing

10

The People's Game? Football Spectatorship and Demographic Change

DOMINIC MALCOLM, IAN JONES
and IVAN WADDINGTON

Spectatorship is something of a neglected area in sports research. A recent review of sport sociology and sport psychology journals, for instance, found that only 4 per cent of studies had focused on fans.[1] One might have expected that, since it has been termed 'the people's game', football would be different from other sports in this respect, and to some extent this is the case.[2] The literature on football spectators is relatively plentiful by comparison with data on spectators at other sports yet, as a number of writers have noted, much of the European research on football crowds has been dominated by the issue of football hooliganism.[3] Consequently, whilst we have detailed information on a minority of football fans, there has been a neglect of systematic empirical research into the majority of the football crowd. As V. Duke has pointed out, this neglect was starkly illustrated in 1990 when the Taylor Report on the Hillsborough stadium disaster had no recent data on the social composition of football crowds in Britain upon which it could draw.[4]

Despite the lack of empirical data, however, there is a widely held perception that the make-up of football crowds has changed considerably in recent years. In large part this notion stems from the debates which arose in response to the Hillsborough disaster. As journalists and administrators reflected on the apparent orderliness of spectators at American sports (not to mention the financial success with which these sports are run), the idea that a similar application of the principles of the free market could be used to reform football in Britain became increasingly influential.[5] The perceived need to improve facilities in general and aspects of safety in particular led, most notably, to the introduction of all-seater stadiums in the top two English divisions. However, in the eyes of the press, this modernization of facilities necessitated not only a change in the relationship between fans and the clubs which they supported, but also a change in the fan base of football itself. 'Fans were to become customers ... [and] the notion of the customer, who paid more for a better service, implied a shift of football support towards more affluent sections of society.'[6] An additional consequence of this changing relationship, it was assumed, would be that, again like the American model, increasing numbers of women and families would attend games. The ideas forwarded in the press were, as King has illustrated, adopted by football club chairmen. Peter Storrie of West Ham articulated this change in marketing strategy very clearly: 'Football is moving towards the family model. There is a strong basis to go forward if we push the family model.'[7]

Thus new marketing strategies started to be implemented with the express purpose of altering what was assumed to be football's traditional fan base. Many journalists have discussed what they perceive to be the resultant changes. For example W. Borrows, writing in the *Guardian* after the 1998 World Cup in France, described what he saw as the new football fan: 'The corpulent middle class tosser who might have delivered a well practised dinner-party excoriation aimed at football supporters two years ago but who will, this season, be asking his secretary to fax Chelsea *re* the availability of a box for the Arsenal game.'[8] Similarly, J. Crinnion argued that for the 1998/99 season, 'more women will be sitting in the stands, watching the box, following the form than ever before. As a spectator sport football is being feminised.'[9] Academic writers have made similar statements. J. Williams, for instance, has stated that 'Football has changed recently … it's suddenly a lot more middle class.'[10] A. King claims that the 'lads' who formed the basis of his research at Manchester United have, in recent years, been restricted and partially excluded from the Old Trafford Ground. This, he concludes, 'constitutes a profound social change'.[11] Finally R. Nash, although initially rather more circumspect in stating that '*it is likely* that those on low incomes, the unemployed, students, the disabled and pensioners, *in so far as they attended previously*, will struggle more and more to meet the cost of seeing many games over the course of the season' (emphasis added), goes on to claim that what seems 'likely' is, in fact, the case. Commenting on the Carling-sponsored surveys of football supporters, he argues that, 'it is essential that researchers find some way to assess the impact on those who now find themselves outside a game they actively followed until recently'.[12]

It is clear that stadiums have been modernized and that admission costs have risen, but the view that the predicted changes in crowd composition have also occurred remains something of an untested assumption.[13] Interestingly, with the partial exception of Crinnion, none of the writers cited above offers any evidence in support of their claims that the composition of football crowds has changed in recent years.[14] The purpose of this essay, therefore, is to take an overview of the available evidence and to examine whether it is correct to assume that there has been a change in football spectator demographics in recent years. More particularly, have the new marketing strategies of clubs succeeded in changing the social composition of football crowds and, if not, how can we account for this resilience to change?

METHODOLOGICAL PROBLEMS

One of the reasons for the paucity of information regarding football crowds is that there are many methodological difficulties in gathering data. Easily identifiable sample groups – season ticket holders, buyers of programmes or fanzines, members of fan groups, and so on – are, almost by definition, distinctly unrepresentative of the crowd as a whole. Moreover, as a great many fans aim to enter the stadium as close to kick-off as they can (survey data indicate that around 50 per cent of spectators aim to arrive in the 30 minutes prior to kick-off, but that a considerably higher proportion actually do so), interviewing is highly impractical and likely to reflect a bias towards certain groups, namely those arriving earliest. Thus postally returned questionnaires are generally the most appropriate and manageable research tool. Consequently, their distribution is critical to the representativeness of the sample drawn.

This study uses data drawn from a range of questionnaire surveys administered between 1984 and 1997. Various distribution methods have been used, some of which have resulted in low response rates (Preston North End, 1988;[15] Carling Survey, 1993/94)[16] and others which have resulted in the over-representation of specific groups (that is, season ticket holders at Rangers in 1990,[17] programme buyers in the 1993/94 Carling Survey). Some distribution methods have resulted in samples biased towards older fans (Rangers, 1994)[18] and other surveys, having been undertaken as part of an investigation of particular issues, are likely to have an over-representation of those spectators with a particular interest in the subject being addressed (Coventry City, 1983; Watford, 1987;[19] Carling Survey, 1996/97).[20] On the face of it, this methodological variety makes comparison difficult but, quite simply, these surveys constitute the only data source at our disposal. Until more adequate information becomes available (and some recommendations to this end are provided at the end of this essay) these surveys are the only means through which we can examine the academic theories outlined earlier regarding demographic trends in football spectatorship.

AGE AND SEX

The claim that football is now attracting a family audience implies that, increasingly, those who are stereotypically considered to be traditional fans (i.e. adult males) are increasingly bringing their wives and children to matches. However, from an examination of the age structure of football crowds over the 14 years covered by the surveys it is very difficult to identify any particular pattern of change (see Table 10.1). The proportion of the youngest supporters (those under the age of 20) varied from a high of 25 per cent at Aston Villa in 1992 to a low of 11 per cent in the 1996/97 Carling Survey.[21] Likewise, the proportion of the oldest supporters (those over 50 years of age) varied from a high of 23.9 per cent at Luton Town in 1997 to a low of 14.1 per cent in the 1993/94 Carling Survey. It would appear that between clubs and between surveys there is as much variance in findings as there has been over this period of time.[22] There is, therefore, nothing in this review of data to indicate that the age composition of crowds has altered in recent years, and thus no indication that an increasing

TABLE 10.1
THE AGE STRUCTURE OF FOOTBALL CROWDS (%)

Year	Coventry City 1983	Watford 1987	Preston N.E. 1988	Glasgow Rangers 1990	Aston Villa 1992	Arsenal 1992	Carling Survey 1993/94	Glasgow Rangers 1994	Carling Survey 1996/97	Luton Town 1997	National Profile 1991 Census
Age											
<20	22	17	21	17	25	17	14.9	under 25 19.4	11	15.8	25.3
21–30	27	23	19	29	28	33	27.8	25–40, 46.9	21	17.6	15.4
31–40	21	23	25	24	20	20	26.5		30	22.3	13.9
41–50	10	17	14	14	13	13	16.6	18.1	21	20.4	13.5
50+	20	21	21	16	15	18	14.1	15.2	17	23.9	31.8

TABLE 10.2
THE SEXUAL COMPOSITION OF FOOTBALL CROWDS (%)

Year	Coventry City 1983	Watford 1987	Preston N.E. 1988	Glasgow Rangers 1990	Aston Villa 1992	Arsenal 1992	Carling Survey 1993/94	Glasgow Rangers 1994	Carling Survey 1996/97	Luton Town 1997
Sex										
Male	88	87	89	90	89	90	87.3	93.2	87.7	88.7
Female	12	13	11	10	11	10	12.7	6.8	12.3	11.3

number of young people are now attending matches; indeed the only survey to be repeated (i.e. the Carling Surveys) suggests a significant decrease.

Similarly there is little to suggest that more women are now attending games; indeed the most striking feature of the data regarding the sexual composition of football crowds is its highly uniform nature. Leaving aside the Glasgow Rangers (1994) findings,[23] we can see that over a 14-year period surveys conducted in Great Britain have consistently found that females constitute between 10 per cent and 13 per cent of the crowd (see Table 10.2). Not only is there no indication that this figure has increased in recent years, but surveys from a variety of Western European countries, over a number of years, have produced very similar results.[24] Thus there is no evidence to suggest that the new marketing strategies of football clubs have succeeded in this respect and, given the distinct lack of evidence of change in both the age and the sexual composition of football crowds, there is little to support the contention that football is increasingly becoming a family game.

These findings are interesting because, of all the perceived changes in football crowd demographics, those changes related to sex have received the most attention. In particular, two related claims have been made: a) that a relatively high proportion of those who have recently been attracted to the game are female; and b) that smaller, 'provincial' clubs tend to attract a larger proportion of female support.[25] From the findings of the 1994/95 Carling Survey, Williams notes that 'more than one quarter (25.8 per cent) of fans – twice the proportion of women in the national sample – who have been attracted to football since the change to all-seater stadia are female'. This, we are told, is 'the first conclusive evidence, beyond the anecdotal, that more female supporters are indeed being attracted to Premiership matches'.[26]

Yet, as evidence from the surveys reviewed here shows, this is clearly a false conclusion to draw; there is no reliable evidence to indicate that women constitute a greater proportion of football spectators than was previously the case. However, an examination of the relationship between the age and sex of football supporters provides an explanation of this Carling Survey finding which is consistent with the overall picture. Those who have recently been attracted to football are, as one would expect, comparatively younger than football fans in general.[27] Furthermore, at the three clubs for which we have cross-tabulated data – Aston Villa, Arsenal and Luton – the sample of female supporters was considerably younger than the sample of male supporters (see Table 10.3, p.135). At Arsenal, 64 per cent of females but only 48 per cent of males were aged 30 or under, whilst at Luton the corresponding figures were 43.1 per cent of females and 32 per cent of males. The pattern was most marked, however, at Aston Villa where 70 per cent of females but only 50 per cent of males were from this age group. It is also significant that considerably fewer female than male spectators are married; at Arsenal under 35 per cent of female fans were either married or living with a partner, compared to almost 54 per cent of men, while at Aston Villa the comparable figures were 31 per cent for women and 47 per cent for men. It may be that marriage restricts the attendance of women at football matches to a much greater extent than it does that of men; in this connection, Jennifer Hargreaves has argued that women's 'responsibilities in the home and for children restrict leisure activities outside the home and so, not surprisingly, sport is a minority activity. When women marry, they usually stop participating in sport, even if they previously had an interest.'[28] In this regard, it is striking that only 0.9 per cent, 0.2 per cent and 0.6 per cent at Arsenal, Aston Villa and Luton Town respectively described themselves as housewives.

The second claim – that smaller, 'provincial' clubs tend to attract a larger proportion of female support – is also problematic. Evidence for this claim was drawn from the 1994/95 Carling Survey in which females constituted a low of 8.4 per cent at Everton and a high of 17.2 per cent at Sheffield Wednesday and Norwich City and from the 1996/97 Carling Survey where the proportion of season ticket holders who were female varied from 5 per cent at Newcastle to 17 per cent at Nottingham Forest. Firstly, it is not entirely clear what constitutes a 'provincial' club. In what ways are Everton (based in Liverpool) and Newcastle less provincial than Sheffield or Nottingham? Moreover, the surveys reviewed here do not support the claim which Williams makes. Whilst the findings at Watford (13 per cent) constitute the largest proportion of female support (Watford would probably fall within most definitions of a 'provincial' club), the results of the two surveys conducted at similarly small clubs – that is at Preston North End in 1988 and Luton Town in 1997 – do not show a particularly high proportion of female fans (see Table 10.1). Our data, therefore, do not indicate a larger presence of female support at small, provincial clubs. Furthermore, whilst conclusions in this respect must be tentative, these findings illustrate one further interesting point about the marketing of the game. Williams argues that 'the changing image of the sport, improved spectator facilities, changes in the atmosphere in and around the ground, and the changes in the way in which the sport is promoted and marketed, were all cited by "new" female fans, younger and older, as contributing to their recent interest in the FA Premier League'.[29] This claim reveals something of a paradox. If we are to claim that facilities and new marketing strategies have succeeded in changing the fan base of football clubs, one would expect a greater proportion of female supporters at the larger football clubs (which have been most affected by these changes), and not at those smaller clubs which might be described as 'provincial'. The findings in this respect are unclear but this example does serve to illustrate how some of the claims made with regard to the changing composition of football crowds can be both contradictory and unsubstantiated.

OCCUPATIONAL AND EMPLOYMENT STATUS

As we saw earlier, in addition to claims that football is attracting a new 'family audience', others have argued that in recent years football has started to attract an increasingly middle-class support.[30] Concurrently, it is claimed, other groups, such as the unemployed, students and the retired, have been increasingly excluded from the game. Longitudinal comparison of these data is rather more difficult than for, say, age and sex because the occupational structure of the country is subject to rather more regular and pronounced changes than are the former. For instance, in comparison with the 1980s, the 1990s have seen a large increase in the number of students continuing in full time education after the age of 16 and, in part related to this, significantly lower government figures for those registered as unemployed. Given these changes one would expect a greater range of findings in these demographic categories yet, surprisingly, this is not borne out from the surveys reviewed here. With the exception of the 1983 survey at Coventry City (11 per cent), the number of unemployed people attending football matches has remained relatively constant at around 4–6 per cent (see Table 10.3). Additionally there does not appear to be any evidence of the increasing exclusion of retired spectators. The lowest recorded figures (6 per cent) are from Coventry in 1983 and Arsenal in 1992 and the highest recorded figures are from Preston (11 per cent) in 1988 and from Luton (10.3 per cent) in 1997. Interestingly these are the two clubs from the lower divisions. Whilst unemployed spectators do not appear to be any more numerous at clubs from lower divisions, there is limited evidence that at these clubs retired spectators constitute a relatively high proportion of the overall crowd.

TABLE 10.3

THE AGE AND SEXUAL COMPOSITION OF FOOTBALL CROWDS (%)

		<20		21–30		31–40		41–50		50+	
		male	female	male	female	male	female	male	female	male	female
Aston Villa	1992	23.1	40.5	27	29.7	20.4	16.5	13.2	8.8	16.2	4.6
Arsenal	1992	15.1	29.9	32.9	34.1	20	14.8	12.9	12.4	19	8.8
Luton Town	1997	14.7	22.4	17.3	20.7	22.8	19.0	21.1	15.5	24.1	22.4
National Profile	1991										
	Census	25.3		15.4		13.9		13.5		31.8	

Although the findings for the unemployed and the retired have remained relatively constant, there is some evidence to suggest that students have decreased as a proportion of football crowds in recent years. The two lowest figures from the surveys are 9.5 per cent at Glasgow in 1994 and 9.0 per cent from the Carling Survey of 1996/97. In the surveys which preceded these, if we exclude the 1990 Glasgow survey (the sample of which was heavily biased towards season ticket holders), the proportion of students in football crowds ranged from 12 per cent to 17 per cent. Thus, despite the increase in the overall number of students in the 1990s, fewer seem to be attending live football matches. It may be that such changes are a consequence of the increase in ticket prices and the game's

TABLE 10.4
FOOTBALL CROWDS AND OCCUPATIONAL AND EMPLOYMENT STATUS (%)

	Coventry City	Watford	Preston N.E.	Glasgow Rangers	Aston Villa	Arsenal	Carling Survey	Glasgow Rangers	Carling Survey	Luton Town
Year	1983	1987	1988	1990	1992	1992	1993/94	1994	1996/97	1997
Occupation										
Employed	67	77	68	78	69	72	74.2	75.8	76	71.6
Unemployed	11	2	4	4	6	5	5.3	7.1	4	5.1
Full-Time Education	14	12	15	10	17	15	12.4	9.5	9	13.0
Retired	6	9	11	7	8	6	7.0	6.8	9	10.3
Employment Status										
Professional	7	15		7	6	15	12.2		15.6	6.6
Intermediate	15	15		21	24	28	21.6		23.9	31.7
Skilled non-manual	29	37		27	22	23	33.5		26.9	25.9
Skilled manual	35	27		30	27	17	22.4		24.6	10.5
Semi skilled manual	12	4		12	19	15	9.0		7.0	18.7
Unskilled	2	2		3	2	1	1.3		2.0	6.6

marketing but, it should be noted, during the 1990s the economic position of students has declined noticeably with, firstly, the freezing of the student grant and the advent of student loans in 1990 and latterly the introduction of tuition fees in 1998. These broader changes may be equally significant in explaining the decline in the number of students at football matches and illustrate how wider demographic trends need to be considered in this context.

In line with the idea that these groups have been, post-Hillsborough, excluded from football grounds is the assumption that football spectatorship is increasingly a middle-class phenomenon. Table 10.4 contains the employment status details from the surveys.[31] From these figures we can see that there has been a considerable diversity in the research findings. If we take the admittedly crude technique of distinguishing between the working and middle class on a manual/non-manual basis, then the proportion of middle-class spectators has varied from a low of 51 per cent at Coventry in 1983 to a high of 67 per cent at Watford in 1987. However, there is no smooth trajectory over time in this regard and it would appear that regional differences may be more significant than longitudinal changes. That is to say, it might be more relevant to contrast geographically similar clubs, such as comparing the West Midlands findings at Coventry City (51 per cent) with those at Aston Villa (52 per cent) in 1992 and the Home Counties findings at Watford (67 per cent) with those at Luton Town (64.2 per cent) in 1997. Furthermore, given the differences in occupational make-up of regions in the country it would seem wise to avoid making sweeping claims about the changing class composition of football crowds. From the data reviewed here, there appears little to support the theory that football is increasingly attracting a middle-class spectatorship. Indeed, the two nation-wide Carling Surveys reviewed actually show a slight decrease in the proportion of middle-class spectators watching Premiership football between 1993/94 and 1996/97.

ETHNICITY

The final demographic category to be addressed here is ethnicity. Tellingly the surveys from the 1980s did not address this question and so again longitudinal comparison is difficult. However, throughout the 1990s and despite the increasing prominence of race and ethnicity as issues addressed by the footballing authorities, surveys have continually found that only a very small proportion of football spectators define themselves as coming from minority ethnic groups.[32] The major anomaly in this respect was the Arsenal survey of 1992 which revealed that 7.9 per cent of supporters described themselves as Jewish and a further 3.8 per cent described themselves in non-'white' categories. The 1996/97 Carling Survey, however, found a range of non-'white' spectators from 0 per cent at Sunderland to 2.8 per cent at Arsenal. Of all the demographic categories addressed in this essay we have the most limited information on ethnicity and our conclusions about trends over time are necessarily tentative. However, it appears that football attracts relatively few spectators from minority ethnic backgrounds and there is little evidence to suggest that there have been any marked changes in this pattern in recent years.

THE ENDURING NATURE OF FANDOM

The key question raised by our analysis of crowd surveys is how can we, given the predicted shift towards the 'affluent customer' rather than the 'traditional fan', explain the relatively stable patterns of attendance? How is it that a 'product' which has undergone such significant change in terms of both environment and marketing strategy in recent years finds little or no change in its 'consumers'? The answer to this question lies, we would suggest, in the nature of football fandom itself. To illustrate this, we will examine some of the findings from the most recent of the surveys, that carried out at Luton Town which, unlike the other surveys, was part of a larger, more in-depth piece of research into football fandom.[33] It is important to note, however, that we are not suggesting that football crowds have not changed at all; new fans have been, and will continue to be, attracted to the game. Rather, in this section we wish to explain the resilience of the majority of existing fans, and how the changes in the marketing and presentation of the game have had a relatively minor impact on the way they consume and/or support their team.

One of the major findings of the Luton study was that fandom was characterized by a particularly strong level of commitment. To many of the fans at Luton their fan identity was a central component of their overall conception of the 'self'. Even at a 'less fashionable' club such as Luton, 88.4 per cent of fans scored highly on a scale to measure their level of identification as a fan.[34] Almost three-quarters (73 per cent) saw themselves 'very strongly' as fans of the club and a similar percentage (71 per cent) felt that their friends would probably describe them in similar terms. Further evidence of the strength of fandom emerged in comparison to other sources of identity. Approximately a third of fans interviewed suggested that being a fan was the most important facet of their identity. A further 40 per cent suggested that being a fan was at least equal to any other factor (for instance, their work or family relationships) as a source of identity. For many, being a fan of a football team was one of, if not the most important thing in their life.

Fans at Luton also displayed a strong sense of bonding with other fans; that is to say, they shared a common identity as supporters of Luton Town FC. Supporters showed high levels of 'bonding' with fellow fans purely on the basis that they were seen by each other as part of the same group. Strong cohesiveness resulted in displays of localism (for example, notions that Luton fans were 'better' than other fans) which led many fans to display pride in belonging to the group. Consequently a sense of loyalty was evident which led to what might be described as a 'monogamous' commitment to the club. 81.6 per cent of fans at Luton described themselves as supporting only one club. All other local or rival teams were seen as universally 'worse' in some way, and generally spoken of in a derogatory manner. To show signs of fandom for another club was seen to be 'disloyal'. This, combined with the importance of supporting the geographically 'local' club (cited by 53 per cent of fans questioned at Luton), means that it is highly unlikely that fans will shift allegiance very easily.

To bolster their supportership, Luton fans exhibited behaviours which could broadly be categorized under the term 'ego-enhancement strategies' which served to perpetuate fandom as a 'positive' experience. The initially surprising conclusion drawn from the Luton study was that to a large extent success and failure have no influence upon fandom. Although all fans tended to show elements of 'basking in reflected glory', or increasing their association with the team after success ('we won'), the converse reaction, that of 'cutting off reflected failure', or disassociating from a losing team ('they lost') was found to be rare, and was generally a characteristic of less committed fans. Fans who viewed themselves as strongly committed were likely to maintain their identification with the team, but show compensatory characteristics, such as to emphasize that their team was better in some way (for instance, in that they had played the more entertaining football), or attributing defeat to an external influence such as refereeing bias, or simply 'bad luck'. Thus fans often utilize strategies designed to 'rationalize' seemingly negative experiences in order to justify their continued 'strong' identification.

This brief discussion of the characteristics of fandom can also be used to explain why recent changes in English football, such as the introduction of all-seater stadiums and new marketing policies, have had a relatively minor effect on spectator demographics. The Luton study, supporting the findings of Coalter, concluded that changes in facilities, such as the introduction of seating, have little or no influence on the composition of the crowd.[35] As Coalter suggests, the physical environment appears to be relatively unimportant compared to the other aspects of fandom. Given the strength of fandom measured at Luton and the importance of loyalty, it could be argued that the physical environment and changes in the presentation of the game are simply not important enough to fans to affect their fandom. In this respect the findings can be compared with those of A. Tomlinson *et al.* who suggest that the 'social opportunity', or chance to mix with other fans, is more important than the environment within which such interaction takes place.[36] The key point is that such changes do not affect the experience of fandom *per se*, rather they affect the context within which football fandom is enacted. Indeed, as King has shown, fans can very effectively adapt the context to create the experience of supportership which they want. King has described how, following Manchester United's Premiership title win of 1993/94, whilst the majority of the crowd celebrated in a club-orchestrated, relatively restrained fashion, an alternative celebration of 'extraordinary frenzy' was simultaneously occurring in a bar area behind the K-stand.[37] Thus, changes such as all-seater stadiums may not be significant enough to alter radically the sense of group membership which fandom involves. The strength of loyalty to the club, and to other fans, suggests that fandom will endure. These characteristics may also help us account for the relative length of support at a relatively 'unsuccessful' club such as Luton (the mean length of support at Luton was 21.9 years).

To conclude this section, the picture which emerged at Luton was one of a relatively long-standing crowd, especially among those who identified more highly with the club. The importance of fandom was located within the sense of shared identity, an identity which could be enhanced through success but, perhaps more importantly, was protected from failure. These characteristics of fandom make it unlikely that the composition of the crowd will change rapidly, given that the majority of the crowd will be highly committed to the club, other spectators and fandom as a source of identity. Given this commitment, it seems unlikely that relatively cosmetic changes will have a particularly significant impact on the majority of the crowd. Certain strategies may attract new fans, but overall the majority of the crowd will show considerable stability over time – supporting their team 'through thick and thin' – and regardless of changes to the physical environment.

CONCLUSION AND RECOMMENDATIONS FOR FUTURE RESEARCH

The findings presented here represent the first systematic longitudinal analysis of football spectatorship. Given the adequacy of the information available definitive statements about the typical composition of football crowds have not – and perhaps should not – be made. Clearly there is a need to improve our knowledge and understanding in this area but, as a precondition to this, it is vital that we have an element of consensus over what constitutes good methodological practice. A certain amount of debate about the appropriate methodologies for performing crowd surveys has begun and we hope, in this final section, to make a few additional constructive suggestions.[38]

A by-product of the examination of these surveys is that through comparing methodologies we can begin to establish some principles of good methodological practice. In particular, it seems that the surveys undertaken at Arsenal and Aston Villa in 1992 and at Luton in 1997 were particularly good. Firstly, the response rates for each of these surveys was relatively high (57 per cent, 56 per cent and 48.2 per cent respectively). This, in part, reflects the relatively simple nature of the questionnaires, the incentive for fans to return the questionnaire (entry into a prize draw, for instance) and, more particularly, the careful planning which went into the distribution of the questionnaires. The questionnaires were relatively simple partly because they were not sponsored by a commercial company nor sought views on particular footballing issues. Questionnaires were either posted directly to supporters or distributed by hand. In each case, based on club estimates of the likely total match attendance, questionnaires were distributed proportionately between the individual sections of the ground. Where questionnaires were distributed by hand, this was undertaken by the respective researchers and postgraduate students as opposed to relying on club personnel who may have little interest in the success of the research and are likely to be unfamiliar with the importance of the accuracy of the distribution method.[39] Questionnaires were handed to every Kth supporter with no targeting of particular groups. If the questionnaire was refused, then that subject was ignored, the questionnaire handed to the next entrant, and every Kth spectator after that.[40] In the case of the Arsenal and Aston Villa surveys, as a means of testing the representativeness of the respondents, the clubs provided details of the total attendance in each section of the ground. The distribution of responses from different sections corresponded very closely with the actual distribution of fans within the ground on the day of the match. This precision of sampling, it is argued, may reasonably be expected to have translated into accuracy of findings and reliability of results and we would recommend that similar methodologies are utilized in future.

Future research should aim to build on our current knowledge base whilst also attempting to uncover some of the complexities and diversities of football crowd composition. One feature of the surveys reviewed here is that, in general, they have employed similar categories for analysing data such as age and class. This has facilitated comparison and is essential for meaningful longitudinal analysis. There are, or course, problems with using the Registrar General's scale to classify occupations and perhaps other systems might fruitfully be used, but these should be used in addition, so that both comparison and more adequate data can be generated.[41] A further aim should be to discover something of the regional and divisional differences in crowd make-up. Which clubs attract the most women and why? Which clubs have the largest middle- and working-class spectator bases? These are some of the issues which we would recommend are addressed in future football crowd surveys.

A considerable amount of work has been done with regard to the inclusion and exclusion of particular social groups from sports participation. Spectatorship, though equally if not more significant in terms of numbers, has long been a neglected subject. We hope that this paper will act as a catalyst for more and different research in future.

NOTES

1. D. Wann and M. Hamlet, 'Author and Subject Gender in Sport Research', *International Journal of Sport Psychology*, 26 (1995), 225–32.
2. See J. Walvin, *The People's Game* (London: Allen Lane, 1975).
3. See, for instance, A. Tomlinson, *Explorations in Football Culture* (Proceedings of 1982 BSA/LSA Workshop, Sheffield, 1983); V. Duke, 'The Sociology of Football: A Research Agenda for the 1990's', *Sociological Review*, 39 (1991), 627–45; I. Waddington, D. Malcolm and R. Horak, 'The Social Composition of Football Crowds in Western Europe: A Comparative Study', *International Review for the Sociology of Sport*, 33 (1998), 155–69.

4. Duke, 'The Sociology of Football'.
5. A. King, 'New Directors, Customers and Fans: The Transformation of English Football in the 1990s', *Sociology of Sport Journal*, 14 (1997), 224–40.
6. A. King, 'New Directors', 232.
7. Ibid., 234. See also Pierpoint's contribution to this collection.
8. W. Borrows, 'Action Stations', *Guardian Guide*, 25 July 1998, 20.
9. J. Crinnion, 'A game of two sexes', *Guardian*, 13 August 1998, 16.
10. *The Sunday Telegraph*, 1 September 1996.
11. A. King, 'The Lads: Masculinity and the New Consumption of Football', *Sociology*, 31 (1997), 329.
12. R. Nash, 'Research Note: Concept and Method in Researching the Football Crowd', *Leisure Studies*, 16 (1997), 127.
13. See for instance J. Williams, 'English Football Stadia after Hillsborough', in J. Bale (ed.), *The Stadium and the City* (Keele: University of Keele Press, 1995). Between 1988/89 and 1992/93 ticket prices at Old Trafford rose by 222.9 per cent.
14. Crinnion states that 30 years ago females constituted one in 50 spectators at first division matches. Although the focus of her article is changes in the game post-Heysel and post-Hillsborough, she offers no 1980s/1990s comparison.
15. P. Murphy, E. Dunning and J. Williams, *Preston North End Crowd Survey: Preliminary Report* (Leicester: Sir Norman Chester Centre for Football Research [SNCCFR], University of Leicester, 1988).
16. Sir Norman Chester Centre for Football Research, *Carling Premiership Fan Surveys, 1993–94: General Sample Report* (Leicester: SNCCFR, University of Leicester, 1994).
17. J. Williams and T. Bucke, *Seven Years On: Glasgow Rangers and Rangers Supporters, 1983–1990* (Leicester: SNCCFR, University of Leicester, 1990).
18. H. Moorhouse, *Survey of the Crowd at Rangers F.C., Glasgow, Scotland* (Glasgow: Research Unit in Leisure, Culture and Consumption, University of Glasgow, 1995).
19. J. Williams, E. Dunning and P. Murphy, *'All Sit Down': A Report on the Coventry City All-Seated Stadium 1982–83* (Leicester: SNCCFR, University of Leicester, 1984). The Coventry City survey, investigated responses to the proposal to convert the Highfield Road ground into an all seater stadium. J. Williams, E. Dunning and P. Murphy, *Football Spectator Behaviour at Watford: 'The Friendly Club'* (Leicester: SNCCFR, University of Leicester, 1988). The Watford survey was done as a means of monitoring and helping to develop the club's 'community activities'.
20. Sir Norman Chester Centre for Football Research, *F.A. Premier League National Fan Survey 1996/97: Summary* (Leicester: SNCCFR, University of Leicester, 1997). The Carling Surveys contain large sections on the purchase of consumer goods.
21. For details of the methodology of the Aston Villa and Arsenal surveys see I. Waddington, D. Malcolm and R. Horak, 'The Social Composition'.
22. What can be said, however, is that, compared to the age profile of the nation as a whole, those between that ages of 20 and 50 are over-represented among football crowds.
23. Moorhouse specifically notes that questionnaires mailed to season ticket holders were not sent to children. As we discuss below, there is a distinct pattern in terms of the age and sexual composition of football crowds. The fact that many children were excluded from the Rangers survey is likely to mean that a disproportionate number of females fans were also excluded.
24. For an overview see Waddington *et al.*, 'The Social Composition'.
25. J. Williams, 'Surveying the Social Composition of Football Crowds: A Reply to Waddington, Dunning and Murphy', *Leisure Studies*, 15 (1996), 217.
26. SNCCFR, *FA Premier League Fan Surveys, 1994–95: General Survey Report* (Leicester: SNCCFR, University of Leicester, 1995), p.14.
27. I. Waddington, E. Dunning and P. Murphy, 'Research Note: Surveying the Social Composition of Football Crowds', *Leisure Studies*, 15 (1996), 209–14.
28. J. Hargreaves, 'The Promise and Problems of Women's Leisure and Sport', in C. Rojek (ed.), *Leisure for Leisure* (Basingstoke: Macmillan, 1989), p.136.
29. J. Williams, 'Surveying the Social Composition of Football Crowds', 218.
30. Borrows, 'Action Stations'; King, 'The Lads'.
31. There are no figures provided from the 1988 Preston NE survey (for which employment details were not sought) or the 1994 Glasgow Rangers survey (which utilized slightly different occupational categories than were used in the other surveys).

32. Following various fan-led anti-racist campaigns, the Professional Footballers' Association and Commission for Racial Equality launched the Let's Kick Racism Out of Football campaign to coincide with the 1993/94 season. See Football Task Force, *Eliminating Racism from Football* (London: Stationery Office, 1998).

33. I. Jones, 'Football Fandom: Football Fan Identity and Identification at Luton Town Football Club' (unpublished Ph.D. thesis, University of Luton, 1998).

34. For a more detailed discussion of the sport spectator identification scale see Jones, and D. Wann and N. Branscombe, 'Sports Fans: Measuring Degree of Identification with their Team', *International Journal of Sport Psychology*, 24 (1993), 1–17.

35. F. Coalter, 'Crowd Behaviour at Football Matches: A Study in Scotland', *Leisure Studies*, 4 (1985), 111–17.

36. M. Tomlinson, F. Buttle and B. Moores, 'The Fan as Customer: Customer Services in Sports Marketing', *Leisure Studies*, 14 (1995), 97–106.

37. A. King, 'The Lads', 336.

38. See for instance, I. Waddington, E. Dunning, and P. Murphy, 'Research Note'; J. Williams, 'Surveying the Social Composition of Football Crowds'; R. Nash, 'Research Note'.

39. Williams, 'Surveying the Social Composition of Football Crowds', 217, notes that the initial Carling surveys were administered by clubs under the guidance and supervision of Sir Norman Chester Centre for Football Research staff. However, as problems with this arose, in 1996 the SNCCFR started to select and directly mail season ticket holders itself.

40. For a discussion of this see G. Kalton, *Introduction to Survey Sampling* (Sage University Series on Quantitative Applications in the Social Sciences No. 35. London: Sage, 1983).

41. Defining class solely or primarily according to occupation, though useful and, given limited resources, unavoidable in a practical sense, is unsatisfactory in that such a generalized category as occupation is unable to include all relevant groups (such as housewives/husbands, the unemployed, retired or those in full time education) or capture the subtleties or dynamic properties of human relationships such as those we describe as 'class'.

11

The Hooligan's Fear of the Penalty

JON GARLAND and MICHAEL ROWE

The tail-end of the 1998/99 football season witnessed several incidents which suggested that hooliganism has continued to be a significant feature of the game. Outbreaks of disorder during the Celtic–Rangers fixture in May 1999 saw the referee being hit by a missile thrown from the crowd, several pitch invasions, violence between rival fans after the match and a total of 100 arrests being made by police. In England, disturbances followed Newcastle United's defeat by Manchester United in the FA Cup Final. The fact that this violence occurred in Newcastle city centre, hundreds of miles from Wembley Stadium, indicates something of the changing nature of football spectating. A combination of flexible licensing laws and the frequent televising of live games means that football spectating in pubs and bars is, for some, the main way in which football is consumed. The volatile mixture of extended drinking and the passions aroused by major matches has, unsurprisingly, resulted in violence in many locations far removed from the stadium. Such incidents of unrest were widely reported across the country after the England team exited from Euro '96 following its loss against Germany.[1]

The physical dislocation of these incidents from football stadiums raises particular problems for the police and other authorities in that they may find it extremely difficult to predict where unrest might occur. It also raises questions about how 'football hooliganism' is defined and where the boundary might be drawn between this and other kinds of violence, such as that which occurs relatively routinely in and around pubs and clubs. If a distinction is to be drawn between explanations of football-related hooliganism and other manifestations of violence then it might be that some reclassification of events is necessary. It could be more instructive to distinguish between football violence involving relatively organized and committed actors, and more or less spontaneous unrest that occurs in a football-related context, which may be more akin to other kinds of public disorder. One of the aims of this essay is to explore the nature of 'unorganized football hooliganism' and to consider the relative inability of the police to counter it. Put simply, it is argued that recent policing strategies have been fairly successful in tackling dedicated hooligans who orchestrate their activities in tandem with rival 'firms' from other clubs, those whom we categorize as organized groups. What is more difficult to police is the *ad hoc* violence that may involve fans who are not determined hooligans but come to be involved in disorder relatively spontaneously. It is quite difficult to identify who is likely to engage in 'unorganized football hooliganism', and when and where it may erupt. One implication of this distinction is that further attention needs to be paid to structural and cultural factors that continue to incline certain groups to engage in violent and disorderly conduct. Strategies against 'rational choice' hooligans may have enjoyed some success but it remains the case that many others become involved in certain circumstances, even though they may not have been consciously intent on so doing. Factors such as 'aggressive masculinity', nationalism and xenophobia – which are not directly amenable to direct policing intervention – must still be addressed if a more fundamental solution to hooliganism is to succeed.

A feature of the media discussion of hooliganism that occurred during the 1998 World Cup was the high profile such stories were given, in contrast to the way that incidents of disorder during the domestic season had been almost ignored.[2] Of particular interest were two highly ambiguous stories that appeared to praise England's hooligan fans – 'Two Nil' exclaimed the *Sun*[3] over pictures of England captain Alan Shearer and a defiant England hooligan, whilst the *Daily Star*[4] claimed 'First Blood' in an article about the initial disorder. Dunning has argued that the profile of football hooliganism largely depends on the machinations of the media agenda rather than the extent of the problem in any empirical sense, and it may be that the 'amplification' of the hooliganism stories was simply regarded as a 'good angle' for what otherwise might have been a fairly routine story.[5] Even so, that the media are able to adopt this stance indicates something of the remarkable cultural rehabilitation of football during the last ten years. Other contributors to this collection discuss the revival in football's fortunes in the 1990s but this essay will focus on one central dimension – the changing methods of policing football which have contributed to a reduction in football's reputation for violence.

It would be a gross simplification to attribute the transformation of football solely to the apparent success that the police and other authorities have had in tackling hooliganism. However, claims that the problem of crowd violence has been solved in England have gained considerable currency in recent years. Commenting on plans for the policing of the 1998 World Cup, the French Director of Security claimed that 'the English model is fantastic! ... The English may have invented the poison of hooliganism, but they have also invented the remedy for this poison.'[6] Similar sentiments were expressed in the English Football Association's bid for the 2006 World Cup, which suggested that 'England's new breed of fully trained safety officers, inspectors and stadium managers have ensured that "fortress football" is no more. Our new generation of welcoming, fan-friendly and family-oriented stadiums are safe, secure and accessible to all.'[7] Such conceptions are shared, it seems, by many of those at the other end of the football hierarchy. Survey results from season 1995/96 found that 81.5 per cent of supporters felt that there had been a decline in the problem of hooliganism over the preceding five-year period.[8]

Recent high-profile incidents of disorder in other European countries may give further credence to the view that the English model of policing hooliganism is more 'progressive' than other methods. For example, the trouble at the Italy versus England Word Cup qualifier in Rome in 1997 was widely held to have been exacerbated by the aggressive and inappropriate reaction of the Italian police to minor scuffles, an allegation often made against the police in England in the 1980s. As pockets of trouble flared inside the stadium, it was widely held by eye-witnesses and attendant media that the Carabinieri's violent response, including attacking English supporters with truncheons, aggravated an already tense situation.[9] This event followed on from another much-publicized incident, when Manchester United fans in Turkey for a fixture against Galatasaray maintained that inflammatory tactics by Turkish police were out of proportion to the problems that were occurring.[10] In England, overly aggressive police tactics are generally associated with the 1970s and 1980s, before the Taylor Report refocused the policing emphasis upon issues of crowd safety and security.[11]

This study sets out to review the key dimensions in the apparent success story of the English policing methods. Critical analysis is especially important since many of the measures introduced in the context of football, such as closed-circuit television (CCTV) and an increased employment of private police, are also advocated as solutions to problems of crime and disorder in society more generally. In the final part of the essay it is argued that the problem of hooliganism has certainly not been eliminated, and that the occurrence of spontaneous disorder inside stadiums needs to be addressed. It is suggested that the authorities might have successfully confronted orchestrated football violence, at least in the environs of football grounds, but that 'unorganized hooliganism' is a significant issue and a form of disorder that is much more difficult to police.

THE CHANGING FACE OF POLICING FOOTBALL

As political debate in recent years has often focused on the possibilities of privatizing or 'civilianizing' certain roles and responsibilities of the police,[12] football has become something of a role model for other spheres. A Home Office report[13] echoed the earlier recommendation of the Taylor Report into the Hillsborough Stadium disaster of 1989, suggesting that private sector personnel ought to supplant many of the activities traditionally undertaken by the public police. In keeping with these reports there has been an increasing absence of uniformed police officers from stadiums. Although the police remain responsible for maintaining order in public areas outside stadiums, private sector personnel are now often solely responsible for the safety of the public inside football grounds and regularly there are games played with no internal police presence whatsoever. The emergence of a private sector security industry has occurred in various contexts in Britain during recent years, in the case of football this process has been closely allied to a shift in emphasis from the maintenance of public order to the promotion of public safety. The discursive change reflected in a move towards a safety culture both reflects and influences the wider rehabilitation of the game that has seen an emphasis on the creation of a sanitized 'family atmosphere'.

As P. Stenning has observed, the relations between private and public police can be considered against a spectrum which ranges from out-and-out hostility to mutual co-operation and collaboration.[14] Often, he argued, the initial reaction of public police forces has been to disparage the professional credentials and ability of private sector operators. While there continue to be grounds for concern about the efficacy of some private sector personnel, as discussed below, it is clear that there are few, if any, a priori reasons to prefer the public over the private. Stenning observed in general terms that 'many private police organisations often have considerably longer experience (and in some cases greater success) than most public police organisations in addressing almost all of the key issues which are now said to confront our public police organisations. This proposition ... does not sit very well with many public police officials.'[15]

Recognition that stewards can play a professional and effective role within football grounds, and that they can provide a service that is preferable to that offered by the police, has grown within the football industry. Independent pressure groups such as the Football Supporters' Association (FSA) have welcomed the erosion of the 'heavy-handed' policing culture which previously dominated the game. A police football liaison officer commented on the relative proficiency of the two sectors:

> I could show to you several club stewards at my club who are very competent at doing their job, and then I could show half a dozen police officers who have never been to a football match before and yet, because of their uniform, you would have the impression that the police officers knew what they were doing, when in fact they wouldn't.[16]

Despite these positive attitudes there are reasons to be cautious about the abilities of some stewards to carry out their duties capably, and to some extent these might arise from the unregulated status of private sector police in Britain and the lack of control on recruitment and training that this allows. Some clubs employ their own stewards, who might be recruited through word of mouth, and who are often 'friends' of the club and are familiar with many of the spectators they are supervising. This creates its own problems, and anecdotal evidence suggests that some stewards are reluctant to reprimand those who are known to them personally. Other clubs contract private security companies, who may set higher standards in their methods of recruitment and training of personnel. In some environments a combination of club and private company stewards work together, creating a more complicated policing framework. This framework appears to be independent of the status or wealth of a club, as research conducted by the authors indicates that cost has no real bearing on the decision as to the hiring of club or private company stewards, either because there are little significant differences in cost, or because other factors – such as perceived effectiveness – are regarded as equally important.[17]

Whether club or private company personnel, the training and recruitment of stewards to work at football matches is an issue of concern. Serious questions have been expressed about both of these aspects of stewarding.[18] The suitability of stewards who support the club that employs them to supervise 'away' fans is questionable, as anecdotal evidence suggests that on rare occasions stewards have provocatively celebrated home goals in front of opposition fans, and have even attacked visiting supporters! A less stark but probably more common difficulty is the employment of stewards who are unsuitable, for a variety of reasons, for the job. One journalist who reported on his experience of stewarding at an England fixture suggested that his colleagues were typical casual workers, with little dedication to the job:

> Everyone I spoke to had come to see the game and certainly not for the money which, at £3.50 an hour failed to generate many feelings of job responsibility. Our minibus included temping agency lifers, drifting from order-picking jobs in the supermarket warehouses to early starts 'on the bins', and students, either struggling to balance night-shifts and engineering degrees – or those just out for a laugh.[19]

Recognition of the variable standards of stewarding led, in 1995, to various agencies within the game producing a guide to assist clubs in the training and management of stewards.[20] Whilst this document established some useful principles surrounding the role of stewards, it remains the case that agreed common standards are yet to be established, and local authorities retain considerable discretion in certifying that clubs provide appropriate training. The relatively recent introduction of NVQ-level qualifications for stewards has helped to provide relevant training, but again these are not mandatory and serve only to complement the exiting training packages.

Since stewards are employed primarily to ensure crowd safety and enforce ground regulations, rather than to deal with disorder, they are more likely to eject troublemakers from the stadium than arrest them. This difference between the manner in which stewards deal with crime compared to the police illustrates one tension between the contrasting cultures of safety and law enforcement. The lesser power of stewards *vis-à-vis* the police may also explain the declining number of arrests made in grounds over recent seasons, a decrease made even more stark when increasing overall attendance is taken into account.

As has been mentioned, an important change in the policing of football since the disasters of the 1980s has been the shift towards an emphasis on crowd management and safety, a shift that has driven the move to employ more stewards. The resultant low profile of public police within stadiums may create environments more conducive to outbreaks of disorder, as security personnel are untrained, or unable (as it is not their function to deal with violent disturbances) to cope with events, as the Football Liaison Officer of a First Division club commented: 'If there's trouble, the stewards' duty is to alert the safety officer, then summon the police. If there are no police inside the ground, stewards have to call 999 like anyone else.'[21]

At a fixture between West Bromwich Albion and Bristol City in season 1998/99, a serious outbreak of disorder did occur inside the stadium, where no public police were on duty. The resultant violence, reportedly involving hundreds of supporters, lasted for 15 minutes before some semblance of order was restored. Interestingly, although the police were summoned to deal with the incident, it was the stewards who managed, eventually, to quell the disorder on their own.

This case throws into sharp relief many of the issues discussed in this essay. For example, did the lack of a public police presence inside the stadium mean that supporters were not deterred from disorder? Did the relatively long time that it took to bring the disturbance under control signify that the stewards cannot be left to police matches on their own, or did the fact that the stewards managed to cope on their own mean that their role should be widened to encompass public order situations?

Another question posed by the above incident is that it occurred within full view of closed-circuit television cameras. An increasing reliance on technology and environmental design has been another important development in the policing of football. The 'electronic panacea for crime'[22] that is CCTV was introduced in football ahead of other areas in society – in much the same way that private sector policing made an early appearance in the sporting environment. Coupled with technological assistance to crowd-control techniques has been the post-Taylor development of all-seater stadiums. Together these moves have made the identification of individuals considerably easier than during the era when supporters were packed together on terraces. Previous research by the authors found that CCTV was almost universally regarded by the authorities as beneficial to policing the game and fan surveys suggest that supporters also welcome this development, as other surveys have suggested the public more generally welcome its introduction.[23] The capacity of CCTV cameras to prevent crime may be enhanced by the use of computer software which can match individual faces against a database of offenders, but the lack of audio facilities means that such apparatus is of limited use in the prevention and detection of other crimes, such as 'racialist chanting' (an offence under Section Three of the (1991) Football Offences Act), for example. Furthermore, disorder inside grounds continues to occur regularly despite the deterrence supposedly offered by CCTV, and disturbances such as those during a Leicester City versus Chelsea match in 1996, clashes between Ipswich Town and Norwich City supporters in 1998, and pitch invasions during matches at Barnsley and Millwall indicate that violent behaviour is not entirely prohibited by cameras.

The panoptican capabilities of CCTV have led to concern that increasing regulation of crowd behaviour threatens to undermine legitimate fan cultures regarded as inimical to the interests of the contemporary football industry. Attempts to rid the game of racist chanting, for example, are often predicated on the use of technological and other means to identify offenders and either prosecute them through the courts, eject them from stadiums, and, more rarely, to introduce long-term bans from grounds.[24] While there appears to have been some success in reducing racist chanting, although other dimensions of racism continue to exist within football, it is clear that conceptually the problem is regarded as closely aligned to the broader issue of anti-social behaviour. Interviews and observation carried out by the authors provide a strong impression that club officials, stadium managers and the police often regard racist chanting or abuse as offensive to 'family audiences' in much the same way as vociferous swearing, for example, might deter some spectators from regular attendance. The football fans' pressure group Libero! has been particularly critical of attempts to control elements of supporters' behaviour which has been central to the atmosphere and culture of the game.[25] It seems clear that the prohibition of behaviour deemed to be 'antisocial' will damage features of the football 'experience' treasured by some supporters. Whether such control can be justified if it serves to encourage the attendance of spectators who might otherwise be deterred poses a difficult question beyond the scope of this study.

Despite these concerns it appears that, as in other areas of policing, technology will continue to play a major role in the surveillance of fans. The growth of the use of CCTV has coincided with the increased use of police intelligence-gathering in the context of football. Evidence about the behaviour and future intentions of committed hooligans is gathered by football intelligence officers associated with all professional clubs and collated by the Football Intelligence Unit of the National Criminal Intelligence Service. Information is shared between forces internationally when clubs or national teams play abroad.

The experience of the 1998 World Cup highlights limitations of an intelligence-led approach, even in circumstances where there appears to have been considerable collaboration between the French and English police. Prior to the tournament, efforts were made by the British Home Office to discourage from travelling to France ticketless fans and/or those intent on hooliganism. Advertisements were carried on television and in newspapers warning that the sophisticated ticketing arrangements devised for the tournament meant that there was little chance of those unable to purchase tickets in advance attending games with those bought from touts. In addition the Home Secretary claimed in February 1998 that 'the football hooligan is a violent criminal. He's a coward who hides behind the good name of the decent supporter. My message to the hooligan is simple – we know who you are, we know what your plans are, and we will do everything we can to stop you.'[26]

In the event, a large number of fans did travel to France without tickets for matches, and bought them from touts, on many occasions in front of police officers who, it is claimed, turned a 'blind eye'.[27] The tournament was marked by scenes of violence involving English supporters, principally in Marseilles, and British newspapers and politicians once again demanded that the authorities take tough action against those involved (see, for example, the *Daily Mirror* editorial 'Blair Must Crush These Sick Thugs').[28] Several points arise from this episode which are of particular significance for policing football hooliganism. First, it is clear that the small number of tickets available through legitimate channels, and warnings against travelling to France without one, appear not to have deterred supporters from journeying to the tournament. The broader emphasis on free movement within a borderless European Union appears to have been inimical to efforts to stop the migration of potentially disorderly fans. For example, it seems to have been particularly problematic for French authorities to prevent German supporters associated with far-right political groups crossing into France and engaging in violence at Lens. In addition, it appears that some English fans known to the police travelled into France via other European countries, thus evading controls and surveillance at Anglo-French crossing points.

TABLE 11.1

ARRESTS OF ENGLAND SUPPORTERS AT THE 1998 WORLD CUP BY OFFENCE

Offence	Number of Arrests	Per cent*
Public Order	246	86
Criminal Damage	16	6
Drunk/drunk and incapable	11	4
Other†	13	5
Total	286	101

* Figures are rounded and so do not add up to 100 per cent.

† Other offences include theft of tickets, travelling without a ticket, theft, credit card fraud, entering private property, robbery, ticket touting, assaulting a police officer, and murder.

Source: National Criminal Intelligence Service.

Data relating to those English fans arrested in France during the 1998 World Cup reveal further limitations to the intelligence-led strategy. Of the total number of arrests, 86 per cent were for public order offences (see Table 11.1). Yet, given the Home Secretary's claim referred to above, it is revealing to note that only 35 out of the total of 286 arrested (12 per cent) were classed by NCIS as category C supporters (see Figure 11.1) – considered as organized hooligans.[29] A further 17 were recorded as 'known category B' fans, namely not determined hooligans but those liable to become involved in disturbances should they occur. These totals suggest 234 of the 286 England fans arrested in France, some 82 per cent, were not known to the police. Of course arrest figures such as these must be treated with considerable caution as they do not reflect convictions, although in the absence of other data they do provide some ground for suggesting that the conceptualization of football hooliganism as organized premeditated violence committed by dedicated perpetrators – the kind of behaviour which might be susceptible to surveillance and intelligence gathering – needs to be reconsidered.

FIGURE 11.1

NCIS STATUS OF ENGLISH FANS ARRESTED DURING WORLD CUP 1998

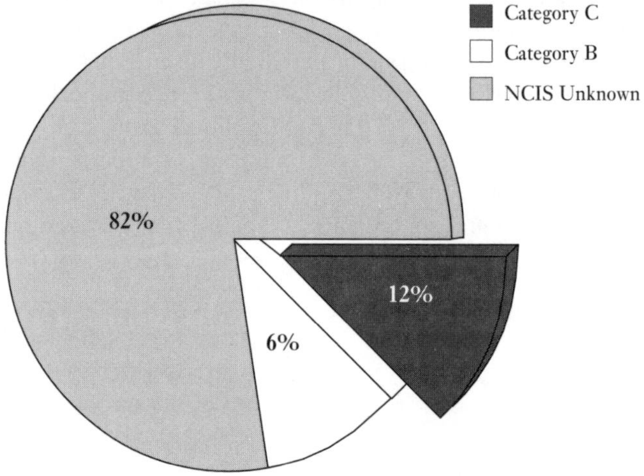

The lack of category C supporters may suggest that the police have had some success in tackling highly organized football violence, and that these types of supporters were deterred from engaging in disorder in France. Conversely, the figures may suggest that category C fans are better at avoiding detection than less 'experienced' troublemakers. It may even be that the known organizers of hooliganism have simply 'retired' from the hooligan 'scene'. The suspicion lingers, however, that much of the disorder was engaged in by fans who were not involved in organized football-related violence in England, or had not taken part in such violence before. Some of the disorder, like that which occurred during England's opening match on a beach, in front of a giant television screen, was sparked by a reaction to England's first goal, and did not appear premeditated. It is to an analysis of unorganized hooliganism that this essay now turns.

ORGANIZED OR UNORGANIZED HOOLIGANISM?

Although factors such as the increasing reliance on stewards may partly explain the decrease in arrest figures, it might also be that there has been a genuine reduction in such behaviour, especially in the context of an overall increase in attendances.[30] However, the experience of the 1998 World Cup as well as a number of other incidents which have occurred within the domestic game during the last few seasons caution against complacency. As the historical perspective offered by E. Dunning *et al.* indicates, apparent changes in the extent of football hooliganism have been related to the rise and fall of the problem on the media agenda, as much as the actual level of disorder in any objective sense.[31] More recently Dunning has argued that the rehabilitation of football has meant that political authorities and the media prefer to emphasize the success of policing strategies, rather than the continuing problem of hooliganism.[32] The high-profile, politically sensitive campaigns to secure the 2006 World Cup for England have created a context in which emphasis on the successful resolution of the hooligan problem coincides more closely with the interests of the English Football Association and the Labour government than it does with the actual reality of the situation

Notwithstanding the media and political profile of hooliganism there is considerable anecdotal and statistical evidence that football violence has not disappeared, either as a result of improved policing methods or because, as has been suggested by J. Williams and also by S. Redhead, of a cultural shift in the behaviour of supporters. Williams proposes that the impact of football fanzines, with their anti-violence and anti-racist stances, have, along with more political developments such as the growth of the FSA, challenged the hooligan agenda.[33] It is said that other developments, such as the inflatables craze of the late 1980s and other humorous and irreverent activities, have also helped.[34] Redhead refers to changes in youth cultures, and in particular to the spread of 'Rave Culture' in the 1980s, as a cause for the decrease in violence, and claims that this 'carnivalesque' transformation of football fandom resulted in the terraces experiencing 'their own "summer of love"' in the late 1980s and early 1990s.[35] Also, the FSA has successfully undertaken campaigns on behalf of 'ordinary' supporters, and fan cultures have become more light-hearted, more self-mocking and, for the most part, less willing to tolerate hooliganism and racism. In some ways fanzines have provided a voice for ordinary fans that they lacked in the 1980s, and, if nothing else, helped supporters to combat the slightly hysterical response to any outbreak of disorder from the authorities and the media. Whether they had any effect on those who were dedicated to causing trouble is open to debate, and Moorhouse casts doubt on how truly they reflect wider fan opinions.[36] It could be argued that fanzines, more often than not, merely 'preach to the converted'. Whatever their actual readership demographics, fanzines do reflect some of the changes in fan attitudes and behaviour over the last decade, and their influence should not go unacknowledged. It would certainly seem that they have provided the media with a source other than the stereotypical 'yobbo fan', and maybe this too has contributed to a de-amplification of the hooligan issue.

According to arrest figures published in the summer of 1998, season 1997/98 witnessed a decrease in arrests, down to 13.4 per 100,000 spectators compared to 15.7 in 1996/97.[37] However, the number of violent offences increased, according to the official NCIS figures, over the same period although an officer suggested that 'over half the arrests took place outside football grounds and so knowing the intentions and plans of the hooligans remains a priority'.[38] However, during the 1998/99 season NCIS announced that there had been an increase in arrests for affray, violent disorder and throwing missiles compared to the same period in the previous season, causing the head of NCIS Strategic and Specialist Intelligence Branch to comment, 'The number of people involved do remain comparatively small but it is a hard-core, well-organised and hell-bent on causing mayhem, that is using football matches as a cover for its criminal activities.'[39] However, particular incidents of unrest referred to by NCIS did not appear, at least as far as they were reported, to be 'well organized' or of the kind alluded to above. Instead, many of them seemed to be relatively spontaneous incidents caused by fans meeting by chance. One of the most serious occurrences of violence highlighted by NCIS, at a Millwall versus Manchester City fixture, may not have been as orchestrated as the police suggested. One eye-witness account reinforces a point made above that some violence which is centred around football may not be very different from that which occurs elsewhere in society: '… the club [Millwall] continues to be a focus for anyone with bad intentions and an evening to spare. For the Man City … fixture, the sections of the ground that are normally almost deserted were suddenly brimming with mobs of young men … the transgressors at the City game were no more than 14 years old …'[40]

The response from Government to recent hooligan incidents, and especially those at France '98, was the announcement of new proposals to combat known trouble-makers. These included: strengthening curbs on foreign travel; toughening existing powers to stop convicted hooligans from travelling to domestic games; and the introduction of new measures to stop unconvicted but known hooligans from travelling abroad.[41] Again, the focus is on organized hooligans, whether convicted, or, potentially draconianly, unconvicted, which could fail to affect many of those who engage in disorder in the late 1990s. The remainder of this study argues that suggestions that the problem can be resolved via improved intelligence-gathering and stronger controls reveal a fundamental misconception of football violence.

CONCLUSION

Much of the policing strategy held to have cured the 'English disease' is akin to broader crime prevention strategies which emphasize the importance of deterrence and reducing the opportunities for crime. Research by the authors has revealed that the employment of CCTV has often been cited as one of the key factors behind the reduction in disorder inside stadiums, as it has been praised for its effectiveness in town and shopping centres. The quality of CCTV systems and the pictures produced, as well as the placement of cameras, affect its usefulness. A number of club safety officers, when surveyed by the authors of this piece, felt that their CCTV system was too slow and cumbersome in reacting to flashpoints of disorder, and consequently missed these types of incident. Others felt that some supporters 'played-up to the cameras', and fans, in the heat of the moment, forget that cameras are present, and become involved in disorder regardless.

Surveillance and the use of technology have meant, conventional wisdom has it, that committed football hooligans have had to go ever greater lengths to fulfil their desire for trouble and this is one reason why venues far removed from football stadiums have become sites for violent confrontation. The fact that such events are relatively co-ordinated does at least offer the police the possibility of controlling and preventing this type of disorder, just as intelligence-gathering and surveillance might be used against drug-traffickers, paedophile rings or other organized criminals. Such strategies remain limited though, since much football-related violence appears to be relatively unorganized and *ad hoc*, and not the product of highly organized groups, and is therefore very difficult to prevent using the kinds of approach detailed here. It is important to acknowledge that the patterns of hooligan behaviour have changed and evolved, so that the idea that the highly organized, highly mobile fighting 'crews' of the 1980s are still dominant needs to be reassessed. Elements of such gangs do still exist, and undoubtedly many of those involved are among the 6,500 or so names on the NFIU hooligan database. The police have, through the strategies outlined above, developed effective systems for monitoring and containing these groups, and it is these systems that have attracted the praise from abroad.

Explanations which refer to notions such as 'aggressive masculinity' and draw attention to the importance of violence to the identity of participants, or discuss the centrality of xenophobia and nationalism to understandings of the disorderly behaviour of hooligans following the English national team, do not readily lend themselves to particular policy solutions and there may be a tendency for practitioners to reject what is no doubt often regarded as the 'incessant chatter' of academics.[42] The crime prevention approaches outlined above assume that football hooliganism will occur and address how it might be thwarted, whilst paying relatively little attention to social, political, economic or cultural factors that underpin this behaviour. Images of disorder which have filled the media from time to time in recent seasons may have been presented as the reappearance of a problem that had been policed out of existence, but it is important to realize that the deeper causes of such violence remain to be addressed.

NOTES

1. J. Garland and M. Rowe, 'War Minus the Shooting? Jingoism, the English Press and Euro '96', *Journal of Sport and Social Issues*, XXIII, 1 (1999), 80–95.

2. See J. Garland and M. Rowe, *Racism and Antiracism in British Football* (London: Macmillan, forthcoming) for an analysis of the newspaper coverage of the disorder during France '98.
3. *Sun*, 16 June 1999, 1.
4. *Daily Star*, 16 June 1999, 4–5.
5. E. Dunning, 'The Social Roots of Football Hooliganism: a Reply to Critics of the "Leicester School"', in R. Giulianotti (ed.), *Football Violence and Social Identity* (London: Routledge, 1994).
6. *Le Monde*, 'Comment la Coupe De Monde Joue La Securité'. (http://www.lemonde.fr/football. securite.model.htm, 19 September 1997).
7. Football Association, *World Cup England 2006* (London: The Football Association, 1997).
8. FA Premier League, *FA Premier League Fan Survey 1995–96* (Leicester: Sir Norman Chester Centre for Football Research, 1996).
9. J. Troup, 'Shame of Italy's Thug Cops', *Sun*, 13 October 1997, 6–7; R. Syal, 'England Reach World Cup Finals', *Sunday Times*, 12 October 1997, 1.
10. A. King, 'One Hell of a Trip', *When Saturday Comes*, 83 (1994), 6–7.
11. Lord Justice Taylor (Chairman), *Inquiry into the Hillsborough Stadium Disaster: Final Report* (London: HMSO, 1990).
12. L. Johnston, *The Rebirth of Private Policing* (London: Routledge, 1992); R. Morgan and T. Newburn, *The Future of Policing* (Oxford: Clarendon Press, 1997).
13. Home Office, *Review of Police Core and Ancillary Tasks: Final Report* (London: Home Office, 1995).
14. P.C. Stenning, 'Private Police and Public Police: Toward a Redefinition of the Police Role', in D. J. Loree (ed.), *Future Issues in Policing: Symposium Proceedings* (Ontario: Canadian Police College, 1989), pp.169–92.
15. Stenning 'Private Police', 170.
16. Interview with Football Liaison Officer conducted March 1997.
17. A survey of 70 professional clubs showed that there was no identifiable correlation between income from gate receipts and whether club, private company or a combination of stewards were employed.
18. Channel Four Television (London), 'Terror on the Doorstep Dispatches', 26 October 1994.
19. J. Lee, 'Game for a Laugh at Wembley', *Observer*, 11 January 1998, 7.
20. Football League, Football Association, Premier League, Football Licensing Authority, and the Football Safety Officer's Association, *Stewarding and Safety Management at Football Grounds* (London: Football League *et al.*, 1995).
21. Interview with Football Liaison Officer conducted February 1997.
22. A. Beck and A. Willis, *Crime and Security: Managing the Risk to Safe Shopping* (Leicester: Perpetuity Press, 1995), p.180.
23. J. Garland and M. Rowe, 'Racism at Work – a Study of Professional Football', *International Journal of Risk, Security and Crime Prevention*, I, 3 (1996), 195–205.
24. J. Garland and M. Rowe, 'War Minus the Shooting?'; Advisory Group Against Racism and Intimidation (AGARI), *Alive and Still Kicking: A Report by the Advisory Group Against Racism and Intimidation* (London: Commission for Racial Equality, 1996).
25. Libero! *Offence* (London: Libero, 1998).
26. Home Office, *UK Shares World Beating Experience of Policing Football* (London: Home Office Press Release 076/98 27 February 1998).
27. E. Brimson, *Tear Gas and Ticket Touts: With the England Fans at the World Cup* (London: Headline, 1999).
28. *Daily Mirror*, 16 June 1998, 6. See also P. Webster, 'Blair calls for jailed fans to be sacked', *The Times*, 18 June 1998, 7.
29. National Criminal Intelligence Service, *Football Intelligence Unit Arrest Sheet World Cup 98* (NCIS: Private Correspondence, 1998).
30. NCIS arrest statistics for 1997/98 show that, when considering all four professional divisions together, arrests per 100,000 spectators have decreased from 22.2 in 1992/93 to 13.4 in 1997/98.
31. E. Dunning, P. Murphy and J. Williams, *The Roots of Football Hooliganism* (London: Routledge, 1988).
32. E. Dunning, 'The Social Roots'.
33. J. Williams, 'Having An Away Day', in J. Williams and S. Wagg (eds.), *British Football and Social Change: Getting into Europe* (Leicester: Leicester University Press, 1991).
34. For a while, it became 'fashionable' to bring inflatable objects to matches, a fad started by the supporters of Manchester City who adopted large bananas as their 'inflatable'.
35. S. Redhead, 'An Era of the End, or the End of an Era? Football and Youth Culture in Britain', in J.

Williams and S. Wagg (eds.), *British Football and Social Change: Getting into Europe* (Leicester: Leicester University Press, 1991), pp.145–59.

36. H. Moorhouse, 'From Zines Like These? Fanzines, Tradition and Identity in Scottish Football', in G. Jarvie and G. Walker (eds.), *Scottish Sport in the Making of the Nation: Ninety Minute Patriots?* (Leicester: Leicester University Press, 1994).

37. D. Adams, 'NCIS Figures Show Increase in Violence at Football Matches', *Police Review*, 14 August 1998, 9.

38. D. Adams, 'NCIS Figures'.

39. J. Butler, 'Alarm Over Increase in Hooliganism', *Sporting Life* (http://www.sporting-life.com/soccer/news/, 27 November 1998).

40. L. Bellers, 'Backs to the Wall', *When Saturday Comes*, 142 (1998), 12.

41. ITN, 'New Crackdown on Football Hooligans', ITN Online (http://www.itn.co.uk/britain/brit19981127/112705.htm, 1998).

42. J. Young, 'Incessant Chatter: Recent Paradigms in Criminology', in M. Maguire, R. Morgan and R. Reiner (eds.), *The Oxford Handbook of Criminology* (Oxford: Clarendon Press, 1994), pp.69–124.

12

Taking Offence: Modern Moralities and the Perception of the Football Fan

CARLTON BRICK

the characterization of fandom ... supports, and justifies elitist and disrespectful beliefs about our common life.[1]

According to J. Jensen, discourses on fandom are 'haunted by images of deviance'.[2] However, in the ten years since Hillsborough and the Taylor Report there has been a dramatic 're-centring' of the 'fan' within socio-political discourse. The death of 96 Liverpool fans at Hillsborough in April 1989 has been identified as a key moment whereby dominant socio-political discourses on fandom (hooliganism and its 'threat' to law and order) became politically unsustainable.[3] The exhaustion of these discourses is often counterposed to the emergence of new and vibrant discourses from 'within' the football subculture.[4]

The 'fan' in the 1990s has come to be seen as a very different animal from that of the 1970s or 1980s. Fan groups have acquired respectable media and political profiles. The role of organized fan pressure groups won unanimous media and political applause in influencing Secretary of State, Stephen Byers' decision to uphold the Monopolies and Mergers Commission's recommendation to block the proposed merger between satellite broadcaster BSkyB and Manchester United Football Club. However, this process is not without its tensions. A week after the Department of Trade and Industry's announcement, the House of Commons debated the second reading of The Football (Offences and Disorder) Bill which is, potentially, the most authoritarian legislation concerning the regulation of football fandom ever proposed by a British government.

This essay is concerned with the contemporary construction of fandom within political discourses, and examines the relationship between notions of deviancy and fandom reflected in the legislative and discursive regulation of spectatorship. The football-related legislation of the last 10–15 years has led to a form of regulation that is neither dependent on, nor constrained by, the formal demands of legislative and legal frameworks. Increasingly, regulation exerts itself through the construction of highly moralistic discourses which act as a fetter on the behaviour of the fan. As such the power of regulation is exercised through discursive forms, or 'speaking', rather than through legislation or law (although such regulations are, of course, not mutually exclusive).

These forms are manifest in the emerging discourses of crowd management and safety that have been a feature of the post-Hillsborough period, and recast and transform the meanings and content of what is considered to be social deviancy. S. Redhead has suggested that discourses on football-related deviancy have proliferated at a time when deviancy itself seems to have been 'disappearing from public view',[5] but whilst I am sympathetic to Redhead's meaning, his conceptualization of the construction of discourses of deviancy is flawed. To argue that football-related deviancy is disappearing reflects a rather fixed notion of what should, and what should not, be considered as deviant. The process of labelling behaviour as deviant has, historically, proven to be a much more fluid process. Football-related deviancy has not disappeared as such; rather, it has become something else. The concept of deviancy is itself redefined and expanded.

Thus, despite the apparent transformation of fandom within socio-political discourse, its conceptualization as a deviant activity still peppers both the political and social imaginations, albeit in more mediated form. This I hope to illustrate through the course of this essay.

MORALITY AND FANDOM

Legislative interventions into football fandom have occurred at a time when issues of social regulation more generally have taken increasingly 'moralistic' forms.[6] As A. Giddens has noted, there is 'a fundamental impetus towards a remoralizing of daily life' within society.[7] Whilst moralizing, 'civilizing' and social welfare goals are not new features in football's historical development,[8] a central contemporary shift is seen to be the move from a 'traditional' consumption to a 'new' consumption.[9] These types or styles of consumption, it is maintained, are in conflict. As such, the regulation of the stadiums and spectators is driven by a physical transformation of the football culture and experience. New styles of consumption and 'new' fans are encouraged in order to usurp the 'traditional' fan and associated style of consumption.

The reinvention of the football culture, it is argued, de-centres the traditional 'sporting tophilia' embedded within the football ground.[10] Geographer John Bale, who has developed the study of football and fandom to incorporate notions of space, refers to the football stadium and its environment as a 'sense of place' – an entity embedded with notions of 'tradition' and 'ways of doing' – rather than simply a physical space where sporting activity is watched.[11] As a place rather than just physical space, the football stadium implies emotional and sentimental attachment; features of which are central to the way in which contemporary fan identity is constructed. In this respect, Bale has talked of the 'sporting tophilia' as an 'extension of the self', or 'self-image'.[12]

A feature of the development of collective fandom in the post-Hillsborough period has been the self-conscious incorporation and articulation of the notion of a 'traditional' or 'authentic' tophilia as a form of resistance to the new consumption of fandom. Although, strictly speaking, there is no one definitive tophilia (rather there are multifarious physical and emotional relationships embedded within the football stadiums and the types of consumption that exist therein), the incorporation of the notion of the sporting tophilia as a self-conscious identity implies otherwise. The 'authentic' tophilia is presented as a cultural way of life that is under threat from the fad and fashion of the styles and consumption patterns of the new and inauthentic fandom. As such, 'long-standing cultural tradition has been altered in numerous ways beyond mere attendance at the ground. The whole process from ticket purchase through socialising before and during the game, to conduct inside the ground has irrevocably changed.'[13] Similarly, E. Horton argues that football's official institutions are operating 'a policy of social cleansing, of making football suitable for the better-off by the simple means of removing the lower orders from the stands'.[14]

Developments in the forms and technologies of regulation that have emerged in the post-Hillsborough era are presented by some critics of regulation as the results of the dynamic to disrupt and actively replace relationships within the environment of the stadium that have been born of the traditional sporting tophilia. Encroachment on the traditional tophilia is interpreted as a contestation of moral and behavioural standards, whereby the 'new' fans with their 'own dress codes and etiquette' usurped those of the 'traditional' fan.[15] But this resistance is only formal. The substance of my argument here is that in its content, resistance to the new consumption of fandom is actually compliant, rather than contestant, with the new moralities of football. Similarly, the argument that forms of regulation are the results of the changing patterns of consumption raise a number of serious shortcomings. Based on mythical notions of fandom, there is little appreciation of the historical link between football, spectatorship and social regulation. Instead, the problem is perceived as one set of fans versus another – the 'traditional' fan and the 'new' fan – rather than the legislative and discursive renegotiation of the relationships of power between the State and the individual.

The formal articulation of resistance to the 'new' moralities of consumption are an integral part of organized fandom, reflected in fan campaigns and 'representative' bodies.[16] For example, Richard Kurt, the 'unofficial' chronologer of Manchester United's recent history writes: 'Old Trafford is being Americanised, swabbed with the antiseptic of family values, deproletarianised, stuffed with the slick, plastic fast food of the stadium gig … you can stop this by standing up, shouting fuck a lot and singing your hearts out for the lads forever!'[17] The new moralities are understood by critics to be the consequence of the commercial expediency of the clubs in attracting the 'new' fan and their patterns of consumption. The assumption of tensions between changing patterns of consumption and the 'trad' fan is implicit in the quotation from Kurt. Also implicit is the need for 'trad' fans to resist the new consumption through a reassertion of a notion of 'authentic' fandom and its style. Such resistance, however, tends towards a partial and self-selecting romanticization of the football tophilia but, nevertheless, this romanticization remains at the core of many fan campaigns. Campaigns for the reintroduction of terracing, singing sections and even demands for lower admission prices are predicated upon the rather naive assumption that the problem lies with the 'new' fan.

'The songs and chants that used to make the English football match an intensely passionate experience are more subdued', is a sentiment shared by many critics of the regulation of fandom.[18] Yet, unfortunately, the majority of the critiques start and stop with the narrow issue of football's economic gentrification. This is insufficient as a critique, and has fed into the pronounced romanticization of the 'traditional' fan culture. Ironically, this romanticized view has in turn resulted in a new form of commercialization of fandom, manifested, for example, through the commodification of the football chant. This is reflected in the growing number of books devoted to the 'lost tradition' of the football terrace. One such example is Adrian Thrills' *You're Not Singing Anymore*.[19] Subtitled *A Riotous Celebration of Football Chants and the Culture that Spawned Them*, the chants and songs contained within are actually as sanitized and as censored as the new culture that the book claims to define itself against. Thrills states that 'Many chants have been omitted due to their racist or sectarian content. Some, such as the songs about the Munich Air Disaster that have been directed at Manchester United fans, are absent on grounds of common decency.'[20] Here lies the greatest irony. Whilst formally oppositional to the new moralities of the football stadiums, the discourses of resistance are an implicit acceptance and appropriation of the new discourses of regulation that have been a feature of the policing and regulation of post-Hillsborough football fandom. Indeed, The Football Party, formed by author and former hooligan Dougie Brimson, seeks 'the removal of intimidation in all its forms, be it racial, verbal or physical, from the game'.[21] Such aims have become the norm amongst fan organizations. Thus we are left with a rather bizarre, but none the less real contradiction. The fandoms of resistance that have emerged in response to the sanitization of the traditional fan culture are entirely consistent with, and compliant in, the development of new discursive and legislative regimes of regulation.

A TYRANNY OF SAFETY

F. Furedi argues that the concept of safety became a 'fundamental value of the 1990s', and gave new meaning to a wide range of human activity.[22] As the concept is drawn on in recasting the issue of the football offence, Furedi's argument is equally applicable in the sphere of football. As gestures and styles of fandom have been problematized, a perceived crisis of atmosphere has arisen. In April 1997 the FA Premier League commissioned a report on how to remedy the problem (that is, the lack) of crowd atmosphere.[23] Whilst the report tentatively suggests that there is a need to cultivate atmosphere areas in stadiums, there are grounds for arguing that such interventions will not, and cannot, remedy the perceived atmosphere crisis; that is to say, they will only create more confusion and uncertainty. The atmosphere at football, like that at most live spectator sports, is largely dependent on the spontaneity of the relationships and interactions between spectators and between spectators and the spectacle. Now, however, these relationships and interactions are so heavily regulated that atmosphere is robbed of its spontaneity and its potential for passion. Consequently, it is little wonder that the modern football stadium is considered by many to be a rather sterile and silent arena. Yet if the atmosphere is increasingly the subject of schemes to manufacture it, the essential ingredient – spontaneity – is reduced, or even lost. The fact that it is perceived as necessary for atmosphere to be cultivated – to the extent that it becomes institutionalized as a part of the football experience in the form of singing sections, and so on – also means that it becomes subject to increasingly more intrusive regulatory codes and rules which define what type of behaviour is deemed permissible. Moreover, a consequence of the 1997 FA Premier League survey's proposal would be that different types of behaviour are deemed acceptable and unacceptable in different parts of the stadium. The report states that fans who buy tickets to these designated singing areas 'should be told in advance what the code of conduct for that section of the stadium is. By buying tickets they implicitly agree to adhere to that code.'[24] That the behaviour of fans will be restrained even in attempts to encourage 'spontaneous' support indicates that regulation remains a prominent issue.

The theme that draws these issues together is safety. The implementation of the Taylor Report has involved a culture of regulation that has been articulated and rationalized in these terms and has resulted in policing methods quite different from those previously employed. A regime of regulation now exists that is maintained through the language of care rather than confrontation. Through the construction of discourses on safety, aspects of human behaviour are problematized. Human acts and their motives become increasingly suspect and conceived in terms of the potential risk posed to others. This dynamic is codified and finds expression in the emergence of 'new etiquette(s)'[25] or codes of conduct which emphasize the necessity of self-restraint.[26]

Football clubs now exercise a great deal of control over the behaviour of spectators. Through the establishment of codes of conduct, often printed in the match-day programme, the fan is regularly warned that transgression will result in ejection, or a possible ban, from the ground. Typically, the guilty fan has no redress in law. In this respect the football club acts as a quasi-juridical institution, regulating and disciplining the supporter outside of traditional legal avenues with their procedures for appeal. Furthermore, regulation of this type takes an increasingly moralistic form. Take, for example, discourses pertaining to all-seater stadiums. The seat has been perceived as a significant tool in the normalization of deviant behaviour; perceived to be able to transform and restrict the range of possible behaviour. Indeed the introduction of all-seater stadiums was first rationalized as a matter of safety.

Similarly discourses concerning notions of the family and women share this dynamic. Both conceptualizations are intrinsically bound up with the regulation of assumed types of behaviour. In January 1999 the *Sunday Mirror* launched a campaign to 'cut out the foul language which is driving families away from the game'.[27] Whannel has argued that discourses on the football-going family developed during the late 1960s as a response to the hooligan, and have played a key role in the amplification and labelling of certain behavioural forms as deviant.[28] The construction of the family within socio-political discourse becomes a mode of discursive regulation in and of itself. The family has become a highly moralized and normative concept which assumes fixed modes of behaviour. The FA Premier League recently launched a high profile poster campaign entitled 'Keep the Passion, Lose the Language'. Its central motif was that football-watching families do not use bad language (and are offended by those that do), do not behave in abusive or offensive ways, and, above all, do not support their teams in the ways that other fans do. This is, of course, a ludicrous suggestion but it has, nonetheless, become one of the key themes in the policing of spectators.

Moreover, significant attention has focused on the phenomenon of the female fan. A significant element of discourses on female fans has been their 'civilizing' influence on masculine aggression; that is to say, the feminization of football has been interpreted not as a reflection of the changing social position of women, but as a regulatory tool.[29] As a consequence the regulation of the masculine by the feminine becomes a definition of what it is to be a woman at a football game. By implication women do not enjoy and should not be involved in aggressive or offensive behaviour. Through the application of normative gender stereotypes the behaviour of both men and women becomes the subject of repressive regulatory discourses. Whilst the masculine is contrasted with the feminine, both become confined within a regulatory process bound up in non-legislative forms, which predominantly present themselves as issues of safety.

THE LEGISLATIVE ENCROACHMENT AND JURIDIFICATION OF FANDOM

These discourses of safety are also incorporated into the legislative regulation of fandom. The legislative regulation of fandom has taken both football-specific and non football-specific forms: the Football Spectators Act 1989; the Football (Offences) Act 1991; the 1985 Sports Events (Control of Alcohol) Act; and the Criminal Justice and Public Order Act 1994. The 1989 Act gave courts the power to impose restriction orders on those individuals convicted of football-related offences to prevent them from travelling abroad, and gave magistrates powers to make orders against those convicted of corresponding offences in certain other countries. The 1991 Act created three new football related offences – throwing missiles, racist or indecent chanting, and going on to the pitch without permission – despite there being ample provision in existing criminal and common law to punish the specific acts criminalized under the Act.[30] This move suggests that the increasing trend towards the legislative regulation of behaviour within wider society owes much to the continued demonization and criminalization of football fandom.

In terms of non-specific legislation, The 1985 Sporting Events (Control of Alcohol) Act made it a specific offence for football fans to consume alcohol while travelling to a game, or on entry to a ground.[31] The Act also made it an offence to enter a ground when drunk, be in possession of alcohol, or to be drunk during the period of a match. The Act gave the police increased powers of search and arrest, allowing them to search coaches and trains carrying football fans, and anyone 'reasonably' suspected of committing an offence under the Act (drinking alcohol on a train, for example).

The Criminal Justice and Public Order Act 1994 further criminalized the activities of football fans. Under provisions of the Act ticket 'touting' became an offence, and the 'unauthorized' selling of tickets (whether an act of 'touting' or not) was made a criminal act. Furthermore S. Greenfield and G. Osborn draw specific attention to provisions of the Act which brought what they consider an 'integral part of supporting and fandom' – singing and chanting – under threat.[32] Schedule 154 of the 1994 Act created a new Schedule 4A of the 1986 Public Order Act, whereby:

> A person is guilty of an offence if, with intent to cause a person harassment alarm or distress, he –
>
> a) uses threatening, abusive or insulting words or behaviour, or disorderly behaviour, or
>
> b) displays any writing, sign or visible representation which is threatening, abusive or insulting, thereby causing that or another person harassment, alarm or distress.[33]

Following disorder involving England supporters during the 1998 World Cup, the Labour government issued a 29-measure consultation document.[34] The Football (Offences and Disorder) Bill is an attempt to implement them as law. It is the third piece of fandom-specific legislation that may find its way onto the statute books in the last ten years but the first piece of legislation that seeks to extend the scope of domestic regulations to cover football overseas, thereby expanding the sphere of legislation and the regulation of fandom still further; this time beyond national boundaries.

Clause 1 of the proposed Bill amends section 15 of the 1989 Football Spectators Act. The current provision for courts to impose 'restriction orders' on individuals convicted of football related offences, is replaced with an 'international banning order'. The Bill proposes that provision should exist for an individual to be banned from travelling to designated matches overseas, for an 'offence' committed domestically, if a court is 'satisfied that there are reasonable grounds to believe that making the order would help prevent violence or disorder at or in connection with designated overseas football matches'.[35] Clause 2 of the Bill expands the list of 'offences' in respect to which a court may make a banning order. The clause seeks to incorporate section 5 of the Public Order Act 1986, with respect to behaviour causing harassment, alarm or distress. This also includes the incorporation of Part III of the 1986 Act relating to issues of 'racial hatred'. The Bill seeks to make these football-specific offences. Furthermore, within the expansion of the schedule of 'offences', Clause 10 of the Football (Offences and Disorder) Bill seeks to extend section 1666 of the 1994 Criminal Justice and Public Order Act, which will make it a criminal offence for 'unauthorized persons' to sell 'tickets for designated football matches' to include matches overseas.

The amendment to section 15 of the 1989 Football Spectators Act in Clause 1 of the Bill – pertaining to the powers of a court to issue an 'international banning order' – lowers the threshold by which a decision of guilt can be made. At present the 1989 Act states that a banning order can only be made if a court is 'satisfied that issuing an order would help to prevent violence or disorder'.[36] The current Bill seeks to change this to 'reasonable grounds to believe that making the order would help to prevent violence or disorder'.[37] The proposed change in wording is highly significant. In law there is a significant difference between 'satisfied' and 'reasonable grounds to believe'. The former involves a much higher degree of objectivity, or burden of proof. 'Satisfied' means that the court, in full knowledge of all the facts, believes that imposing such an order will prevent violence. In effect, the court has to make a decision between the interests of public safety and the liberty of football fans based on a thorough scrutiny of the evidence presented. 'Reasonable grounds to believe', on the other hand, is much more subjective and in practice will often be based on the opinion of a police officer acting on less than adequate intelligence. It will become much easier for the courts to make such orders, as the court will no longer be required to test the opinion of the police and the evidence on which this opinion is based.

The term 'reasonable grounds to believe' also relates to the court having reasonable grounds to believe the evidence which has been presented. For example, if a police officer applies to the court and states that it is his honest belief that football fans travelling abroad are doing so with the intent to cause trouble, then that police officer's 'honest belief' alone could form 'reasonable grounds' to grant such a banning order. Indeed it was hoped that the Bill could be further amended in its Committee stage to extend the power of the courts to issue banning orders and withdraw the passports of 'unconvicted football hooligans'.[38] As such it is a less robust testing of the thoroughness of evidence, and the burden of proof becomes much easier to satisfy.

'WE'RE ALL HOOLIGANS NOW': EXPANDING THE CONCEPT OF DEVIANCY

The proposed amendments to the current Bill expand the meanings of deviancy which have been a feature of previous legislation. Distinctions between football-related offences and other forms of anti-social behaviour are significantly blurred, as are definitions of violence and harm which now include acts of speech. The Bill's extension to cover activities not labelled offences in previous legislation actively expands the category and definition of social deviancy; something which A. Calcutt has identified as a central dynamic in socio-political discourse on crime and social order more generally.[39] Furthermore, Furedi suggests that the expansion of behavioural activity now being classified or perceived as deviant or anti-social reflects a degree of uncertainty and unease regarding society's ability to judge what is permissible and what is not. This uncertainty is reflected and institutionalized in the development of current legislation on football and fandom, where 'a look or gesture may now be interpreted as a routine sign ... of harassment'.[40]

The extension of the sphere of deviancy, to some extent, contradicts the rhetorical premise of the Bill; loosely defined as a legislative effort to 'drive out the hooligan'.[41] Hooligans are defined as 'a small, dedicated minority ... [who] have been determined for far too long to ruin [football] ... by their loutish and illegal behaviour'.[42] By implication these definitions pinpoint the target of the Bill as a 'dedicated minority' whose behaviour is already 'illegal' but who have managed to evade punishment under previous anti-hooligan legislation. Yet, as outlined above, the dynamic of the Bill is actively to criminalize behaviour previously considered non-criminal. The process of problematization and criminalization of behavioural activity embedded within the Bill contradicts the notion of the Bill's minority target.

The implicit motive behind the introduction of the Bill – to extend and develop existing legislation – significantly redefines our understanding of what is meant by the term football-related. The relationship between a football offence and a football match is becoming increasingly tenuous. As it currently stands in the Football Spectators Act 1989, offences are considered to be football-related if they take place:

(i) two hours before the start of a match, or

(ii) two hours before the time at which it is advertised to start, or

(iii) from the time which spectators are first admitted to the premises, whichever is the earliest, and ending one hour after the end of the match.[43]

Here there is at least a recognition that there should be a definable proximity with the organization of a football match to label something as 'football-related'. Changes proposed under the current Bill weakens such a demand. Clause 2 of the Bill seeks to extend the definition of football-related hooliganism to acts committed within 24 hours either side of a match.[44] The Bill further suggests that:

(a) a person may be regarded as having been on a journey to or from a designated football match whether or not he attended or intended to attend the match; and

(b) a person's journey includes breaks (including overnight breaks).[45]

Does this then mean that 'disorder', or acts of violence that happen in transit to, or in a town or city where a match happens to be taking place will be classified as 'football related', regardless of whether those involved had any intention of attending?

Consequently, the category football-related becomes a catch-all term with little real meaning in its practical application. But this lack of clarity is not really that important in terms of what the Bill is trying to achieve. The labelling of types of behaviour as football-related gives them a far better chance of being criminalized than is the case in law more generally, and is often a precursor to a wider social application. Despite the football friendliness of contemporary socio-political discourse, the football hooligan still remains one of society's most potent folk devils. Given the expanded definition of deviancy and 'football-related' we might justifiably ask, are we not all football hooligans?

ONLY WORDS? THE CRIMINALIZATION OF SPEECH

As noted above, Greenfield and Osborn have drawn attention to the criminalization of what they consider an 'integral' part of fandom – the football chant. Although there is criticism of both legislative and moral regulation of this 'essential' activity, critiques are often partial and self-selective. On matters concerning offensive and racial abuse, juridical intervention is often actively condemned for not going far enough.

Initially, taking part in 'chanting of an indecent racialist nature' was made an explicit offence under the 1991 Football (Offences) Act.[46] Furthermore, the 1991 Act defines chanting as 'the repeated uttering of any words or sounds in concert with one or more others'.[47] There is a widespread reluctance to condemn the legislative extension to deal with supporter 'racism'. Indeed, it is the perceived legislative inadequacy to deal with the problem that is often attacked: 'The failure of the various legislative provisions, in terms of both drafting and enforcement, suggests at worse a statutory impotence and at best practical indifference to the issue of the racial abuse of players ... the sad fact is that the resulting statute has in fact been of little assistance in the fight against racial harassment and abuse.'[48] In turn the Football (Offences and Disorder) Bill seeks to amend section 3 of the Football (Offences) Act 1991 accordingly. Clause 9.-(3) of the Bill amends the Act's definition of chanting from 'in concert with one or more others' to 'whether alone or in concert with one or more others'.

In the United States hate speech is a highly contested issue, especially within the country's college and university campuses.[49] In the domestic context the issue of hate speech has become increasingly manifest in football, gaining increasing academic and legislative attention. Within the current legislation, and the proposed amendments suggested in the 1998 Bill, racist abuse is equated with other forms of indecent or offensive behaviour or chanting. Furthermore racism is equated with speech. Given the sensitivity and controversy of this issue, it merits further examination. What then is hate speech? In general hate speech is defined as speech which causes harm. Words themselves have been transformed into a form of assault. Fish argues that hate speech is, in and of itself, oppressive and that speech is not separable from conduct or consequence. He concludes therefore that hate speech should be regulated against and criminalized.

There are a number of key problems contained within such a thesis. Firstly, the regulation of a type of hate speech actively expands the boundaries of illegality and problematizes other types of speech. Whilst those who seek to impose restrictions on speech may have a very narrow range of insults or abuse in mind, the implementation of restrictions and codes has led to a broadening of the types of speech that become classified as abusive. This broadening and blurring has been reflected in legislation, as racial abuse is equated with other forms of abusive speech; a point that the advocates of criminalization are reluctant to take up. Because of the subjective nature of words that cause harm, clear definitions of what constitutes hate speech are impossible (as speech that causes harm, the classification of hate speech is wholly dependent on the opinion of the recipient or victim of the speech, as they are the only ones in a position judge whether or not the speech in question has caused harm). This leads to an expansion in the use of the term. Once one class or area of speech is criminalized others are immediately brought within the boundaries of illegality, or become questionable. Potentially, then, in activities such as watching football, which are dependent on the spontaneity of the relationship between spectators and the spectacle, all acts of speech become potentially harmful and therefore illegal. Whilst the criminalization of other types of speech, such as chants, songs and expressions of emotion associated with football, may not be the intention of the advocates of the regulation of hate speech, it is without doubt a possible outcome.

The second key issue at stake in the debate about hate speech is Fish's premise that words cannot be separated from their consequences. The idea that words are the equivalent of their consequence is central to the notion of hate speech. But, significantly, rather than a discussion about words, hate speech is actually a discussion about people, and their capabilities to live rationally. Words are not harmful in and of themselves. They do not have consequences outside of a social context. The assumed consequences of the words 'I'm going to kill you' has far greater weight when spoken by someone with a loaded gun, than if it was said, say, by children playing a game. The words are the same, but their contexts and consequences are very different. Context determines how people interpret, judge and act on what they have heard. This is important, as it counters the notion that words are in and of themselves harmful. This is true of 'abusive' and 'offensive' speech, whether racist or otherwise.

Through the construction of the notion of hate speech, the issue of racism has been recast as a problem of the way people speak and behave.[50] In effect, racism has become de-politicized. In dominant socio-political discourses there are no meaningful distinctions between racial abuse and other forms of bad behaviour. Seemingly very different racial and ideological outlooks have begun to share increasingly similar definitions. In 1995 the Labour Party published its charter for football, stating that the party 'will not tolerate any racial abuse or anti-social behaviour at football matches'.[51] Similarly Steve Reynolds, chairman of the National Front in London, has been quoted in his support of the 'Kick It Out' campaign, stating: 'I take my children to football and don't want them to listen to racist chanting and I don't want my members doing it.'[52]

The criminalization of speech as hate speech in its moral and legislative forms feeds into a process whereby acts of behaviour undergo a process of problematization. Rather than solving the perceived problem, the legislative institutionalizing of such subjective definitions only serves to problematize other acts of speech, and other aspects of actual and potential behaviour. The very act of spontaneity that is celebrated as 'essential' to fandom is criminalized. Moreover, as the potential for spontaneity is recast as a potential threat to the safety of others, a previously autonomous sphere of human behaviour becomes a legitimate arena for political and legal regulation.

DARK ASSUMPTIONS

As a social institution, modern football is the product of interrelated social and political processes: the regulation and normalization of the 'lower orders', and the creation of an autonomous sphere of social activity. As this autonomous sphere expands, tensions emerge between the political élite's concerns for social control and the autonomy of individuals. The development of mass sport spectatorship in the modern era has resulted in increasingly authoritarian interventions by the authorities of law and order.[53] Whilst mass participation sport and spectatorship have become socially accepted activities, it would be foolhardy to suggest that the tension between social regulation and autonomous activity has been resolved. Far from it. This tension is being recast for the twenty-first century.

Jensen argues that the concept of fandom is full of 'dark assumptions' about modern life, technical progress, moral, cultural and perceived social decay.[54] Fandom's 'dark assumptions' are, she argues, a reflection of elitist fears of modern society; fears particularly bound up with notions of the mob or the masses. Implicit in Jensen's conceptualization is the relationship between state power, a perceived crisis of social order, and the development of technologies of regulation. Similarly, the concept of the hooligan has been consistently deployed as a discursive mechanism to demonize. The hooligan caricatures, which Taylor defined as 'élitist stereotypes', became institutionalized expressions of the political élite's social disquiet.[55] By the late 1970s and early 1980s the football hooligan had become a dominant character of British political and social discourse.

Whilst it has largely been perceived as representative of a break with this conceptualization of the fan as a deviant, the contemporary construction of fandom within socio-political discourse recasts notions of deviancy that are far more wide-ranging and inclusive than before. Today, football's 'dark assumption' has become a fear about the capacity of individuals to interact and function with civility. Attempts to resist the threat to 'traditional' fandom have in fact embraced notions of safety and the new technologies of regulation rather than rejected them. They have become a defining feature in the articulation of new, post-1989 forms of fandom. What were once considered 'élitist fears' or 'élitist stereotypes' have become appropriated and generalized within the new cultures of fandom.

Embedded within these processes are a fundamental renegotiation and moral recasting of relationships between the state and the individual. Furedi argues that this is best expressed in the dramatic ways in which language and speech are perceived as 'harmful'. This, he suggests, indicates a dominant 'social mood' of uncertainty and 'diminished sense of individual control ... when attitudes and ways of behaving can no longer be taken for granted'.[56] The development of the new technologies employed in restricting football fans' sphere of activity is predicated on the perception that behaviour between individuals is potentially dangerous or unsafe, and that as individuals we are unable to cope with this threat. Critiques of the legal regulation of fandom as a consequence of gentrification underestimate this increasingly authoritarian renegotiating of the State's relationship to society and the individual. The Football (Offences and Disorder) Bill formalizes these trends and signals a new phase in the conceptualization of fandom as a deviant activity.

It seems likely that the Football (Offences and Disorder) Bill will become law in the twenty-first century. Political support for the Bill is widespread and critical voices have been partial and self-selecting in their opposition. There is also broad acceptance, particularly within academia and organized fandom, for aspects of the Bill which seek to criminalize 'hate speech' and 'offensiveness'. But this need not necessarily be the case. In order to combat the trends towards legislative regulation and moralization outlined above, fandom requires a much more robust and thorough critique of the cultures of regulation that exist within football. There is a definite need to resist the temptations to romanticize and mythologize certain styles of fandom. There is also a need to question the economic determinacy of the gentrification debate. This achieves nothing other than to blame the cultures of regulation developing within the game on other fans, and masks the dynamic towards much more expansive and inclusive definitions of deviancy. Fandom must also shake off its acquiescence to the contemporary forms of regulation within the game. Fandom is in danger of being complicit with its own criminalization most explicitly through its support of anti-hate speech campaigns and legislation. Whilst recognizing that these are increasingly controversial and sensitive issues, there is a danger that the criminalization and banning of forms of hate speech, abuse and offensiveness become the norm within football. As such the challenge that faces fandom in the new millennium is that it needs to challenge what has been until now largely considered as unchallengable. I hope that this essay will be seen as such a challenge.

NOTES

1. J. Jenson, 'Fandom as Pathology: The Consequences of Characterization', in L.A. Lewis (ed.), *The Adoring Audience* (London: Routledge, 1993), p.10.
2. Ibid., p.9.
3. R. Giulianotti, 'Social Identity and Public Order: Political and Academic Discourses on Football Violence', in R. Giulianotti, N. Bonney and M. Hepworth (eds.), *Football, Violence and Social Identity* (London: Routledge, 1994), pp.10–36; I. Taylor, 'English Football in the 1990s: Taking Hillsborough Seriously?', in J. Williams and S. Wagg (eds.), *British Football and Social Change: Getting into Europe* (Leicester: Leicester University Press, 1991), pp.3–24.
4. I. Taylor, 'English Football in the 1990s', p.2.
5. S. Redhead, 'Some Reflections on Discourses of Football Hooliganism', *Sociological Review*, 39, 3 (1991), 479.
6. F. Furedi, *Culture of Fear: Risk-taking and the Morality of Low Expectation* (London: Cassell, 1997).
7. A. Giddens, *Modernity and Self Identity* (Cambridge: Polity Press, 1991), pp.225–6.
8. See, for example, J. Hargreaves, *Sport, Power and Culture* (Cambridge: Polity Press, 1986); R.S. Gruneau, 'Modernization or Hegemony: Two Views on Sport and Social Development', in J. Harvey and H. Cantelon (eds.), *Not Just a Game: Essays in Canadian Sport Sociology* (Ottawa: University of Ottawa Press, 1988), pp.9–32; G. Armstrong and R. Giulianotti (eds.), *Entering The Field: New Perspectives on World Football* (Oxford: Berg, 1997), p.4.
9. S. Greenfield and G. Osborn, 'The Legal Regulation of Football and Cricket: "England's Dreaming"', in M. Roche (ed.), *Sport, Popular Culture and Identity* (Aachen: Meyer & Meyer, 1998); C. Critcher, 'Football since the War', in J. Clarke, C. Critcher and R. Johnson (eds.), *Working Class Culture* (London: Hutchinson, 1979), pp.161–84.
10. J. Bale, 'Playing at Home: British Football and a Sense of Place', in J. Williams and S. Wagg (eds.), *British Football and Social Change: Getting into Europe* (Leicester: Leicester University Press, 1991), pp.130–44; J. Bale, *Sport, Space and the City* (London: Routledge, 1993).
11. Bale, 'Playing at Home'.
12. Bale, *Sport, Space and the City*.
13. Greenfield and Osborn, 'The Legal Regulation of Football and Cricket', p.202.
14. E. Horton, *Moving the Goalposts: The Exploitation of Football* (Edinburgh: Mainstream, 1997), p.29.
15. Greenfield and Osborn, 'The Legal Regulation of Football and Cricket', p.207.
16. I use the term 'representative' reservedly. Adam Brown has argued, 'it is extremely difficult for any fans organisation to legitimately claim that they represent the views of a majority .... [as] fan organisations are often dominated by an active minority'. A. Brown, 'United We Stand: Some Problems with Fan Democracy', in A. Brown (ed.), *Fanatics! Power, Identity and Fandom in Football* (London: Routledge, 1994), p.64.
17. R. Kurt, *United We Stood* (Cheshire: Sigma Leisure, 1994), pp.112–13.
18. P. Haverson, 'Football Goes to Market', *Prospect* (June 1998) 22.
19. A. Thrills, *You're Not Singing Anymore: A Riotous Celebration of Football Chants and the Culture that Spawned Them* (London: Ebury Press, 1998).
20. Ibid. p.12.
21. The Football Party, 'Representing the Underrepresented', press release, August 1998.
22. Furedi, *Culture of Fear*, p.1.
23. P. Carling, M. Highmore, S. Sillitoe and P. Johns, *Crowd Atmosphere at Premier League Matches* (London: FA Premier League, 1997).

24. Ibid. p.4.
25. Furedi, *Culture of Fear*, p.150.
26. Ibid., p.155.
27. B. McNally, 'Let's Kick out Football's Foulmouthed Yobs', *Sunday Mirror*, 3 January 1998, 79.
28. G. Whannel, 'Football, Crowd Behaviour and the Press', *Media, Culture and Society*, 1 (1979), 1–16.
29. Rather interestingly the conceptualization of the female football fan as a calming, rational influence upon the emotional irrationality of the male contradicts the more common perception of females as 'emotional' and 'irrational'.
30. Greenfield and Osborn, 'The Legal Regulation of Football and Cricket', p.200.
31. Ibid. p.199.
32. Ibid. p.201.
33. Criminal Justice and Public Order Act S154.
34. Home Office, Review of Football-Related Legislation (London: Home Office, 1998).
35. Football (Offences and Disorder) Bill, 1998: Clause 1.-(2).
36. Football Spectators Act 1989, Clause 15.-(2).
37. Football (Offences and Disorder Bill 1.-(2).
38. Simon Burns MP, House of Commons Hansard Debates, 16 April 1999 (pt. 2): Column 475). This has since been dropped in Committee, but it is hoped to be included 'in a future criminal justice bill put forward by the government' (Simon Burns MP quoted in the *Guardian*, 6 May 1999, 9).
39. A. Calcutt, 'Uncertain Judgement: A Critique of the Culture of Crime', in S. Walton (ed.), *Marxism, Mysticism and Modern Theory* (London: Macmillan, 1999), pp.28–60.
40. Furedi, *Culture of Fear*, p.69.
41. Home Office, 'Marking Hooligans Out of the Game', News Release, 468/98, 27 November 1998.
42. Simon Burns, MP, Hansard Debates 16 April (pt. 2): Column 470. (1999).
43. Football Spectators Act 1989 1.-(8) (a).
44. Football (Offences and Disorder) Bill, Clause 2.-(3) (b) and (c).
45. Football (Offences and Disorder) Bill 1998, 2.-(2).
46. Football (Offences) Act 1991. Section 3.-1(1).
47. Ibid. Section 3–(2) (a).
48. S. Greenfield and G. Osborn, 'After the Act: The (Re)Construction and Regulation of Football Fandom', *Journal of Civil Liberties*, 1, 1 (1996), 334.
49. H.L. Gates, A.P. Griffin, D.E. Lively, R.C. Post, W.B. Rubenstein and N. Strossen, *Speaking of Race, Speaking of Sex: Hate Speech, Civil Rights and Civil Liberties* (New York: New York University Press, 1995); S. Fish, *There's No Such Thing As Free Speech: And It's a Good Thing Too* (New York: Oxford University Press, 1994).
50. D. Allirajah, 'Getting a Good Kicking', *Offence* (London: Libero, 1997).
51. Labour Party, *A New Framework for Football: Labour's Charter for Football* (London: Labour Party, 1995), p.8.
52. L. Brown, 'NF Backs New Racism Policy', *South London Press*, 27 February 1998.
53. Hargreaves, *Sport, Power and Culture*, p.84.
54. Jensen, 'Fandom as Pathology', p.15.
55. I. Taylor, 'Soccer Consciousness and Soccer Hooliganism', p.140.
56. Furedi, *Culture of Fear*, p.157.

PART 5
Football Players and Referees

13

Global Sport and the Migration Patterns of France '98 World Cup Finals Players: Some Preliminary Observations

JOSEPH MAGUIRE and ROBERT PEARTON

Elite labour migration is now an established feature of the sporting 'global village'.[1] This involves the movement of workers in a variety of sports both within and between nations and continents. In recent years this phenomenon has attracted increased academic attention, with studies examining several sports including ice hockey,[2] cricket,[3] baseball,[4] basketball,[5] and perhaps most notably, football.[6] This research has focused on differing aspects of the migration process. Firstly, patterns in sports migration have been identified. Secondly, academics have been concerned to explain how and why these patterns occur, and thirdly, an ethnographic approach has been employed to investigate the lived experiences of some sports migrants.

What existing research has established beyond doubt is that élite sports migration cannot be explained solely with reference to an economic analysis. Rather, a complex and shifting set of interdependencies contours the migrant trails of world sport. These interdependencies are multi-faceted and incorporate not only economic, but also political, historical, geographical, social and cultural factors. Thus, in seeking to explain global sport labour migration, a broad approach must be taken. An examination of wider societal processes is more appropriate than a focus on the sports industry. This essay employs just such an approach in its examination of football labour migration and seeks to contribute to continuing research about talent migration in world football at the very élite level.

PUTTING FOOTBALL MIGRATION PATTERNS IN CONTEXT: ISSUES AND DIMENSIONS

Currently, the migration of sports talent as athletic labour is a pronounced feature of European, and indeed, global cultural interchange. This process is interwoven with the commodification of sports within the capitalist world economy. It is not usual for sports devotees to think of sportspeople as workers. They are, however, not unlike other workers who, for various reasons, have to ply their trade in locations outside their country of origin. Again, not unlike their counterparts in other occupations, élite athletes as a group experience varying degrees of exploitation and dislocation, but also enjoy some personal gains.

Such sports labour migration occurs within nation-states, between nation-states located within the same continent and between nation-states located within different continents. A socially and geographically mobile workforce is a feature of most modern societies and the movement of athletes from their 'hometown' to their place of initial recruitment into élite or professional sports clubs within the boundaries of the nation-state is part of this process. There are discernible patterns to the recruitment and subsequent retention of people in sports such as American football, baseball, basketball, cricket, ice-hockey, track and field and football.[7] 'British' sport, for example, reveals several quite specific and more general features of sports labour migration. That is, although Britain is composed of England, Scotland, Wales and Northern Ireland, these 'nations' have, for example, football leagues that contain varying levels of 'indigenous' labour and labour from other 'nations' within the United Kingdom. It was also possible, at least until recently, to point to the former Soviet Union and Yugoslavia as countries where similar processes were at work. That is, sports performers from different republics, such as the Ukraine and Georgia, or Croatia and Bosnia, moved within these former nation-states, to ply their athletic labour for sports teams such as Moscow Dynamo and Red Star Belgrade.

Sports labour migration also occurs between countries located within the same continent. If one considers the 'states' within the United States of America, inter-state migration of sports talent is extremely widespread and is not without controversy.[8] Witness also the involvement of US citizens in Canadian baseball teams and athletes from the Dominican Republic in 'American' baseball teams. In Europe, this sports labour migration takes place in several sports but is, arguably, most pronounced in football where professional players regularly criss-cross the continent of Europe. In this case, talent is purchased, above all, by the national leagues of England, Germany, Italy and Spain. This labour stems from 'donor' countries spread across Europe, including Germany, Holland, the United Kingdom, the Commonwealth of Independent States and the Balkan and Scandinavian countries.

Football labour flows across the continent with the more economically powerful leagues in these countries attracting a standard of player commensurate to the ability to pay 'transfer' fees and, even more importantly, the salaries of the players concerned. Even in countries where the outflow of talent is most evident, the Scandinavian countries for example, players from abroad and less talented players from home are recruited. The opening up of Eastern Europe, with Hungarian, Czech, Slovakian and Romanian players to the fore in the early 1990s, has further complicated this movement of athletic labour, largely involving the outflow of talent from eastern Europe. This process has been enlarged by the movement of Bosnian and Croatian players following the civil wars in the former Yugoslavia.

A similar trend is also evident on a trans-continental level. Movement of sports labour occurs from North America to Europe in sports such as basketball, American football and ice-hockey. By the mid-1990s over 400 Americans were playing in Europe's professional men's basketball leagues, with the higher calibre of players 'residing' in Italy and Spain. Anglo-Canadians and French-Canadians ply their ice-hockey skills in Britain, Germany, France and Switzerland. There is also a flow of sports labour in the opposite direction. North American ice-hockey clubs recruit Scandinavian and East European players.[9] Moreover, American universities have actively recruited European men and women in sports such as track and field, football, rugby, basketball and swimming.[10] These trends have been the subject of critical debate within Canada and the United States with a quota of non-US athletes being proposed.[11] Issues of ancestral links to specific countries and the imposition of quotas on 'foreign' players by particular national sports organizations further complicate the migration process.

The movement of sports labour on a trans-continental level also occurs between Europe and Africa. Africans are prominent in a range of European football leagues. First and second-generation migration patterns emerge. Sport can provide a means of integration into the host society, exemplified by the presence of a continuous stream of 'foreign' footballers into France. Sport, however, does not necessarily aid the cultural assimilation of ethnic groups. Rather, in specific instances sport can serve as a symbol of identification with the cultural heritage of the group from which the individual comes.[12]

The migration of sports labour on a trans-continental level is also evident in the involvement of first and second-generation Afro-Caribbeans in English football. Thus, several current players are the sons of migrants who have settled in the country that was formerly their colonial overlord. Australian, Afro-Caribbean, South Asian and South African players figure prominently in English cricket, and have done so for many decades. In the United States, African track and field talent is recruited through the American university scholarship programme.

Sports workers tend to be 'hired' by a specific club or organization and individuals reside in the host country for a limited period. However, this is not always the case. Some athletes stay on and make the host country their 'home'. This occurs either through marriage to a citizen of that country or through staying 'attached' to a specific country for long enough to qualify for nationality status. Chen Xinhua, a former citizen of the People's Republic of China who played table tennis for Britain during the early 1990s, and Sydney Maree, a South African runner who became a naturalized American citizen to run in international competitions during the same period, are examples. Sometimes, such as in European basketball, individuals begin to play for the country in which they have become resident then subsequently claim 'nationality'.

In certain sports, such as cricket and rugby league, migration has a seasonal pattern. The northern and southern hemispheres offer in sports such as cricket what amounts, in effect, to two seasons of continuous play. Other sports migrants experience a transitory form of migration. Take, for example, the experience of athletes on the European track and field Grand Prix circuit or European and American skiers on the World Cup Alpine skiing circuit. Other such sports include cycling and motor racing ranging from Formula One to motor-cycling. Sometimes, seasonal and transitory migration patterns interweave, as in golf and tennis. Golf and tennis players are arguably the nomads of the sports labour migration system with a seemingly constantly shifting workplace and place of residence.[13] Though both men and women have their global circuits, the enabling and constraining features of this experience may be markedly different. In terms of numbers the global migration of 'sports labour' predominantly, though not exclusively, involves men. Their ability to move over time and across space is based on a patriarchal structure that ensures that it is usually women who perform the domestic labour, whether in the company of their travelling partners or waiting 'at home'.

FOOTBALL LABOUR MIGRATION: A RESEARCH AGENDA

Four main issues can be identified that should arguably form the core of a research agenda in this area. First is that of labour rights. The rights enjoyed by sport migrants, and indeed indigenous sports workers, vary considerably between sports and across continents, and may also have changed considerably over time. The employment rights achieved by players in team sports such as European football are still minimal compared to the freedoms gained by sports people in individual sports, particularly in tennis and golf. Pete Sampras, Martina Hingis, Tiger Woods and Lotta Neumann all enjoy greater control over the production and exploitation of their sports talent than do football players of comparable ability such as Dennis Bergkamp or David Beckham. Of course, not all participants in individual sports enjoy the advantages of tennis players or golfers. Track and field athletes have only recently begun to flex their collective muscle, and pressed the International Amateur Athletic Federation (IAAF) to pay prize money at the 1993 World Championships. Now, the payment of athletes is commonplace.

Within team sports, employment rights also vary across sports played in different continents. Although North American athletes in sports such as American/Canadian football, ice-hockey, basketball and baseball have unionized, conducted negotiations with owners based on collective bargaining and involved themselves in strike action, they have not been particularly successful in gaining greater employment rights.[14] The draft, in which college athletes are 'assigned' to specific teams, still operates in North American sport. In comparison, the free movement of labour is now part of European Union (EU) law. EU nationals are technically free to ply their athletic labour where they wish within the European Union although certain restrictions remain (see Foster's essay in this collection).

However, the very rights for which Bosman sought enforcement are not applicable to all players. Individuals from countries outside the EU are subject to a selection procedure. They have to prove international status in their respective sports. Further, as with migrants more generally, exploitative labour practices also take place. No detailed substantive research on the experience of migrants from less developed countries, for example, African and East European football players, exists. It is evident, however, that lower wages than their EU counterparts is one of the attractions for West European clubs. Indeed, these élite clubs are increasingly investing in 'feeder' or 'nursery' clubs in underdeveloped countries. Sport labour migration is not, then, a uniform experience. It has its own highly differentiated political economy.[15]

This movement of athletic talent involves, in many instances, the de-skilling of 'donor' countries and this issue should arguably form part of a second broad area of inquiry. Latin and Central American countries for example, regularly experience the loss of baseball stars and football players to the United States and Europe respectively. Here, less developed countries have invested in the production of athletic talent. Once this talent reaches maturity, more economically developed leagues cream off the best available talent.[16] Not only is the native audience denied direct access to the talent nurtured and developed in their country, in some cases, as with African national football teams, sports lose some of their quality players when the demands of European clubs clash with international matches. Ironically, if corporate concerns become so dominant, the viability of national teams in general will also surface as an issue facing Union of European Football Associations (UEFA) and Fédération Internationale de Football Association (FIFA) officials.

Questions regarding the impact of sport labour migration on the 'host' culture could form part of a third research area. The social-psychological problems of dislocation and adjustment need consideration. Problems of inter-cultural communication arise for sport migrants – witness the 'babel-like' quality of global sports festivals or tournaments. For sport migrants such a social milieu involves a multi-layered form of inter-cultural communication centring on interaction with fellow players, coaches, officials, the crowd and media personnel in their professional lives, and a variety of new 'others' at a personal level. In the world of European football, Swedes, Norwegians, Dutchmen and Germans appear adept at deploying flexible personal controls and often communicate with ease in several different languages. While some sport migrants may find the move from one culture to another relatively free of culture shock (when Gary Lineker moved to Barcelona, for example), this may not always be the case (when Ian Rush moved to Juventus). The burnout of young women tennis players may, in part, be connected to these processes. Further, the movement of eastern European migrants to Europe and North America may also bring problems of adjustment to free market economic processes. Some élite sport migrants also work in (and inhabit) a specific type of urban space; think of the redeveloped city areas now occupied by sport-work places such as the Skydome in Toronto, the Globe in Stockholm and the Palais Omnisports in Paris.

This labour migration may also engender hostility in the host country. Sport labour unions, such as in European football, have sought to protect indigenous players by arguing for quotas and qualification thresholds to be applied to potential migrants. During 1993 the English Professional Footballers' Association (PFA) called for tighter controls and checks on the playing credentials of foreign players.[17] An attempt by FIFA, the world governing body of football, to remove restrictions on foreign players in European leagues, was met with the threat of a Europe-wide strike by professional players.[18] Following a meeting held in February 1993 between the English PFA, the football authorities and the Department of Employment, tighter restrictions were imposed on foreign players.[19] This concern extends to the development of national teams. The presence of overseas players denies indigenous players access to élite teams and could thus lead to personal and national under-development. Cesare Maldini, the Italian under-21 national coach, highlighted this issue when he noted that 'at youth level, our football is getting worse. We don't have the players any more. The increasing number of foreigners in our game means the opportunities for the youngsters are vanishing.'[20] The French have already introduced a quota system for senior clubs to encourage youth development. England's poor performances in the qualification phase for the 2000 European football championships were linked, in the press, to the presence of some 180 plus foreign players employed by Premier League clubs. Consequently calls were made for restrictions to be placed on the recruitment of overseas players.

In contrast to these sentiments, major European football club owners seek to strengthen their position at every opportunity. The ascendancy in the mid-1990s of AC Milan exemplifies this process. Its then owner, Silvio Berlusconi, argued for no restrictions on sport migration. As part of this process, which he viewed as already underway, Berlusconi concluded that 'the concept of the national team will, gradually, become less and less important. It is the clubs with which the fans associate.'[21] In this approach, the fortunes of the national team become secondary. Corporate success is what counts. Yet, as both Euro '96 and France '98 highlighted, national identity politics still underpins global football.[22]

This reference to the success of national teams raises a fourth issue that could form part of a research agenda examining sport labour migration and globalization. Questions of attachment to place, notions of self-identity and allegiance to a specific country are significant in this connection. Reference to the de-monopolization of economic structures in the world economy shows that such processes led to the concomitant deregulation and globalization of markets, trade and labour. Similarly, the introduction of market imperatives has become a pronounced feature of the sports world over the last decade. Consequently, the amateur ideology of élite sports administrators have been superseded in the need to compete in the market-place.

A new generation of agents and organizations, such as Mark McCormack and his International Marketing Group, and media–sport production executives, have created sport spectacles by employing élite sport migrants to perform exhibition bouts or contests. Elements of an Americanization process are evident. A range of sports have been forced to align themselves to an American-style sports model in order to survive in the global media-market place.[23]

The new generation of sport migrants may have little sense of attachment to a specific space or community. Such arguments have been used by fans and reporters who have been critical of the recruitment of football migrants by traditional English clubs like Liverpool and Newcastle United. Highly rational and technical criteria determine their status and market value. Just as the migrant workers in North American law firms whom Dezalay studied – a group he termed 'hired guns' – stress technical competence, aggressive tactics and a meritocratic ethos, so sport migrants embrace the ethos of hard work, differential rewards and a win at all costs approach.[24] Aggressive and violent tactics characterize the occupational subculture of some élite sport migrants (in ice-hockey, for example). The 'rebel' cricket and rugby union tours to South Africa highlight how sport migrants can likewise act as mercenaries for 'big business'.

In this process nationality has become more flexible. Canadian ice-hockey players and American basketball players have represented Great Britain and a range of other European countries in Olympic qualifying tournaments. In referring to these examples we do not wish to underestimate the pull of national traditions. On the contrary, global sporting festivals, such as the World Cup and the Olympics, owe their unrivalled popularity to the fact that they are prestige contests between nations. However, we suggest that national identity and traditions are not necessarily always as fixed as they sometimes appear.[25] Questions of national/cultural identity also relate to the process of globalization. At this stage, let us turn attention to how the migration patterns evident at the France '98 World Cup finals reflect and reinforce these broader global sport issues and dimensions.

FIFA AND THE 1998 WORLD CUP FINALS

FIFA is the governing body of world football and administrator of the global competition known simply as the World Cup. It was formed in 1904 with seven member nations (France, Sweden, Denmark, Switzerland, the Netherlands, Belgium and Spain) but has since grown into a massive global organization, with 201 full, provisional and associate member nations in 1998.[26] World football is sub-divided into six confederations that are not members of FIFA *per se* but are in practice represented within FIFA by their member states. Of the six confederations, UEFA (Europe) is the most powerful, as although it has only about 25 per cent of FIFA member states within its borders, these nations generate around 80 per cent of FIFA's annual revenue.[27] The qualifying rounds for the World Cup finals take place within the confederations. Table 13.1 details these confederations and the number of teams from each at the World Cup finals of 1998.

TABLE 13.1

COUNTRIES REPRESENTING FIFA CONFEDERATIONS IN THE WORLD CUP, 1998

UEFA	15
CONMEBOL	5
CONCACAF	3
CAF	5
AFC	4
OFC	0

CORE PATTERNS TO ELITE TALENT MOVEMENT

In examining the migration patterns evident with regard to the national squads playing in France in 1998 five main questions guided our research. First, how much of the process underpinning the patterns identified could be explained in economic terms? Second, what dimensions in conjunction with the economic appear to play a part in contouring and shaping these migration patterns? Third, what combination of factors appear most central in explaining relations between global football regions? Fourth, what are the main networks, power relationships, enabling and constraining features and labour inequalities involved in the processes described? Fifth, what conceptual and sport policy implications follow from the findings uncovered in this study? Due to the limitations of space, not all of the broader conceptual and sociological issues will be dealt with in this study.

The clearest feature which can be determined from the data is that Europe (UEFA) is still football's 'core economy'.[28] This is demonstrated by Figure 13.1, which shows where the 704 players at France '98 make their living in club football.[29] It demonstrates that 62 per cent (436) of these players work in Europe. Four of the other five FIFA confederations are represented, with no players making their living in the Oceania Football Confederation (OFC) area. This is due to the facts that OFC had no representatives at the World Cup finals, with Australia just missing out to Iran, and that none of the clubs in OFC attracts players from countries outside the confederation.

From the available data it is clear that UEFA attracts most players from other federations, 122 in total, and has the most movement within the confederation itself. Although there is movement of players between the countries that make up the Confederación Sudamericana de Fútbol, or CONMEBOL (South America), there are no World Cup players from any of the other confederations playing there. The Confédération Africaine de Football, or CAF (Africa), similarly attracts no players from other confederations. The Asian Football Confederation (AFC) and the Confederación Norte-/Centroamericana y del Caribe de Fútbol,

FIGURE 13.1

WHERE WORLD CUP PLAYERS MAKE THEIR LIVING, BY COUNTRY

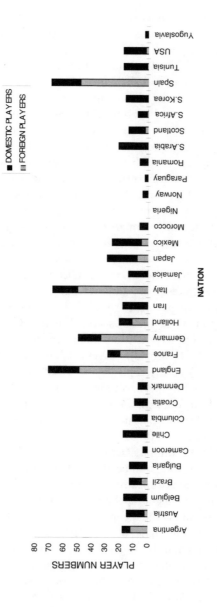

or CONCACAF (North and Central America and the Caribbean), have only nine players between them from other federations within their club systems. These figures thus emphasize the centrality of Europe in the international football labour market.

The most popular destinations for migrant World Cup players are the English, Italian and Spanish leagues with the German Bundesliga also prominent. Clubs in these four leagues together employed 270 of the players taking part in the World Cup finals. Five countries (England, Japan, Mexico, Saudi Arabia and Spain) had all 22 members of their squad playing at 'home'. In contrast, Nigeria had no players in its national team playing club football domestically, let alone any migrants. This is attributable in part to the under-development of football in Nigeria but also due to the continuing political unrest that is prevalent in that country. Let us now outline some of the main features evident at the confederation, European and national levels.

CONMEBOL (South America) had five of its member nations at the World Cup finals (Brazil, Argentina, Paraguay, Colombia and Chile). Thus 110 players from South America were present. Of these 110 players, 41 (37.3%) play their club football outside South America. Thirty of these 41 players (74%) earn their living in the 'Latin' countries of Italy and Spain. Portugal, England and Germany are their other European destinations. In total 83 per cent of the South Americans playing outside CONMEBOL work in UEFA countries. A further ten per cent play in Mexico and, presumably, linguistic and geographical issues are significant. The remaining seven per cent 'work' in the affluent, though not high status, Japanese and North American soccer leagues. CAF (Africa) also had five representatives at France '98 (Cameroon, Morocco, Nigeria, South Africa and Tunisia); again a total of 110 players. Clubs outside Africa employ a large proportion (67.3%) of these players. Overall, migration by African players is overwhelmingly to European countries, with just 4 per cent of the migrants playing outside UEFA. Of the 74 African migrant players, 58 per cent are located in nations with Mediterranean coastlines (France, Italy, Spain, Greece and Turkey), with France (19%) and Spain (18%) being the most popular destinations. Whilst economic factors are relevant this is also due to the fact that these nations have historical and colonial links with North Africa. The position of Turkey is unclear and requires further study.

The east European talent pipeline, as we have already noted, has been a feature of several sports since the people's revolutions of the late 1980s. Western European football clubs have been some of the principal beneficiaries of this continuing phenomenon. Of the 88 Eastern European players representing four nations (Bulgaria, Croatia, Romania and Yugoslavia) at France '98, 56 (63.6%) played outside Eastern Europe. Only 6 per cent chose to play for, or were recruited by, non-Western European clubs. Spain is their most 'popular' destination, nearly a third (29%) play for Spanish clubs. Germany, Italy and Turkey were also popular, arguably for geographical reasons, as all share borders with former 'Iron Curtain' nations. From the data presented it is impossible to deduce whether the popularity of certain destinations is a function of player preference, club economics, and/or coach selection policies. More qualitative research is required to complement this preliminary account.

IMPORT STRATEGIES AND NATIONAL STEREOTYPES

To establish a fuller picture of 'very élite' football migration, it is also necessary to investigate the import of football talent. The immigration patterns of the four most popular destination countries – England, Italy, Spain and Germany – were examined on two levels to enable both broad and more specific analysis. This was achieved by considering both the confederation origin and the national origin of their immigrants. Let us turn attention to this aspect of the migration process. Germany can be considered the most 'cosmopolitan' nation as among its 35 World Cup immigrants, five FIFA federations are represented. England has four federations among the 54 immigrants to the Premier League, with no representatives from the AFC (Asian) federation. Italy and Spain have similar patterns of immigration in terms of federation origin, neither having migrant players from AFC (Asia) or CONCACAF (North and Central America and the Caribbean). Both nations also have around half their immigrant World Cup players from UEFA. Italy, however, has a larger percentage of migrants from South America (37%) than Spain (22%), while the Spanish Liga employs more Africans (26%) than does Italy's Serie A (14%).

England also has the largest proportion of migrants from fellow UEFA countries, with 74 per cent of migrants in English club football being from Europe. Almost half come from just three countries. Nineteen per cent are from Norway – a long-established migrant trail.[30] Fifteen per cent originate in Scotland, which can be explained by the fact that these two footballing nations belong to the same nation-state, and a further 13 per cent are from Jamaica. This is due to the historical colonial links between the two nations, and the presence of the British-born sons of a large immigrant population from Jamaica in England. A single Colombian was the only South American presence, while four players from Nigeria and South Africa represent Africa – arguably a function of the colonial links these two countries have with England.

Thirty-seven per cent of World Cup migrants in Italian football are from South America – principally Argentina (21% of the total) and Brazil (12%). In terms of other UEFA nations, Serie A imports more players from France than from any other country (13% of total). This pattern differs from that identified in earlier work by J. Maguire and D. Stead (on migration patterns in EU countries) who found Holland to be the principal nation from which Serie A clubs recruited.[31] Sixteen per cent of World Cup migrants in Italy come from eastern Europe – specifically Yugoslavia and Croatia. This is probably due to the geographical proximity of the countries and the recent war that has engulfed the Balkans.

Spain attracts players from the largest number of World Cup Finals nations, with 19 of the 32 countries having players from the Spanish club system. Eastern Europeans constitute 34 per cent of the World Cup migrants playing in the Spanish Liga which supports the earlier findings of Maguire and Stead.[32] There were also 13 African players among the 50 World Cup migrants in Spain, with all five of the African countries playing in France '98 having representatives in Spanish football. As yet, there is no evidence available as to why this specific pattern has developed. Seventeen different World Cup finals nations are represented by the 35 migrants playing in the Bundesliga, making it arguably more cosmopolitan than the Spanish Liga, whose 50 migrants are represented by 19 countries. Not surprisingly, given linguistic and geographical considerations, Austrians (14%) form the highest percentage of World Cup migrants recruited by Bundesliga clubs. Bulgarians are also prominent with 11 per cent, perhaps for geographical reasons but also, perhaps, in part connected to the more general process of east European migration.

DISCUSSION

Several key findings can be identified in the case study presented above. Firstly, UEFA (Europe) is confirmed as the core economy within world football. Europe is the principal destination for the 'very élite' players who took part in the 1998 World Cup finals. Secondly, a pattern of top-level player recruitment within Europe is evident which arguably differs from migrant trails at a slightly lower level. In this study, the affluent English, Italian and Spanish clubs, which can afford the best of the élite, were found to be the major importers of football talent. These findings contrast with those of Maguire and Stead who looked at a slightly lower playing level in considering football migration in the EU.[33] They identified, in the 1994/95 season, Belgium, Germany and France as the biggest recruiters of foreign football talent ahead of England, Italy and Spain. Officials of clubs located within Serie A, the Premier League and the Spanish Liga prefer to spend large sums of money on fewer, very élite players – those competing at the World Cup finals. In contrast, Belgian, French and German clubs may spread their resources by buying more players of a slightly lesser standard.

The rise of England as a major purchaser of élite football talent is confirmed in this study. This is a function of the increased economic power possessed by Premier League clubs since their alliance with Rupert Murdoch's Sky TV network. This process may gather momentum in the future with the Murdoch-owned company purchase of shares in several Premier League clubs including Leeds United and Manchester United. This process has also been fuelled by the re-entry of English clubs into European competitions following the ban of the late 1980s. But for migrant football players, as shown in a study of élite cricketers, the desire to compete at the top level is also an important motivating factor. With regard to England, the study presented here further confirms the well-established migrant links between Nordic countries and Britain/England.[34] Many of the Norwegian and Danish squad members at France '98 play their club football in England and Scotland. This pattern would have been further emphasized if Sweden had qualified for the World Cup finals.

As identified in previous work by Maguire and Stead, the North–South European divide is evident within the recruitment of World Cup players.[35] It involves the discrepancy between the number of northern Europeans recruited by southern European clubs as compared with southern Europeans recruited by northern European clubs. It is argued that northern European (especially Nordic) players are attractive purchases as they are perceived as having a strong work ethic, excellent language abilities and the ability to assimilate easily into their new surroundings. Southern Europeans, alternatively, appear to be not as popular with coaches as they are perceived as conforming to the 'Latin' stereotype – temperamental, hotheaded and individualistic. However, this may now be changing with the recent influx of Italians to Chelsea FC under the influence of firstly Ruud Gullit and then Gianluca Vialli.

A dominant feature of the migration patterns identified in the case study was the number of South Americans playing in Italy and Spain. This phenomenon is a function of several factors. Firstly, it is Brazilians and Argentinians who make up the majority of South American 'immigrants' to Spanish and Italian leagues. These nations have historically done very well in the World Cup and produced very talented and very well-known players. Thus they would be an attractive proposition for the economically powerful clubs of Italy and Spain. Secondly, there is a linguistic and cultural link between many of the South American nations (except Brazil) and Spain because of their colonial past. This makes the assimilation of migrant players into Spanish culture much easier. This is arguably also a factor for migrants to Italy from South America. Thirdly, perceived playing styles may have an influence on player selection. South American football is stereotypically renowned for its skill and flamboyancy. According to this stereotype, it is better suited to the playing styles of the 'Latin' countries of Italy and Spain than to those of northern Europe.

Maguire and Stead point out that Spanish clubs tend not to recruit from other west European nations.[36] The case study here supports this. Spanish clubs seem to prefer to gain players principally from eastern Europe, South America and Africa. It is not clear why this is the case. The destinations of African players seem to have changed. Previous research had identified them as being prominent in English, French, Belgian, Portuguese and Dutch football, but this study found African players predominantly in Spain and Italy, as well as, though to a lesser degree, in France.[37]

From the results presented it is evident that it would be impossible to explain élite talent migration in football by recourse solely to an economic theory.

Although economics play a crucial part in determining the patterns of football migration, they are by no means the only factor involved. Rather, sets of interdependencies contour and shape the global sports migration. The findings presented here are evidence of this, demonstrating that politics, history, geography and culture all affect the structuring of football migrant trails. Viewing these as interconnected processes will enable the researcher to more adequately grasp how football migration patterns are likely to develop in the twenty-first century.

NOTES

1. J. Maguire, *Global Sport: Identities, Societies, Civilizations* (Oxford: Polity Press, 1999).
2. J. Maguire, 'Blade Runners: Canadian Migrants, Ice Hockey and the Global Sports Process', *Journal of Sport and Social Issues*, 20 (1996), 335–60.
3. J. Maguire and D. Stead, '"Far Pavilions"?: Cricket Migrants, Foreign Sojourn and Contested Identities', *International Review for the Sociology of Sport*, 31 (1996), 1–25.
4. A. Klein, *Sugarball: The American Game, the Domincan Dream* (Yale: Yale University Press, 1991).
5. J. Maguire, 'Preliminary Observations on Globalization and the Migration of Sport Labour', *Sociological Review*, 3 (1994), 452–80.
6. C. Bromberger, 'Foreign Footballers, Cultural Dreams and Community Identity in some North-western Mediterranean Cities', in J. Bale and J. Maguire (eds.), *The Global Sports Arena: Athletic Talent Migration in an Interdependent World* (London and Portland, OR: Frank Cass, 1994), pp.171–82; P. Lanfranchi, 'The Migration of Footballers: The Case of France', in Bale and Maguire, *The Global Sports Arena*; J. Maguire and D. Stead, 'Border Crossings: Soccer Labour Migration and the European Union', *International Review for the Sociology of Sport*, 33 (1998), 59–73.
7. Bale and Maguire, *The Global Sports Arena*.
8. Ibid.
9. Maguire, *Global Sport*.
10. Bale and Maguire, *The Global Sports Arena*.
11. *US Today*, 2 January 1992.
12. Maguire, *Global Sport*.
13. Ibid.
14. Ibid.
15. Maguire and Stead, 'Border Crossings'.
16. Klein, *Sugarball*.
17. *Mail on Sunday*, 24 January 1993, 95.
18. *Guardian*, 25 November 1992, 16.
19. *Guardian*, 27 February 1993, 16.
20. *Daily Mail*, 1 March 1993, 47.
21. *World Soccer* (April 1992), 10.
22. J. Maguire and E. Poulton, 'European Identity Politics in Euro '96: Invented Traditions and National Habitus Codes', *International Review for the Sociology of Sport*, 34 (1999), 17–30.
23. Maguire, *Global Sport*.
24. Y. Dezalay, 'The Big Bang and the Law: The Internationalization and Restructuration of the Legal System', *Theory, Culture & Society*, 7 (1990), 279–98.
25. Maguire and Stead, '"Far Pavilions"?'
26. J. Sugden and A. Tomlinson (eds.), *The FIFA Story* (Cambridge: Polity Press, 1998).
27. Ibid.
28. Maguire and Stead, 'Border Crossings'.
29. The data used in this paper was taken from the *Guardian*, 'World Cup Supplement', 10 June 1998. It detailed the football clubs that the 704 players taking part in the World Cup finals played for at that time. Thus the data contained within this essay will have changed since the World Cup, as the football transfer market is extremely dynamic. Although the data used in this research constitute only a 'snap-

shot', the analysis of the case study presented here is still a valid contribution to academic debate regarding élite talent migration in football – and sport more generally.

30. Maguire and Stead, 'Border Crossings'.
31. Ibid.
32. Ibid.
33. Ibid.
34. Ibid.
35. Ibid.
36. Ibid.
37. Maguire, 'Preliminary Observations on Globalization'.

14

Racism in Football:
A Victim's Perspective

RICHIE MORAN

Unlike many of the other contributions to this collection, this essay is written from a unique perspective: I am a black ex-professional footballer who actually quit playing the game because of the direct, indirect, overt and covert institutionalized racism that exists within the sport. Although my experience of racism is by no means isolated, as a number of current and ex-players will testify,[1] that I felt I had to stop playing the game that I had loved since I was young because of this racism is a terrible indictment of the football industry. This essay will begin by describing my background and my own experiences of racism in an 'everyday' context. I shall then outline some of the events which made me take such a drastic course of action, and assess the current levels of racism within football and the efficacy of the game's antiracist initiatives.

Born in London, I was adopted by a white family and so although the majority of my primary education was spent living with my natural mother in south-east London (which I still regard as and where I feel more at home), virtually all my secondary education and beyond was spent living in Gosport in Hamsphire where, after attending schools in Bermondesy and New Cross with their diverse ethnic mix of pupils I was suddenly one of only three black kids in a school of 1200 with all that that implies.

I am still based in this area but have lived in places as diverse as Tokyo, Tenerife and Birmingham. I have also travelled extensively in Britain and abroad. Linguistically I can get by in Japanese, French and I have a smattering of Spanish and I believe these factors, especially the fact that I spent a vast amount of time living in almost exclusively white communities, have given me an extensive overview of English/British people's racial attitudes both at home and abroad. That said I feel I have to point out that of all the places I have lived and/or worked I find Portsmouth the most racist, not to mention sexist and homophobic city of all.

As a football-mad kid growing up in south-east London, I spent many an afternoon on the terraces at Millwall's old Den and, after moving to the south coast, Portsmouth's Fratton Park. As a nine-year-old at Millwall I was scared by the overt hostility towards me even though I was supporting the home team; this occurred particularly if the opposition had a black player. During the late 1970s and early 1980s, when my support of Portsmouth was at its peak, there was a huge resurgence of National Front activity in the area. Believe me, standing in the middle of thousands of people giving the Nazi salute is not my favourite way of spending a Saturday afternoon.

Inevitably, I have had several altercations with Portsmouth fans over the years about racism. One of the most memorable was when, after remonstrating with fans who were abusing black striker John Fashanu on his Wimbledon debut, they informed me that 'It's OK mate, you're one of our niggers.' Interestingly enough, years later when speaking to fellow black professionals, both Fratton Park and the old Den were two of the grounds where they least liked playing, owing to the crowd's abuse and hostility.

Living as I do now in such an overwhelmingly white area I have had a whole range of experiences of racism. In the period when the 'sus' laws were in force I was regularly arrested, abused and even beaten up in police cells. A neighbour of mine conducted what I can only describe as a sustained campaign of abuse, harassment and intimidation which involved calling my son's mother 'a nigger lover', slashing her car tyres, and making allegations about me at work (resulting in my having to take three months' 'paid leave' whilst they were investigated). He later admitted in a police statement that these were fabrications. In addition to this he had me arrested (charges dropped) for punching him and his wife, and, worst of all, he actually made monkey noises at my son in the street. After writing to the Chief Constable of Hampshire, I eventually gave a huge dossier of events to the police. The police sent the files to the Crown Prosecution Service which declined to prosecute for lack of evidence.

Over the years I have become tired of being asked if I have any drugs to sell every time I am in a nightclub, tired of my white girlfriend being asked with a nudge and a wink if it's true what they say about black men, tired of the appalling attitudes of many Portsmouth bus drivers and 'men in white vans', and tired of sometimes just getting 'that look'. Worse than any of this is the abuse from children. A boy aged around three once pointed at me and said 'Look mummy, there's a nigger.' She did not even chastise him. I have also been called a 'black c***' by a girl no older than seven.

It always disturbed me when playing professionally that when I looked on the terraces and saw the features of middle-aged men contorted with hate racially abusing me, that self-same man was often standing with his arm around his eight or nine-year-old son who was quite often calling me the same thing!

RACISM IN FOOTBALL: MY OWN EXPERIENCE

I had an unusual route into the professional game as I did not become a professional player until I was 25 (having not played at all from the ages of 16 to 20). In the course of my football career I played at all levels, from parks upwards. As the bulk of my non-professional career was spent playing in predominantly white leagues, I experienced the whole range of racist behaviour: from the idiot on the sideline on a Sunday morning, who became irate and abusive every time I sped through his team's defence to score, to the loudmouths at the semi-professional grounds where I could still hear every comment they made.

I remember playing at Trowbridge for Gosport Borough in a cup game (we were then in the Beazer Homes League) when a home supporter shouted: 'Why don't you go back to Jamaica, you black bastard?' As we were 4–0 up at the time, I replied with a beatific smile (which disguised the fact that I wanted to punch his lights out) that I was actually Nigerian by origin and so therefore if I was to 'go back to Jamaica' I would be going several thousand miles out of my way.

On one occasion at this level I went into the opposition's changing room after the match to confront a player who had been abusing me all game, in front of his team-mates. Needless to say, he did not show up in the bar afterwards for a post-match drink and a chat.

These two incidents, though upsetting, are mild compared to the physical attacks on the likes of Clint Eastman whilst playing in the Olympian League in Watford and the experiences of Santos FC, a west London-based team of mainly African-Caribbean origin, and Bari FC in 1998, a predominantly Asian side competing in the South Essex Sunday League. Both teams suffered appalling verbal abuse which led to violent attacks on their players.[2]

In the case of Santos, after experiencing a pitch invasion by thugs, one of whom was wielding a knife, the team decided to complain about the incident, but were later denied information on their opponents by the Hertfordshire County FA which subsequently refused to acknowledge their involvement in the competition.

Bari, who had entered the field to the cry of 'It's a Paki-bashing spree' from 'fans' of opponents Romside FC, eventually retaliated in the face of repeated verbal and physical violence (two Romside players were sent off for violent conduct). Astonishingly, Bari were fined and suspended for their part in the ensuing fracas by the Essex County FA which declined to investigate or acknowledge the racist nature of the violence.

PROFESSIONAL FOOTBALL

The forms of racism that exist within football range from the open and aggressive abuse, such as that mentioned above, through to the underlying and subtle racism that drips away like a tap. At amateur levels it is easier to leave it behind you, because you are playing only for fun and not on a full-time basis, but when it becomes part of your everyday working life it is impossible to ignore. Casual use of racist invective in the dressing room or on the training ground is dismissed as 'banter', and 'jokes' about the size of your manhood and how it is directly related to the colour of your skin are almost relentless.

Abroad, I experienced forms of racism similar to those that I felt in England. During my playing spell in Japan I was the victim of racism even from my own team-mates, and the alacrity with which I learned Japanese, and therefore understood their terms of abuse, came as something of a surprise to them on more than one occasion. While in Belgium, investigating the possibility of signing for a club, I had an extremely nasty experience in a hotel. The Belgian player who was accompanying me had a heated discussion with the hotelier and then told me in English that the hotel room I was after was double-booked. I replied in French that I had heard the hotelier say that he did not want any blacks in his hotel!

Notwithstanding these incidents, looking back I feel that there were three defining moments in my professional career in English football that made me decide to quit the game. The first major incident took place after I had been sent off in a reserve team game for Birmingham City at Halifax Town. The assistant manager at Halifax followed me into our dressing room and racially abused me. Still upset at my unjust dismissal, I decided that a discussion about racism was not on the agenda, so I punched him. One can debate the rights and wrongs of my actions, and I do not advocate violence as the solution to the problem, but it certainly felt good at the time.

On my return to Birmingham I was called into the office by the management team. After I recounted the aforementioned episode, the gist of their response was that I ought to have tolerated the abuse. My retort – that if the assistant manager had wanted to criticize my ability then he was perfectly entitled to his opinion, but that I should not have had to tolerate abuse based on my skin colour – fell on deaf ears. The management team tried to sack me but could not and so fined me two weeks' wages and ostracized me thereafter.

Later in that season, after a new manager had been appointed, I was summoned to his office one day and asked why I had dreadlocks. Although I did not actually feel that any explanation was necessary, I pointed out that my hairstyle was an affirmation of my African heritage. My explanation was met with derision and I was told to have my dreadlocks cut as they were inappropriate for a professional footballer. I replied that I could think of a certain famous Dutch footballer (Ruud Gullit) with whom the manager would not even think of having this conversation. When I added (tongue firmly in cheek, of course) that his insulting my heritage was akin to me suggesting he take elocution lessons to shed his Scottish accent, I was asked (none too politely) to leave his office. I never played for Birmingham City again.

The final straw for me as a professional footballer occurred during pre-season training at Torquay United. I had already heard terms such as 'nigger' and 'spade' being frequently used at the training ground, and when the assistant manager suggested a 'coons versus whites' five-a-side game I took offence. I confronted him by asking whether he knew my name, and suggested that if he wanted to speak to me I much preferred to be addressed as Richie than by any of the aforementioned terms. I suggested that I would react very badly if he continued in this vein. I never did sign for Torquay, and it was around this time that I decided that I did not want to play professionally any more.

Looking back, my own experiences of racism within football may well pale into insignificance compared to the abuse suffered by earlier black footballers such as Walter Tull, Arthur Wharton, Albert Johanneson, Clyde Best, Cyrille Regis, Brendon Batson and Laurie Cunningham. Nevertheless, I am still left with a sense of irony that a widespread debate about racism within the game was only triggered by the violent reaction against racist abuse by a white player, Eric Cantona, than by any of the incidents of abuse concerning black players. Cantona's infamous 'kung fu kick' aimed at a white spectator who had been racially abusing him for being French brought much condemnation, but also a measure of support, from the football industry.[3]

I should make it quite clear is that I did not quit professional football because I could not tolerate what was going on, but because I felt that *I didn't have to tolerate it*. All my life I have wanted someone to explain to me the reasoning behind the notion that I should 'rise above' racism. I have heard this from teachers, fellow professionals, friends, acquaintances, girlfriends and pub know-alls. Yet, surely, facing up to racism is the best way to counter it, rather than doing nothing by subscribing to an ill-defined and vague notion of 'rising above' it.

In an interview in *Kick It Out* magazine just prior to France '98, Andy Cole stated that he considered it weak to give up football on account of racism.[4] What I actually consider weak is the banal acceptance/apology for racism from leading black players in the game. I understand (although vehemently oppose) that the politics of self-interest dominate in these financially motivated times, but there are enough leading black and foreign nationals in the Premiership and beyond to make a positive statement of zero tolerance towards racism that could have real impact.

For example, I have not heard one leading black player make any statement about the Stephen Lawrence case or the 1999 bombings of communities in Brixton, Brick Lane and Soho. I have never subscribed to the theory that you can only affect change from within, and I feel I have achieved far more through my subsequent work on racism since I left the sport than I ever would have done as a relatively unknown lower division player. Besides, anybody who ever saw me play can testify to the fact that I never changed a thing through my efforts on the pitch!

OTHER INCIDENTS OF RACISM WITHIN FOOTBALL

In addition to the previously mentioned occurrences, there were a number of racist incidents involving players in the late 1990s. The confrontation between the then Wales manager Bobby Gould and black Blackburn striker Nathan Blake is worthy of analysis. Blake withdrew from the Welsh squad in 1997 and subsequently accused Gould of making racist remarks at half-time during a game and on the training ground. Gould was quoted as saying, 'All I said was why didn't somebody pick the big black bastard up, something that has been said many times in many dressing rooms.'[5] This last sentence probably captures the very essence of this essay: that many white people involved in the English game have no conception about racism, or what may constitute racist remarks. For many, racial epithets are 'part and parcel' of the game and so familiar that they cannot see why this type of 'banter' is in any way offensive.

Another recent incident involving a manager was that between Chester City boss Kevin Ratcliffe and black trainee James Hussaney. Ratcliffe was found guilty by an industrial tribunal of racially abusing Hussaney, and Ratcliffe admitted that this had occurred after Hussaney had failed to change the studs in the team's boots before a game. After making the complaint, Hussaney was subsequently released by Chester because, according to Ratcliffe, 'He had neither the technical ability or mental strength to be kept on.' If this was the case, why did club chairman Mark Guterman warn Hussaney's family not to take the matter any further because 'no other club would touch him with a barge pole'?[6]

During the 1997/98 season, Israeli Eyal Berkovic complained about anti-Semitic remarks allegedly received during a game at Blackburn Rovers. Roy Hodgson, then Rovers' manager (and at one time touted as a future England coach) was quoted as describing such events as a storm in a teacup and went on to say that the real controversy of the game surrounded the sending off of Kevin Gallagher, and not what people were alleged to have said.[7]

At the end of February 1998 Aston Villa's Stan Collymore confronted Liverpool's Steve Harkness over alleged racial abuse during a game between the two sides.[8] This incident received wide media coverage for a couple of days whilst other Villa players and Villa's manager John Gregory appeared to back Collymore's version of events. Once again, though, no action was taken and it disappeared from the news pages as quickly as it had arrived.

In October 1999 Arsenal's black French midfield star Patrick Viera made headlines for spitting at West Ham's Neil Ruddock after being sent off. Whilst most of the headlines focused on Viera's actions, he subsequently accused Ruddock of pushing him over and calling him a 'French prat'.[9] Ruddock certainly sprinted a considerable distance to barge into Viera prior to the spitting but virtually every newspaper adopted the moral high ground, with some calling Viera 'scum'. Viera faces severe censure from the FA, and rightfully so, but as I predicted, no disciplinary action was taken against Ruddock.

Football and Racism: The Wider Context

One of the biggest disappointments for me at the time that I decided to quit playing, and even more so since, was the reaction of other players to the racism I suffered. Many, both black and white, told me to keep my mouth shut and just take the money, but this I was not prepared to do. Over the years many people have tried to argue that the use of 'industrial language' and banter is an acceptable part of the game. There are so many derogatory terms for black people, women, gay people and those with disabilities that unfortunately seem to have become acceptable in the English language, but this does not make the use of them right.

There have been many well-documented allegations of racism on the pitch in recent seasons, the most notorious being the Ian Wright–Peter Schmeichel 'affair', when, during a match between Manchester United and Arsenal in 1997 it was alleged that Wright was racially abused by Schmeichel. Schmeichel allegedly called Wright a 'dirty black bastard', an accusation apparently supported by television footage. The main concern this incident raises is not merely that the Football Association did not move to investigate racist allegations against one of the top players from the most well-known club in the country, but that the reaction of the unusually reticent Wright was that he was duty-bound not to get a fellow professional into trouble.

I have noticed that on many occasions in the past Ian Wright has reacted angrily, and vocally, when he feels aggrieved about an issue, yet I remember listening to the tape of his noncommittal response to the Schmeichel incident with dismay, as I felt that Wright would have received great support had he pursued the matter. For myself and many other black people I have spoken to, this is the moment when many of us lost respect for him.

Garth Crooks also leapt to Schmeichel's defence (in *New Nation*) saying that he was prepared to accept that Schmeichel may have said something in the heat of the moment, but that he is the world's best goalkeeper and handles the media like a superb pro. Shall I tell my son as he grows up that as long as he is racially abused in the heat of the moment by someone who is a superb pro that that is acceptable?

Crooks also defended BBC commentator John Motson over his explanation that he was finding it increasingly difficult to commentate on games because most teams now field several black players who look the same.[10] Crooks was very quick to point out that Motson does not have a racist bone in his body, which brings me to an interesting point. In my view, you do not have to be a racist to make a racist comment. Motson may indeed not be a racist, but his excuses in the aftermath of his comments served only to make him look worse. What Motson said was at best crass and insensitive and at worst overtly racist.

In an *Observer* article, black Wimbledon midfielder Robbie Earle stated that we should not overreact to every racial incident that occurs on a football field, and equated verbal racist abuse with the non-racist chants directed at Tony Adams and Paul Gascoigne.[11] In the same article, Earle also stated that he regards racial abuse as a backhanded compliment, meaning that he knew the crowd realized he was playing well. Personally, I fail to see how racist terms can ever be interpreted as complimentary.

Nationalism and Identity

Whilst watching the 1998 World Cup in France on television I was struck by the paternalistic and patronizing way in which commentator Ron Atkinson talked about African teams. He made frequent reference to the fact that these sides could not defend, but had natural attacking flair and speed. Likewise, I found presenter Bob Wilson's comments, before the England versus Argentina game regarding what he saw as the suspect Latin American temperament, offensive. Ironically, it was David Beckham, an Englishman, who was sent off during the game for petulantly kicking an opponent.

The France '98 tournament was one of the best examples of black communities in England visibly supporting the countries of their heritage. Jamaicans and Nigerians wore their national shirts with pride in many towns and cities up and down the country.[12] During the championships I was having a drink in a pub watching Nigeria on television when I was asked in a somewhat unfriendly tone why I was supporting Nigeria. I was asked where I was born, to which I replied London, and what passport I had (British), and my 'accuser' leaned back in 'triumph', thinking that he had won the argument by 'proving' where my loyalties should really be. I then very patiently explained that although this was the case both my natural parents were Nigerian, which made the blood in my veins 100 per cent Nigerian and I was entitled to support whomever I pleased.[13]

Potentially far more threatening for me was being in a pub during Italia '90 for the England versus Cameroon quarter-final fixture. When it looked as if England might lose, the atmosphere became terrible, with racist invective spouted by those watching the game with me. People I had considered friends or at least acquaintances suddenly began to make racist comments. I was so angry I was shaking and I remember being profoundly dejected when Gary Lineker scored the winning goal for England.[14]

From a personal perspective it is incidents such as these, coupled with the things I have learned about black history, that have long since turned me away from supporting the country of my birth, England, and instead I follow the country of my heritage, Nigeria. Having said that, I have no problems about black people supporting England. The significant numbers of black and Asian fans at England matches during Euro '96 had made me hope that this might be the catalyst for a new direction in racial awareness. This hope was boosted by the obvious pride with which such black England players as Sol Campbell, Paul Ince and Ian Wright wear their shirts: pride that sends a clear message to all those black fans who wish to support England.

The influx of foreign footballers into the leagues in England since the *Bosman* ruling in 1995 has met with a degree of xenophobia from some quarters within football.[15] Managers such as Harry Redknapp, Dave Bassett and Joe Kinnear have all expressed some very disparaging views about foreign players and their mentalities. Whilst I do not condone the pushing of a referee to the ground, as Paolo Di Canio did when playing for Sheffield Wednesday against Arsenal during the 1998/99 season, David Batty's manhandling of a referee caused only a fraction of the furore. Pierre Van Hooijdonk acted disgracefully when he went on 'strike' at the beginning of the 1998/99 season by refusing to turn out for Nottingham Forest, but I can think of at least two other English Premiership players who have also 'thrown their toys out of the pram' and been rewarded with multi-million pound transfers, rather than receiving public castigation, as in the case of Van Hoojdonk.

CONCLUSION

Although I have painted a somewhat gloomy picture when describing the racist incidents above, there is reason to be optimistic about the levels of racism within football. For example, I welcomed the formation of the Football Task Force, and its surprisingly astute report *Eliminating Racism from Football*.[16] However, that the Task Force is chaired by David Mellor, someone who was a member of Margaret Thatcher's racist, xenophobic and jingoistic government, deeply disturbs me.

To an extent, racial chanting has disappeared from many grounds, something that the Task Force report noted. This is not to say that it does not happen, as incidents such as those witnessed at Sunderland versus Leicester City in 1998/99, at both Leeds United versus Leicester City fixtures in 1997/98 and Coventry City versus Newcastle United in 1999/00 exemplify. It is still happening far too often for us to become too complacent.

The plethora of recent antiracist initiatives within the game also are worthy of mention.[17] The Commission for Racial Equality's 'Let's Kick Racism Out of Football' campaign, which began in 1993, has enjoyed a measure of success. In 1997 the co-ordination of 'Let's Kick Racism...' was taken over by a new independent organization, Kick It Out (KIO). KIO has targeted many areas, including the marginalization of Asians within the game; the development of grass-roots antiracist campaigns; the production of education material and increasing the involvement of minority ethnic communities in their local clubs.[18] KIO has been praised by the Task Force as 'football's flagship antiracist initiative'.[19]

In 1992 the 'Red, White and Black at the Valley' scheme was launched by the Charlton Athletic Race Equality partnership (CARE), a multi-agency group consisting of representatives from the club itself, supporters' organizations, local authorities and race equality councils, the police and community organizations. The principal aims of CARE were to create a 'safe and welcoming' environment inside the ground, for all sections of the community. The commitment shown by the club is such that the scheme has enjoyed a high profile throughout the organization for several years. By 1996 Charlton had attained its 'best ever racial mix among its supporters'.[20]

Other initiatives, such as 'Football Unites Racism Divides', 'Show Racism the Red Card', fans' groups such as 'Leeds Fans United Against Racism and Fascism' and 'Foxes Against Racism', and others have achieved some success in challenging racism in the game. However, racism in football is merely a microcosm of the problem in wider society, and just as it took the violent reaction of a white Frenchman to instigate a debate about racism in football, it took the tragic and senseless murder of a black teenager, Stephen Lawrence, in south-east London in 1993 to force the white population of this country to examine how racist it and its institutions are.

Football is this country's most popular spectator sport, but approximately only one per cent of supporters at matches are from minority ethnic groups.[21] Survey work has shown that this low attendance figure is due to fear of verbal or physical attack, and should come as no surprise when you examine the wider context.[22] The shocking murder of Stephen Lawrence, the deaths in custody of Shiji Lapite, Ibrahim Sey, Brian Douglas, Wayne Douglas and others, the continuing ordeal of Mal Hussein and the bombings of Brixton, Brick Lane and Soho, plus the racially motivated murders since 1991 of Rolan Adams, Pachadcharam Sahitharan, Navid Sadiq, Mohammed Sawa, Saddick Dada, Sher Singh Sagoo, Michael Menson, Lakhvinder 'Ricky' Reel, Imran Khan, to name but a few, indicate that the levels of racist violence in England are high. Racism within a sport should be challenged from within that sport, but this action is only the very least that should be done. I applaud the antiracism within the game, but there is still much work to be done, both in and out of the sport, before it can be said to have been truly tackled.

NOTES

Dedicated to Kofi Joe Moran, my hero, and Anni Bury, my soulmate.

1. J. Garland and M. Rowe, *Racism and Antiracism in British Football* (Basingstoke: Macmillan, forthcoming).
2. See Kick It Out, *Annual Report 1997/98* (London: Kick It Out, 1999).
3. For an account of the 1995 'Cantona affair' see S. Fleming and A. Tomlinson, 'Football and the Old England' in U. Merkel and W. Tokarski (eds.), *Racism and Xenophobia in European Football* (Aachen: Meyer and Meyer Verlag, 1996), pp.79–100.
4. Kick It Out, *Kick It Out* (London: Kick It Out, 1998), pp.4–5.
5. I. Ross, 'Soccer Star's Fury at Racist Insult', *Guardian*, 5 March 1998, 3.
6. N. Varley, 'Black Trainee 'Racially Abused by Soccer Boss', *Guardian*, 4 November 1997, 8.
7. P. Hayward, 'The Race to Free Football from Poison', *Guardian*, 25 February 1998, 24.
8. I. Ross and P. White, 'Collymore Racist Claims Untrue, Says Harkness', *Guardian*, 6 March 1998, 6.
9. M. Dickinson, 'Racism Inquiry After Garlic Jibe', *Times*, 29 October 1999, 1.
10. O. Bowcott, 'BBC Man and Bus Boss Blunder', *Guardian*, 5 January 1998, 2.
11. R. Earle, 'Racism Hurts, But Not Only Black Players Get Abuse', *Observer*, 28 September 1997, 4.
12. See M. Marqusee, *Anyone But England: Cricket, Race and Class* (London: Two Heads Publishing, 1998) for an analysis of sport, 'race' and identity.
13. L. Back, T. Crabbe and J. Solomos, 'Lions, Black Skins and Reggae Gyals: Race, Nation and Identity in Football', in L. Back, T. Crabbe and J. Solomos, *The Changing Face of Football: Race, Identity and Multiculture in English Soccer* (Oxford: Berg, forthcoming).

14. The result was England 3 Cameroon 2.
15. At the end of the 1998/99 season there were 172 overseas players attached to Premiership clubs, and increase of 111 from the figure in 1995. Of these, the largest contributing nations were Norway (22 players), France (21), Holland (16) and Italy (14).
16. Football Task Force, *Eliminating Racism from Football* (London: Football Task Force, 1998).
17. J. Garland and M. Rowe, 'Field of Dreams: An Assessment of Antiracism in British Football', *Journal of Ethnic and Migration Studies*, 25, 2 (1999), 335–44; D. McArdle and D. Lewis, *'Kick Racism Out of Football': A Report on the Implementation of the Commission for Racial Equality's Strategies* (London: Centre for Research in Industrial and Criminal Law, 1997).
18. Funding bodies for KIO include the FA Premier League, the Commission for Racial Equality, The Football Trust, Professional Footballers' Association and the FA.
19. Football Task Force, *Eliminating Racism from Football*, p.12.
20. Charlton Athletic Race Equality Partnership (CARE*), Tackling Racial Barriers to Watching Football* (Leatherhead: Parker Tanner, 1996).
21. Sir Norman Chester Centre for Football Research, *FA Premier League National Fan Survey 1996/97: Summary* (Leicester: Sir Norman Chester Centre for Football Research, 1998).
22. B. Holland, 'Kicking Racism Out of Football: An Assessment of Racial Harassment In and Around Football Grounds', *New Community*, 21, 4 (1995), 567–86.

15

The 'Letter' and the 'Spirit': Football Laws and Refereeing in the Twenty-First Century

SHARON COLWELL

Ferguson applauds refereeing

The Times, 18 March 1999

This headline might strike readers as somewhat unusual. After all, Alex Ferguson, the Manchester United manager, is not known for his approval of referees. Indeed, football managers in general have a reputation for what might be termed 'referee bashing'. 'Jones Lashes Out in Ref Rage',[1] 'Strachan Faces £10,000 Fine Over Ref Insult',[2] and 'Bad Refereeing Becoming a Plague',[3] are the kind of headlines normally associated with reports on referees and refereeing decisions. Referees at the élite level of the game are under intense scrutiny and, more often than not, that scrutiny results in criticism rather than applause. This essay considers several issues raised in relation to football refereeing in an attempt to understand why refereeing decisions have become such a central focus in the analysis of the game. Initially, the development of the Laws of the Game will be discussed, with reference to notions of the 'spirit' of the game, and the 'spirit' and the 'letter' of the law. The wider context of the football industry will then be examined, with reference to the increasing pressure on élite-level football personnel, and the relationships between referees, players, managers, fans and other football and media personnel. These factors combine to explain why refereeing issues, and in particular criticism of referees, have achieved a relatively high profile in football discussions. Several issues raised by regularly proposed 'solutions' to refereeing problems, in terms of the introduction of various technological aids for referees, are then addressed. Finally, consideration is given to questions about the extent to which these 'solutions' may, or may not, be expected to help resolve refereeing problems as we head into the twenty-first century.

THE DEVELOPMENT OF THE LAWS OF THE GAME

The Laws of the Game may be understood in terms of the related concepts of the 'spirit' of the game, and the 'spirit' and the 'letter' of the law. The notion of the 'spirit' of the game refers to beliefs about the way the game 'should' be played, to ideas about 'fair play' and about 'gentlemanly' – or in the present non-gender specific Laws, 'sporting' – behaviour. The origins of notions about the 'spirit' of the game can be traced back to the public schools in the early to mid nineteenth century, where the game of football developed from its 'folk' or 'mob' football roots into its modern form.[4] The regulation of the game developed, as E. Dunning and K. Sheard argue, in line with the social attitudes of members of the middle and upper classes of Victorian England.[5] As J. Witty has suggested, whilst the 'possibility of damage or even casual injury to the players'[6] was permitted in public school football games during this period, 'It was never even thought that a player would intentionally do anything to hurt an opponent. Such conduct would be "ungentlemanly", and that was an unpardonable offence; ... the lowering of self-control to the depths of ungentlemanly conduct was something which could not be tolerated.'[7]

During this period the responsibility for dealing with such conduct lay in the hands of the offending player's team captain, who would decide any punishment and might order the player from the field. As the number and relative importance of competitions between and within schools increased, so too did the use of umpires. Teams nominated their own umpires, who were required to adjudicate on appeals from the respective team captains. If a decision could not be reached, the umpires then referred it to 'a third man, [the referee] who was seated outside the field; and they were bound to accept his ruling'.[8]

With the advent of the FA Challenge Cup in 1871, the legalization of professionalism for players in 1885, and the formation of the Football League in 1888, football played outside the public schools also became characterized by an increasing seriousness and competitiveness. This was reflected in the way the game was 'policed'. The original rules of the FA Challenge Cup in 1871 required the appointment of two *neutral* umpires and a referee, and Witty notes that 'unsportsmanlike actions of an intentional nature', such as tripping or hacking, were to be penalized with an indirect free kick.[9] Initially, referees were only required to decide on appeals which the umpires were unable to agree on. Gradually, however, referees were required to act autonomously; by 1880 they had the power to send off players who persistently infringed the Laws, and by 1889 they were permitted to 'award a free kick, without any appeal'.[10] By 1891 the referee had moved onto the pitch and had become the sole arbitrator, to be assisted by two linesmen. These changes represented a gradual shifting of power away from players, and captains in particular, to umpires and referees, and eventually to referees alone. In both the *punishment* of breaches of the Laws, and in the *interpretation* of those Laws, there was, then, a shift away from self-regulation to external regulation. Moreover, those regulating the game were also required to make decisions about the way the game was played; that is to say, in terms of the 'spirit' of the game. By the late 1890s *The Referees' Chart* included an instruction to players to 'Play a gentlemanly game. Don't allow yourself to lose your temper; keep a still tongue in your head.'[11] At that time it was part of the referee's role to interpret and, if necessary, penalize any such 'ungentlemanly' conduct.

The changes described above indicate that notions of 'gentlemanly' or sporting behaviour, and notions about 'fair play' and the way the game 'should' be played, have formed an integral part of the rules since the transformation of folk football into a form recognizable as the modern game. Whilst the power to interpret and penalize their infringement has shifted from players to referees, these concepts remain central to both contemporary football discussion, and to the philosophy of football's international governing body, the Fédération Internationale de Football Association (FIFA). FIFA's code of conduct states that 'The characteristic values and norms of fairness in football were essentially those of the English middle and upper classes; they took shape and were defined in Victorian England, and they are in essence the basis of the FIFA code of conduct.'[12]

Included in the code are assertions that 'a fair player accepts the Laws of the Game' and 'does his utmost to win within the Laws of the Game'.[13] Despite their longevity, however, such notions are rather problematic, and indeed are central to explaining some of the problems raised in connection with refereeing. Given the significant social change that has occurred since the early versions of the Laws were devised, and given the changes evident in what might now be described as the global football industry, it is perhaps not surprising that some problems are raised by the inclusion of Victorian ideals in the current Laws and FIFA's philosophy. Further, notions of 'fair play' or the 'spirit' of the game and its Laws are relatively subjective and, therefore, contested concepts which are liable to change over time. What may be deemed to be fair play by one player or referee under certain circumstances may be deemed unfair by others, or by the same player or referee in a different circumstance. There is, then, room for interpretation inherent in the Laws of the Game, and in the application of those Laws by the game's regulators on the pitch: the referees.

THE 'SPIRIT' AND THE 'LETTER' OF THE LAW: ROOM FOR INTERPRETATION

A central tenet of this essay is that the room for interpretation in the Laws is a key element in understanding the reasons why refereeing issues have been, and continue to be, so contentious. Whilst players are expected to play within the 'spirit' of the game, one consequence of the shift of power away from players to referees in regulating the game has meant that referees too are expected to interpret the Laws, and are encouraged to apply them 'in spirit rather than too literally'. Referees are able to facilitate a flowing game by allowing play to go on when 'minor' offences occur, rather than stopping the game for every infringement of the Laws (something which would be required if referees applied the 'letter' of the law). Essentially, the Laws provide for minimum interference from the referee. The referee may avoid continually interrupting the game's flow by striking a balance between the 'spirit' and the 'letter' of the law. This enables a fast flowing game, something which is central to football's appeal in particular in terms of generating excitement. As N. Elias has noted, in drawing up the rules or laws of a sport, 'The problem to be solved, in this case [football] as in that of other sport-games, is how to keep the risk of injuries to the players low, yet keep the enjoyable battle-excitement at a high level.'[14]

When referees allow incidents to go 'unpunished' in order to facilitate a flowing game, critics may argue that they are 'letting the game get out of hand', or that there is a need to start 'clamping down' on offences. Many of the decisions made during the course of a game – both to stop play, or to allow the game to continue – are based on subjective judgements that the referee is required to make. Phrases such as 'in the opinion of the referee' recur in the Laws of the Game, indicating the element of subjectivity inherent in referees' decision-making processes.[15] Further, a range of factors may affect the level of discretion shown by referees. These include the atmosphere and relative importance of the game, and the relationships between the opposing players, both historically or within a particular game.[16] As D. Elleray has suggested,

> If a referee is letting the game flow, he is probably satisfied that he does not need to penalise every foul, that the players are not reacting to being fouled and, therefore, there is limited danger of retaliation ... referees can appear to be inconsistent during a game because they appear to be letting a lot go by and then suddenly bang, bang, bang, bang, bang, everything is being penalised ... People don't always see the overall context.[17]

Because many refereeing decisions are largely subjective, fans, players, managers, commentators and other football personnel may, whilst desiring a fast-paced game, also feel that the referee is not enforcing the Laws strictly enough. Conversely, a referee may be perceived to be applying the rules too rigidly, namely to be sticking to the 'letter' of the law, booking too many players and stopping the game too frequently for infringements which may be perceived to be relatively minor. Under these circumstances, referees are often implored by commentators, fans, players and managers to 'use some common sense', and to interpret the Laws less literally. Yet when we ask referees to demonstrate common sense, we are not really expecting them to do what they think should be done, but to do what we think should be done. In the 1997/98 season Alex Ferguson demonstrated this tendency in his assessment of referee Martin Bodenham's 'liberal' handling of the Arsenal versus Manchester United Premier League game. Bodenham ignored penalty claims when Arsenal's Nigel Winterburn appeared to foul Paul Scholes, of which Ferguson said, 'It was a clear penalty, and you just hope referees stop these type of incidents, but he is the master of not seeing these things.'[18] Of the same game, Ferguson said, 'I don't see why anybody needed to be booked in a game like that.'[19] In this example, Ferguson is insisting, firstly, on the 'letter' of the law – demanding a strict application of the laws, and secondly on the 'spirit' of the law – calling for a more liberal interpretation.

Such calls for common sense, often voiced in discussions about football officials, provide further insight into the reasons why criticism of referees might persist; for, again, views about how appropriate referees' rulings are, and about referees' applications of the 'spirit' or the 'letter' of the Laws, are subjective. The call for common sense, then, does little to resolve the problems raised by the room for interpretation in the Laws, and whilst the desire for referees to exercise the 'spirit' of the Laws remains – in the hope of maintaining the game's flow – disputes about the appropriateness of referees' rulings will inevitably continue. Often whilst demanding a display of common sense from the referee, football personnel will also ask for consistency. As Elleray has argued, 'People in football want two things: consistency and common-sense, but to use consistency one has to reduce the margin for common-sense.'[20] Further, Elleray has identified the levels of consistency demanded of referees: consistency within a game; between games refereed by the same referee; and between games refereed by different referees.[21] To begin to achieve this consistency, referees would need to strictly apply the 'letter' of the law, rather than to interpret the 'spirit' of the law. Further, whether all referees in, for example, the Premier League, would or indeed could achieve such a level of consistency is questionable, for it would require 'referees to perform like clones'.[22]

In the same way that a single incident within a game may be perceived differently by different groups or individuals, the degree of importance we attribute to an incident may also vary. A greater degree of significance may be attributed to decisions that go against 'our' team – as players, fans, managers, and so on – than to those that go in 'our' favour. Again, Alex Ferguson offered some evidence of this trend in the 1998/99 season, in the context of United's European Champions' League games. After a 3–3 draw with Barcelona, during which Barcelona scored two penalties to come back from 2–0 down, Ferguson claimed, 'The first penalty decision was a disgrace and the referee had a real shocker. We have now had three major European games at home where the referee has not been fair.'[23] Ferguson's post-match comments after another of Manchester United's Champions League games, against Internazionale, make an interesting comparison: 'We had our lucky moments, but the referee was fantastic. He called everything correctly.'[24] During the game, two penalty appeals from Internazionale had been turned down by the referee. Sentiments such as those expressed here by Ferguson are familiar themes in post-match interviews. Their prevalence is largely a consequence of the room for interpretation which exists between the 'spirit' and the 'letter' of the law. Referees' decisions can always be questioned, because they do not – indeed, in order to keep the game flowing, are required not to – penalize identical fouls in an identical manner.

Many of the Laws allow little room for interpretation, and are therefore relatively uncontroversial (for example, decisions of 'fact' relating to the ball going out of play). Others, whereby referees are required to make decisions based on 'opinion', offer scope for a wider range of interpretations, and may therefore prove more problematic and controversial. The International Football Association Board (IFAB) meets annually to discuss proposed changes to the Laws or requests for experimentation with the Laws.[25] If any changes are agreed, the game's administrators may, for example, issue instructions to referees to 'interpret' and punish certain incidents in particular ways, in order to achieve a greater level of refereeing consistency. In this sense, referees may, therefore, be constrained to act in certain ways by the game's administrators. The kind of constraints imposed by FIFA – and their effects – were made particularly apparent during the 1998 World Cup tournament. After 20 World Cup games, during which a total of four red cards had been shown, FIFA president Sepp Blatter announced that referees were not acting in accordance with FIFA directives, and that players tackling from behind were not being penalized. He suggested, 'They are not applying the ban on tackles from behind. It is not up to them to decide how fouls should be interpreted.'[26] Michel Platini, president of the French organizing committee (CFO), similarly warned, 'There are referees who do not implement the rule on tackling from behind and they will go home as soon as possible.'[27] In the next two matches, five red cards were shown. The response to this increase in bookings highlights the difficulties referees face in implementing such a change. For, whilst Blatter felt that the referees 'had heard and understood' his message,[28] Platini complained, 'One moment they don't hand out enough cards and the next they hand out too many. The referees need to be a bit more careful.'[29] It is somewhat ironic that the effect of the mid-tournament public criticisms of, and instructions to, referees by FIFA personnel was clearly to reduce the level of consistency between different games – in the sense that the 20 games 'pre-criticism' produced four red cards, and the next two games, 'post-criticism', produced five red cards.

PRESSURE ON REFEREES

Having briefly highlighted some of the problems raised by the room for interpretation in the Laws of the Game, the next section of this essay considers issues relating to the pressures on referees and others involved in the football industry. Some of the reasons why referees receive so much criticism, and why they are under pressure, may be understood if, as well as considering the difficulties connected with the interpretation of the Laws of the Game, the pressure experienced by other football personnel is taken into account. In other words, it is also necessary to examine the relationships between referees and players, managers, club owners, fans and media personnel.

The increasing level of investment in the football industry is often cited by commentators on the game as the cause of most of the problems in the industry, sometimes to the exclusion of other issues. Certainly in recent years the amount of money invested in football clubs, particularly at the élite level, has increased dramatically. This is evident in the rising costs of transfer fees for players, in players' salaries, in the prize money for successful clubs in the Premier League, and in the sale of television rights (see, for example, the essay by C. Gratton in this collection). Whilst the financial rewards for successful clubs and their employees may be great, so too can be the costs to club personnel in their efforts to win or maintain a place in a particular league. As the Annual Reviews compiled by Deloitte & Touche indicate, the financial gap between clubs at élite level and those below them is increasing year on year.[30] Given the financial significance of playing success or failure, it is perhaps not surprising that football managers and players often attempt to locate the reasons for a team's failure to win in terms of a referee's decision, rather than in terms of poor play or team selection. Players' and managers' reputations, and often their jobs, may be on the line when clubs endure a losing streak.

Whilst the increased financial rewards available to clubs and players may contribute to the pressure felt by football personnel, 'money' is without doubt not a new factor. In the 1930s, for example, Arsenal manager George Allison was tagged 'Moneybags Allison' as a result of his tendency to spend relatively large amounts of money on transfers,[31] whilst in 1962/63 Everton were described as the 'chequebook champions'.[32] Nor can 'money' be viewed as the sole cause of pressure, as some commentators on the game have implied. Critics of the financial changes that the Football and Premier Leagues have undergone in recent years, in terms of changing patterns of club ownership, the rewards for success and indeed the costs of a lack of success, tend to ignore the fact that football has long been a relatively highly paid industry, and that factors other than 'money' exert pressure on football personnel. So, whilst one should not underestimate the impact of financial changes, it is also important to consider other factors.

One of the key sources of pressure on players and managers results from the fact that élite level football is essentially representative, and that the fans who are represented have expectations about 'their' team. Expectations about the game being played are bound up with histories of games past, league positions and club records. Fans dissatisfied with the performance of a player, manager, team, club owner or referee can express that dissatisfaction, and thereby exert pressure, in a variety of ways. Physical attacks are probably the most explicit display of dissatisfaction with match officials by fans. There have been a number high profile incidents in recent seasons, such as assistant referee, Edward Martin, being physically attacked by a fan during a Portsmouth–Sheffield United First Division match in 1997/98. The attack occurred after Martin's confirmation of a foul by Sheffield United's goalkeeper, Simon Tracey, resulted in his sending off. In the 1998/99 season at an Oldham–Chelsea FA Cup game, an Oldham supporter threw a hot-dog at referee Paul Durkin while he was discussing a disputed goal with his assistants. In a more serious incident, Scottish Premier

League official, Hugh Dallas, required stitches after fans threw coins at him during the last Celtic–Rangers game of the 1998/99 season, and his home was later vandalized by fans. Such incidents have led to higher security for Premier League referees, to the extent that some now have alarms installed in their homes which are relayed directly to the police.[33] Such attacks are, however, far rarer than they were in the early twentieth century when, as E. Dunning *et al.* note, attacks on the referee, often by scores of fans, were relatively common.[34]

Contemporary fans tend to make their protests in less physical ways than their predecessors.[35] Fans are able to voice their opinions through an expanding range of media outlets, such as football magazines, fanzines, television discussion shows, and local or national radio football 'phone-ins'. Given this exposure, it is not surprising that incidents which are perceived to have been the turning point in a game – a match-winning or losing moment – often provide football commentators, writers and fans with interesting talking points. Radio shows such as Radio 5 Live's *6.06* broadcast almost immediate reactions from players, managers and fans to matches and, in particular, to contentious incidents in games. Such media scrutiny is one of the key sources of pressure for referees. Increased numbers of televised games, commentaries, sports discussion shows and newspaper sports supplements mean that the sights, sounds and sentiments of player or manager turned newspaper columnist, television pundit, or commentator are also familiar. This expanding range of media outlets provides an increasing number of opportunities to discuss football in general and, given their integral role in the game, referees in particular. The current prominence of public criticism about referees may partly be explained by the changing nature of some of this media coverage, and the exposure given to players, managers and other club officials, often at moments when pressure is most keenly felt. Controversial incidents are replayed via alternative camera angles, graphics may provide additional clarity, and we can then watch, listen to, or read the post-match interview, often given within minutes of the final whistle.

Given the emotions which football can evoke, it is perhaps not surprising that such interviews are not always characterized by measured, careful exchanges about the referee's decisions, particularly if those decisions have gone against the interviewee's team and, further, if they have proved to be significant to a game's outcome. So, on one level, players' and managers' views on referees are being sought at often highly emotional and/or tense moments, and they are increasingly required to give their views in a range of formats. On another level, fans have more public opportunities to express their feelings about clubs. One consequence of this combination of factors is that publicity focuses on referees, and therefore pressure on them increases. Further, as suggested, football personnel may well have their jobs 'on the line' if results are unfavourable. Managers losing their jobs in the 1998/99 season, for example, included Roy Evans from Liverpool, Roy Hodgson from Blackburn, and Kenny Dalglish from Newcastle. Clearly, in the search for explanations for a team's defeat, a 'mistake' by a referee may provide an excuse, and a verbal attack on the referee may divert attention away from a poor performance. If we consider these pressures, perhaps we can begin to understand why players, managers and club officials often criticize referees, and why we hear those criticisms so regularly.

In terms of the expanding media coverage of football and football-related issues, however, perhaps the most profound influence on our perceptions of referees has come as a result of television coverage of games. Whilst the history of televised football stretches back over 60 years, television coverage of games has rapidly expanded in recent times, to the extent that during a single season over 60 games are screened live by Sky television alone. The expansion of television coverage – which looks likely to continue given the advent of digital television – with up to 15 cameras present at Premier League games, and up to 30 cameras for each match during 1998 World Cup, has clearly meant that more controversial incidents are captured on camera. More air-time is also available to analyse and dissect them. Given the number of matches shown, and given the time and technology devoted to the scrutiny of matches, it is not surprising that refereeing mistakes are exposed. Games are often repeated, and highlights programmes often provide scope for further, more detailed scrutiny. In these circumstances a referee's decision often provides an interesting 'talking point' for the post-match analysis, and potentially generates more 'entertainment', in terms of the idea that 'controversy makes good television'. Incidents are replayed from a variety of camera angles, in slow motion, and 'expert' views on refereeing decisions from former and current players and managers are offered. More recently, BSkyB has offered its digital customers an option allowing viewers to choose which incidents they replay during games themselves.

Through these channels, refereeing mistakes are captured and given a permanence in our minds.[36] The former player and current television pundit Jimmy Hill has suggested that such replays benefit referees by proving, as often as not, that the referee has made the right decision. However, Hill assumes a neutrality on the part of those involved in football broadcasting, which may not be an accurate assumption. Often the 'wrong' decisions generate interest and discussion, and seem to provide the best talking point for media pundits. Further, the degree of controversy is often increased relative to the importance of the match. Controversial incidents captured on camera in relatively important games in recent seasons include the Middlesbrough–Chesterfield FA Cup semi final in the 1996/97 season, during which referee David Elleray failed to spot the ball crossing the line, and was therefore unable to award the 'goal' which would have given Chesterfield a 3–1 lead, well into the second half of the game. A similar incident in the game between Romania and Bulgaria resulted in the exit of Romania from the Euro '96 competition. Television footage has provided us with the ability to replay these kinds of incident from matches going as far back, for example, as the 1932 FA Cup final, involving Newcastle and Arsenal. In the final, Newcastle scored an equalizer moments after the ball had gone out of play. The

Arsenal players had relaxed, anticipating a goal kick. However, the referee did not see the ball crossing the line, play continued, and Newcastle scored and went on to win the match. Captured by a television camera, the incident was given a relatively permanent place in history and was recalled 66 years later, in the build-up to the 1997/98 FA Cup final between the same clubs. Such replaying and analysis of refereeing decisions and missed incidents inevitably undermine the credibility of referees, and increase the pressure on them. It is perhaps not surprising that, coupled with the expansion in the range of media outlets through which criticisms of referees may be voiced, incidents such as these have led many to question refereeing standards, and to argue for technological assistance for referees. It is these issues which are the subject of the final part of this essay.

THE FUTURE FOR REFEREES

Many football commentators, along with those more directly involved in the game, have come to regard technological assistance as the answer to refereeing problems; as a kind of panacea to refereeing ills. The use of technology is already being considered by the FA, which, having introduced 'three-way communication' via headsets between referees and assistant referees in the 1999/2000 season, is exploring the possibilities of using equipment to ascertain whether or not the ball has crossed the goal-line. The implications for the game, if such technology is introduced, require careful consideration.

Perhaps one of the most fundamental implications relates to the universal nature of the Laws of the Game. Currently, policing of the game at the grass-roots level is very similar in nature to that at the élite level. However, if various technological aids are introduced, it is questionable whether clubs at all levels would be able to afford the technology. In his regular column for *The Times*, Chelsea player Frank Leboeuf has suggested, 'with the amount of money in football, surely it would be possible to have cameras at all professional grounds and someone to watch replays of key moments'.[37] Whilst what Leboeuf suggests may be possible, given the trend towards the concentration of resources at the élite level noted earlier, such a proposal seems unrealistic. It seems that if technology were introduced, one unintended consequence might be that the Laws of the Game would be significantly different for clubs at different levels of the game.

The possible introduction of goal-line technology also raises other questions and challenges. As suggested, many commentators on the game view technology as the 'answer' to refereeing problems. For example, Bob Wilson, the former Arsenal goalkeeper and current television commentator and pundit, recently argued: 'Cricket, rugby league, American football, a host of other sports use technology. Why can't football follow suit? Offside decisions could be cleared up in five to ten seconds; so could goal-line decisions or penalty claims ... We have the technology. We should be attempting to improve the health of the game.'[38]

Examples from other sports indicate, however, that technology may not be the simple solution that Wilson suggests here. Cyclops, or the 'eye on the line' employed in tennis competitions since the late 1980s, demonstrates this point. During tournaments such as Wimbledon, players occasionally 'question' the umpire in relation to the electronic signal emitted by Cyclops. Umpires occasionally decide to overrule Cyclops, or to switch the machine off. Though the introduction of goal-line technology may reduce the occurrence of goals unjustly awarded and disallowed, evidence provided by the use of Cyclops suggests that technology is not infallible. Even with relatively clear-cut decisions, such as those concerning whether or not a ball has crossed a line, problems – and therefore controversy – may remain. Where decisions are less clear-cut, for example where the referee is required to make judgements about legitimate levels of physical contact in a tackle, problems of interpretation remain. As the response to several umpire-related incidents in cricket demonstrates, the use of video replays will not necessarily eliminate contentious decisions by officials. During the 1998 cricket test series between England and South Africa, for example, disputed run-out decisions – made with the aid of video replays – resulted in headlines such as 'Willey: Don't make us victims of TV replay',[39] and 'Ref-er-ee!,[40] whilst the 1999 Ashes series in Australia produced 'World Cup to Act over Ashes Camera Fiasco'[41] and 'Umpire's Snap Decision Points Finger at Cameras'.[42]

The notion of the referee, or a fourth official in the stands having access to video replays of incidents is another commonly proposed solution to refereeing problems. This proposal raises significant questions about potential changes to the way the game is played and regulated. When might referees call for use of the 'third eye'? Who will make the decision on the video replay of the incident? And what are the implications if, after a video replay, a decision still cannot be reached? If referees have access to the 'third eye' during the course of the game, decisions will have to be made about whether, and when, to stop the game and review the incident. Guidelines might be issued, for example, limiting the use of the replay to incidents occurring in the penalty area, in order to limit interruptions to the game's flow. However, often incidents outside the penalty area can prove highly significant to a game's outcome. Some obvious examples include red and yellow card decisions anywhere on the pitch, fouls on players outside the penalty area who are clean through on goal, and free kicks awarded within range of goal. If the pursuit of refereeing accuracy leads both to a greater dependence on technology and a wider range of incidents being defined as 'eligible' for appeal to the video replay, the free-flowing nature of football is likely to be compromised.[43] If such technology is made available, then, given the calls for greater refereeing accuracy, it would be an understandable outcome if referees began to stop the game and check the replay for every close-call decision, as has occurred with run-out decisions in cricket, in order to avoid post-match criticism. A significant unintended consequence of this proposal, therefore, might be to disrupt the fluency of the game. Not only is the need for a free-flowing game seen

211

by many as one of the sport's central attractions, it is also an underlying principle which has traditionally framed football's Laws.

Further questions are raised if we consider who would be viewing video replays and making decisions upon them. If examples in other sports are followed, such as cricket and rugby league, this would involve a fourth official off the pitch reviewing video replays. This may have the effect of reducing the level of refereeing consistency, which is currently achieved in football by having just one individual responsible for decision-making throughout a game. The presence of a decision-making fourth official would be likely to impair the referee's ability to use discretion in her/his application of the Laws of the Game. The referee on the pitch hears exchanges between players, and makes judgements about the need to stop the game if the situation becomes heated, or the need to, instead, 'have a quiet word' and allow play to continue. In other words, the exchanges between players are taken into consideration when the referee uses discretion, and applies the 'spirit' rather than the 'letter' of the law. The fourth official would not be in a position to hear these exchanges, or to exercise such discretion. If such an innovation were employed, we might expect a more strict, less discretionary, application of the Laws of the Game. As noted above, it is this balance between the 'spirit' and the 'letter' of the law that facilitates a free-flowing game with fewer stoppages than might be the case if officials, assisted by technology, were to stick to the 'letter' of the law and to stop play for every foul.

Other questions again relate to the extent to which technology is fallible. Often during televised games even replays of incidents do not prove conclusive. An incident during the World Cup 98 game between Brazil and Norway demonstrates this point. Television pictures appeared to show Norwegian forward Tore Andre Flo diving in the penalty box to win Norway a penalty. Several days later, however, different pictures from Swedish television showed that a Brazilian player, Junior Baiano, had, in fact, pulled the Norwegian down, eventually 'proving' the referee's decision to have been correct. Such is the complexity of the decisions which referees are required to make, it is unlikely that any of the various technological innovations mentioned here will provide the panacea to refereeing ills. Clearly technological innovations may help to increase the frequency of accurate decisions. But the way these issues are resolved may not only have a significant effect on the way the game is refereed, but also on the nature of the game itself, on the way it is played.

The notion of players diving, as shown by the incident in the Brazil–Norway game, raise one final point to be considered here. Players' attempts to deceive the referee in order to gain a greater or lesser advantage are deeply embedded in football culture. This is perhaps most often apparent in the relatively clear-cut instance of a ball going out of play and players from both sides appealing for the throw-in, goal kick or corner. The 'professional' foul by a defender, or the dive by an attacker to gain a penalty, for example, are to a large extent also accepted as part of the game. The pressure on players, described above, often means that they will exploit the Laws of the Game and the referee in their efforts to gain an advantage. Fans, players, managers and club owners do not invariably care a great deal about the manner in which a game is won, particularly if the result sees their team through to the next round of the Cup, or avoiding relegation. During the 1998/99 season FIFA and the FA directed referees to clamp down on players feigning injury and diving. Similarly, The FA has also carried out experiments with the 'rugby-style' ten-yard penalty for encroachment at free kicks. In Jersey in the 1998/99 season this practice succeeded in reducing dissent toward the referee and encroachment during free kicks.[44] However, if such pressures to win remain a feature of the élite game, attempts to 'mislead' the referee will continue. Consequently, refereeing decisions will not become any easier to make.

Much of the analysis of the proposals for various technological aids in this essay has ended where it began – on a discussion about the 'spirit' of the game, and the 'spirit' and the 'letter' of the laws by which it is regulated. As we begin the twenty-first century, few refereeing problems seem to be close to resolution. Given the structural characteristics of modern, élite football it seems likely that refereeing will continue to be a contentious issue. The introduction of, for example, technological innovations are likely to alter the course of the existing debate, but are unlikely to result in its tidy conclusion, for most of the proposed 'solutions' discussed in this study simply recreate the ever-present 'spirit' and 'letter' dilemma.

NOTES

This essay is dedicated to the memory of Betty Kerr.

1. *Daily Mirror*, 29 November 1998.
2. *Daily Mirror*, 29 January 1998.
3. *Daily Telegraph*, 6 June 1996.
4. The transformation of the game from its folk origins to its modern form is discussed by E. Dunning and K. Sheard, *Barbarians, Gentlemen and Players* (Oxford: Martin Robertson, 1979) and J.R. Witty, 'The History of Refereeing', in A.H. Fabian and G. Green (eds.), *Association Football, Volume 1* (London: The Caxton Publishing Company Ltd., 1960), pp.180–4.
5. Dunning and Sheard, *Barbarians, Gentlemen and Players*.
6. Witty, 'History', p.180.
7. Ibid., p.180.
8. Ibid., p.183.
9. J.R. Witty, 'The F.A. Frames its Laws', in Fabian and Green, p.154.
10. The FA Laws of the Game, 1889, cited in J.R. Witty 'History', p.184.
11. Ibid., p.183. Witty refers to a 'very early edition' of *The Referees' Chart*, possibly the second edition, published in 1896.
12. http://www.fifa.com/fifa/pub/magazine/fm8-97.4.html. 30 September 1999.
13. Ibid.
14. N. Elias, 'Introduction', in N. Elias and E. Dunning, *Quest for Excitement: Sport and Leisure in the Civilizing Process* (Oxford: Blackwell, 1986), p.51.
15. The example given appears in Law XI Offside. Other similar phrases include '…in a manner *considered* by the referee to be careless…' (Law XII Fouls of Misconduct), and, 'In his *opinion*…' (Law XII Fouls of Misconduct) (emphasis added). In the Preface to the Laws of the game, it states that the male gender is consistently used 'for simplification'.

16. D. Elleray, 'The Third Team; Patrick Murphy Interviews David Elleray, Spokesman for the Premier League Referees', in P.J. Murphy (ed.), *The Singer and Friedlander Review: 1997–98 Season* (London: Singer and Friedlander Investment Funds, 1998), p.22.

17. Ibid., p.22.

18. *Daily Telegraph*, 11 November 1997. It should be noted that Alex Ferguson is not atypical of football managers in this respect; rather, the prevalence of examples involving him relates, in part, to the greater press coverage which Manchester United games receive.

19. Ibid.

20. *Daily Telegraph*, 2 February 1996.

21. Elleray, 'The Third Team', p.22.

22. Ibid., p.22.

23. *The Times*, 15 October 1998.

24. *The Times*, 18 March 1999.

25. The IFAB is constituted of four delegates each from the Football Association (FA), in England, The FA of Wales, the Scottish FA, the Irish FA and FIFA. Proposed changes to the Laws are voted upon by the Board, and changes can only be made if threequarters of the Board agree on them.

26. *Independent*, 17 June 1998.

27. *Daily Telegraph*, 17 June 1998.

28. *Daily Telegraph*, 19 June 1998.

29. Ibid.

30. G. Boon (ed.), *Deloitte & Touche Annual Review of Football Finance 1996–97 Season* (Manchester: Deloitte & Touche, 1998), and G. Boon (ed.), *Deloitte & Touche Annual Review of Football Finance 1997–98 Season* (Manchester: Deloitte & Touche, 1999).

31. N. Barrett, *The Daily Telegraph Football Chronicle*, Third Edition (London: Ebury Press, 1996), p.60.

32. Ibid., p.106.

33. *Daily Mirror*, 10 August 1999.

34. E. Dunning, P.J. Murphy and J. Williams, *The Roots of Football Hooliganism: An Historical and Sociological Study* (London: Routledge, 1988).

35. Other expressions of dissatisfaction with football personnel, namely club owners and directors, during the 1997/98 season included fan protests at the grounds of Stoke, Sheffield United and Newcastle United, and in 1998/99, at Portsmouth, for example.

36. The definition of what is or is not a 'mistake' by a referee is not straightforward. It is often contested, relatively subjective and subject to change over time. Some 'mistakes' are relatively clear-cut – for example, the referee does not see the whole of the ball crossing the line, and so cannot award a goal, whilst the video replay shows that the whole of the ball did, in fact, cross the line, and that a goal should have been awarded. Other incidents are much more difficult to assess in terms of whether or not a referee has made a 'mistake,' because, as noted previously, referees do not have to punish identical incidents in an identical manner. Where possible I have drawn upon examples of this rather more clear-cut nature to illustrate my argument.

37. *Times*, 30 January 1999.

38. *Daily Telegraph*, 26 December 1997.

39. *Daily Mirror*, 5 August 1998.

40. *Guardian*, 26 July 1998.

41. The *Daily Telegraph*, 17 January 1999. The article continues; 'the move follows a spate of disputed third-umpire decisions ... including the run-out reprieve for Australian Michael Slater ... which effectively killed off England's hopes of squaring the Ashes series'.

42. The *Times*, 12 December 1998.

43. The Rugby Football Union referees' development officer, Nick Bunting, reported that in trials on preseason National (American) Football League matches in the United States, where 'television playback adjudication' was used, eight additional cameras had been required and, 'The playbacks added an average of 25 minutes to each game and confirmed 98 per cent of the judgements were correct. Just one decision in the whole trial had to be overturned.' *Times*, 21 October 1998.

44. David Davies, the then acting Chief Executive of the FA, suggested, 'Such an innovation has seen cases of dissent fall spectacularly and this is a rule which could well become more widespread in the future'. *Daily Telegraph*, 21 February 1999.

Select Bibliography

The Peculiar Economics of English Professional Football
Chris Gratton

J. Cairns, N. Jennett and P.J. Sloane, 'The Economics of Professional Team Sports: A Survey of Theory and Evidence', *Journal of Economic Studies*, 13 (1986)

Deloitte & Touche, *Deloitte & Touche Annual Review of Football Finance* (Manchester: Deloitte & Touche, 1998)

M. El-Hodiri and J. Quirk, 'An Economic Model of a Professional Sports League', *Journal of Political Economy*, 79 (1971)

T. Hoehn and S. Szymanski, 'The Americanisation of European Football', *Economic Policy*, 28 (April 1999)

Monopolies and Mergers Commission, *British Sky Broadcasting plc and Manchester United plc: A Report on the Proposed Merger* (London: The Stationery Office, 1999)

W. Neale, 'The Peculiar Economics of Professional Sport', *Quarterly Journal of Economics*, 78, (1964)

J. Quirk and R.D. Fort, *Pay Dirt: The Business of Professional Team Sports* (Princeton, NJ: Princeton University Press, 1992)

'Heads above Water': Business Strategies for a New Football Economy
Barrie Pierpoint

A Brown (ed.), *Fanatics! Power, Identity and Fandom in Football* (London: Routledge, 1998)

Deloitte & Touche, *Deloitte & Touche Annual Review of Football Finance* (Manchester: Deloitte & Touche, 1998)

D. Hudson, *The Position and Role of Marketing in Professional Football Clubs* (Leicester: De Montfort University, 1997)

A. Fynn and L. Guest, *Out of Time: Why Football Isn't Working* (London: Simon & Schuster, 1994)

Sir Norman Chester Centre for Football Research, *FA Premier League National Fan Survey 1996/97: Summary* (Leicester: Sir Norman Chester Centre for Football Research, 1998)

S. Redhead, *Post-Fandom and the Millennial Blues: The Transformation of Soccer Culture* (London: Routledge, 1997)

Lord Justice Taylor (Chairman), *Inquiry into the Hillsborough Stadium Disaster: Final Report* (London: HMSO, 1990)

Football and European Law: Who's in Charge?
Ken Foster

European Commission, *The Development and Prospects for Community Action in the Field of Sport* (European Commission Staff Working Paper, DG X, Brussels, 1998)

European Commission, *The Fight against Doping, the European Model of Sport, Relations between Sport and Television* (European Commission, DGX, Brussels, 1999)

N.K. Raber, 'Dispute Resolution in Olympic Sport: The Court of Arbitration for Sport', *Seton Hall Journal of Sport Law*, 8 (1998)

S. Szymanski and T. Kuyers, *Winners and Losers: The Business Strategy of Football* (London: Viking, 1999)

FIFA and the Men Who Made It
Alan Tomlinson

S. Inglis, *League Football and the Men Who Made It* (London: Willow Books/Collins, 1988)

J. Sugden and A. Tomlinson, *FIFA and the Contest for World Football: Who Rules the People's Game?* (Cambridge: Polity Press, 1998)

J. Sugden and A. Tomlinson, 'FIFA and the Marketing of World Football', in G. Lines, I. McDonald and U. Merkel (eds.), *The Production and Consumption of Sport Cultures: Leisure, Culture and Commerce* (Eastbourne: Leisure Studies Association Publications, 1998)

J. Sugden and A. Tomlinson, 'Global Power Struggles in World Football: FIFA and UEFA 1954–1974, and their Legacy', *The International Journal of the History of Sport*, 14, 2 (1997)

J. Sugden, A. Tomlinson and P. Darby, 'FIFA versus UEFA in the Struggle for the Control of World Football', in A. Brown (ed.), *Fanatics! Power, Identity and Fandom in Football* (London: Routledge, 1998)

A. Tomlinson, 'FIFA and the World Cup: The Expanding Football Family', in J. Sugden and A. Tomlinson (eds.), *Hosts and Champions: Soccer Cultures, National Identities and USA World Cup* (Aldershot: Arena/Ashgate, 1994)

A. Tomlinson, 'Going Global: The FIFA Story', in A. Tomlinson, *The Game's Up: Essay's in the Cultural Analysis of Sport, Leisure and Popular Culture* (Aldershot: Arena/Ashgate, 1999)

D. Yallop, *How They Stole the Game* (London: Poetic Publishing, 1999)

Democracy and Fandom: Developing a Supporters' Trust at Northampton Town FC
Brian Lomax

A. Brown (ed.), *Fanatics! Power, Identity and Fandom in Football* (London: Routledge, 1998)

Football Task Force, *Investing in the Community* (London: Football Task Force, 1998)

J. Garland and M. Rowe 'Field of Dreams: An Assessment of Antiracism in British Football', *Journal of Ethnic and Migration Studies*, 25, 2 (1999)

S. North and P. Hodson, *Build a Bonfire: How Football Fans United to Save Brighton and Hove Albion* (Edinburgh: Mainstream, 1997)

S. Redhead, *Post-Fandom and the Millennial Blues: The Transformation of Soccer Culture* (London: Routledge, 1997)

R. Taylor, *Football and its Fans: Supporters and Their Relations with the Game, 1885–1985* (Leicester: Leicester University Press, 1992)

P. Vasili, *The First Black Footballer: Arthur Wharton 1865–1930* (London and Portland, OR: Frank Cass, 1998)

P. Vasili, 'Walter Daniel Tull, 1888–1918: Soldier, Footballer, Black', *Race and Class*, 38, 2 (1996)

The Changing Face of Football: Stadiums and Communities
John Bale

J. Bale, *Sport, Space and the City* (London: Routledge, 1993)

J. Bale, *Landscapes of Modern Sport* (Leicester: Leicester University Press, 1994)

A. Burnett, 'Community, Local Politics and Football', in John Bale (ed.), *Community, Landscape and Identity: Horizons in a Geography of Sport* (Keele: Keele University Department of Geography, 1994)

R. Everitt, *Battle for the Valley* (London: Voice of the Valley, 1994)

E. Hague and J. Mercer, 'Geographical Memory and Urban Identity in Scotland: Raith Rovers FC and Kirkaldy', *Geography*, 83, (1998)

C. Mason, and A. Moncrieff, 'The Effect of Relocation on the Externality Fields of Football Stadia: The Case of St. Johnstone FC', *Scottish Geographical Magazine*, 109 (1998)

Exploring Future Relationships between Football Clubs and Local Government
Sean Perkins

T. Crabbe, *Going for Goals!! An Evaluation of the Tower Hamlets Drug Challenge Fund Project* (Goldsmiths College, London: Centre for Urban and Community Research, 1998)

Football Task Force, *The Community Role of Football Clubs* (London: Football Task Force, 1998)

Football Task Force, *Improving Facilities for Disabled Supporters* (London: Football Task Force, 1998)

Kick It Out, *Annual Report 1997/98* (London: Kick It Out, 1998)

S. Perkins and J. Williams, *Local Authorities and Football Club Partnerships: Some Research on New Developments* (Leicester: Sir Norman Chester Centre for Football Research, University of Leicester, forthcoming)

J. Williams and S. Perkins, *Leaving the Trackside: Facilities for Disabled Fans at British Football Stadia, post-Hillsborough* (London: The Football Trust, 1997)

J. Williams and R. Taylor, *The National Football in the Community Programme: A Research Report* (Leicester: Sir Norman Chester Centre for Football Research, University of Leicester, 1994)

Football in the Community: 'What's the Score?'
Neil Watson

J. Williams with R. Taylor, *The National Football and the Community Programme: a Research Report* (Leicester: Sir Norman Chester Centre, 1994)

N.K. Denzin, *The Research Act in Sociology* (London: Butterworths, 1970)

N.K. Denzin, *Sociological Methods: A Sourcebook*, 2nd ed. (New York: McGraw-Hill, 1978)

D.A. de Vaus, *Surveys in Social Research*, 3rd ed. (London: Allen & Unwin, 1991)

The Football Association Technical Department, *Football Education for Young Players, A Charter for Quality* (London: Football Association, 1997)

N. Gilbert, *Researching Social Life* (London: Sage, 1993)

C. Glesne and A. Peshkin, *Becoming Qualitative Researchers: An Introduction* (New York: Longman, 1992)

M. Hammersley and P. Atkinson, *Ethnography: Principles in Practice* (London: Routledge, 1989)

P. McNeill, *Research Methods* (London: Routledge, 1992)

H.W. Smith, *Strategies of Social Research: The Sociological Imagination* (Englewood Cliffs, NJ: Prentice Hall, 1975)

The People's Game? Football Spectatorship and Demographic Change
Dominic Malcolm, Ian Jones and Ivan Waddington

I. Jones, 'Football Fandom: Football Fan Identity and Identification at Luton Town Football Club' (unpublished Ph.D. thesis, University of Luton, 1998)

A. King, 'The Lads: Masculinity and the New Consumption of Football', *Sociology*, 31 (1997)

A. King, 'New Directors, Customers and Fans: The Transformation of English Football in the 1990s', *Sociology of Sport Journal*, 14 (1997)

I. Waddington, E. Dunning and P. Murphy, 'Research Note: Surveying the Social Composition of Football Crowds', *Leisure Studies*, 15 (1996)

I. Waddington, D. Malcolm and R. Horak, 'The Social Composition of Football Crowds in Western Europe: A Comparative Study', *International Review for the Sociology of Sport*, 33 (1998)

The Hooligan's Fear of the Penalty
Jon Garland and Michael Rowe

E. Dunning, P. Murphy, and J. Williams, *The Roots of Football Hooliganism* (London: Routledge, 1988)

Football League, Football Association, Premier League, Football Licensing Authority, and the Football Safety Officer's Association *Stewarding and Safety Management at Football Grounds* (London: Football League *et al.*, 1995)

Home Office, *Review of Police Core and Ancillary Tasks: Final Report* (London: Home Office, 1995)

J. Garland and M. Rowe, 'Racism at Work – a Study of Professional Football', *International Journal of Risk, Security and Crime Prevention*, 1, 3 (1996)

J. Garland and M. Rowe, 'War Minus the Shooting? Jingoism, the English Press and Euro '96', *Journal of Sport and Social Issues*, 23, 1 (1999)

R. Giulianotti (ed.), *Football Violence and Social Identity* (London: Routledge, 1994)

L. Johnston, *The Rebirth of Private Policing* (London: Routledge, 1992)

R. Morgan and T. Newburn, *The Future of Policing* (Oxford: Clarendon Press, 1997)

Lord Justice Taylor (Chairman) *Inquiry into the Hillsborough Stadium Disaster: Final Report* (London: HMSO, 1990)

Taking Offence:
Modern Moralities and the Perception of the Football Fan
Carlton Brick

D. Allirajah, 'Getting a Good Kicking', *Offence*, 1 (London: Libero, 1997)

S. Fish, *There's No Such Thing As Free Speech: And It's a Good Thing Too* (New York: Oxford University Press, 1994)

F. Furedi, *Culture of Fear: Risk-taking and the Morality of Low Expectation* (London: Cassell, 1997)

H.L. Gates, A.P Griffen, D.E. Lively, R.C. Post, W.B. Rubenstein and N. Strossen, *Speaking of Race, Speaking of Sex: Hate Speech, Civil Rights and Civil Liberties* (New York: New York University Press, 1995)

S. Greenfield and G. Osborn, 'The Legal Regulation of Football and Cricket: "England's Dreaming"', in M. Roche (ed.), *Sport, Popular Culture and Identity* (Aachen: Meyer & Meyer, 1998)

R. Giulianotti, 'Social Identity and Public Order: Political and Academic Discourses on Football Violence', in R. Giulianotti, N. Bonney and M. Hepworth (eds.), *Football, Violence and Social Identity* (London: Routledge, 1994)

Home Office, *Review of Football-Related Legislation* (London: Home Office, 1998)

Home Office, *Football (Offences & Disorder) Bill* (London: Home Office, 1998)

J. Jensen, 'Fandom as Pathology: The Consequences of Characterization', in L.A. Lewis (ed.), *The Adoring Audience: Fan Culture and Popular Media* (London: Routledge, 1993)

G. Whannel, 'Football, Crowd Behaviour and the Press', *Media, Culture and Society*, 1 (1979)

Global Sport and the Migration Patterns of France '98 World Cup Finals Players: Some Preliminary Observations
Joe Maguire and Bob Pearton

J. Bale and J. Maguire (eds.), *The Global Sports Arena: Athletic Talent Migration in an Interdependent World* (London and Portland, OR: Frank Cass, 1994)

A. Klein, *Sugarball: The American Game, the Domincan Dream* (Yale: Yale University Press, 1991)

J. Maguire, *Global Sport: Identities, Societies, Civilizations* (Oxford: Polity Press, 1999)

J. Maguire, 'Blade Runners: Canadian Migrants, Ice Hockey and the Global Sports Process', *Journal of Sport and Social Issues*, 20 (1996)

J. Maguire, 'Preliminary Observations on Globalization and the Migration of Sport Labour', *Sociological Review*, 3 (1994)

J. Maguire and D. Stead, 'Border Crossings: Soccer Labour Migration and the European Union', *International Review for the Sociology of Sport*, 33 (1998)

J. Maguire and D. Stead, '"Far Pavilions"?: Cricket Migrants, Foreign Sojourn and Contested Identities', *International Review for the Sociology of Sport*, 31 (1996)

J. Sugden and A. Tomlinson (eds.), *FIFA and the Contest for World Football: Who Rules the People's Game?* (Cambridge: Polity Press, 1998)

Racism in Football: A Victim's Perspective
Richie Moran

L. Back, T. Crabbe and J. Solomos, 'Lions, Black Skins and Reggae Gyals: Race, Nation and Identity in Football', in L. Back, T. Crabbe and J. Solomos, *The Changing Face of Football: Race, Identity and Multiculture in English Soccer* (Oxford: Berg, forthcoming)

Charlton Athletic Race Equality Partnership (CARE), *Tackling Racial Barriers to Watching Football* (Leatherhead: Parker Tanner, 1996)

Football Task Force, *Eliminating Racism from Football* (London: Football Task Force, 1998)

J. Garland and M. Rowe, *Racism in British Football* (Basingstoke: Macmillan, forthcoming)

J. Garland and M. Rowe, 'Field of Dreams: An Assessment of Antiracism in British Football', *Journal of Ethnic and Migration Studies*, 25, 2 (1999)

B. Holland, 'Kicking Racism Out of Football: An Assessment of Racial

Harassment In and Around Football Grounds', *New Community*, 21, 4 (1995)

Kick It Out, *Annual Report 1997/98* (London: Kick It Out, 1999)

Kick It Out, *Kick It Out* (London: Kick It Out, 1998)

D. McArdle and D. Lewis, *'Kick Racism Out of Football': A Report on the Implementation of the Commission for Racial Equality's Strategies* (London: Centre for Research in Industrial and Criminal Law, 1997)

Sir Norman Chester Centre for Football Research, *FA Premier League National Fan Survey 1996/97: Summary* (Leicester: Sir Norman Chester Centre for Football Research, 1998)

The 'Letter' and the 'Spirit':
Football Laws and Refereeing in the Twenty-First Century
Sharon Colwell

E. Dunning, P. Murphy and J. Williams, *The Roots of Football Hooliganism: An Historical and Sociological Study* (London: Routledge, 1988)

N. Elias and E. Dunning, *Quest for Excitement: Sport and Leisure in the Civilising Process* (Oxford: Blackwell, 1986)

D. Elleray, 'The Third Team; Patrick Murphy Interviews David Elleray, Spokesman for the Premier League Referees', in P.J. Murphy (ed.), *The Singer and Friedlander Review: 1997–98 Season* (London: Singer and Friedlander Investment Funds, 1998)

K. Sheard and E. Dunning, *Barbarians, Gentlemen and Players* (Oxford: Martin Robertson, 1979)

J.R. Witty, 'The F.A. Frames its Laws', in A.H. Fabian and G. Green (eds.), *Association Football, Volume 1* (London: The Caxton Publishing Company Ltd., 1960)

J.R. Witty, 'The History of Refereeing', in A.H. Fabian and G. Green (eds.), *Association Football, Volume 1* (London: The Caxton Publishing Company Ltd., 1960)

Notes on Contributors

John Bale is Professor of Sports Geography at Keele University. He has lectured throughout Europe, in North America and Australia and has been a Visiting Professor at the University of Jyväskylä, Finland. He has authored many articles on spatial, regional and environmental aspects of sports and among his books are *Sport, Space and the City* (1993) and *Landscapes of Modern Sports* (1994).

Brendon Batson was born in Grenada and moved to England at the age of nine. He played for Arsenal for four years, having signed as a professional with the club at the age of 17, he then transferred to Cambridge United and then West Bromwich Albion. While at West Bromwich he won three England 'B' caps. He began his association with the Professional Footballers' Association as a 20-year-old player at Cambridge United and has been Deputy Chief Executive since 1984, when a knee injury brought his playing career to an end.

Carlton Brick is a member of the Centre for Sports Development Research at Roehampton Institute London. He is also Network Co-ordinator of *Libero* and editor of the football fanzine *Offence*.

Sharon Colwell, a graduate of the University of Birmingham, is currently completing a doctorate about football refereeing. The research, funded by the merchant bankers Singer and Friedlander plc, is being undertaken at the Centre for Research into Sport and Society, University of Leicester. Sharon has contributed several articles about referees to the annual publication *The Singer and Friedlander Review*, and has recently published an article examining the relationships between feminisms and figurational sociology in the *European Physical Education Review*.

Patricia Day OBE joined the Football Association in 1965, at the age of 17, as a junior secretary. Her initial attraction to the job was primarily because she had been a football fan since the age of 11 and a supporter of her local club, Enfield. She had spells as secretary to Allan Wade, Denis Follows and Ted Croker, until in 1974, she left to broaden her experience. In 1977 Ted Croker invited her to return as his personal assistant. In 1989 Graham Kelly appointed her administrative manager and in 1994 she became the Deputy Chief Executive of the FA.

Ken Foster was educated at Manchester University and now teaches in the Law School at the University of Warwick. He teaches Sports Law at both undergraduate and postgraduate level. He has written on several aspects of Sports Law and is currently researching issues of governance in international sports federations and the impact of legal intervention on these organizations.

Jon Garland is a Research Fellow at the Scarman Centre, University of Leicester. He has published widely in the areas of racism and football, and is currently writing a book on the subject with Michael Rowe. His research interests include racism, xenophobia and sport; policing and crowd control; ethnicity and identity, and crime and the 'information society'.

Chris Gratton is Professor of Leisure Economics and Director of the Leisure Industries Research Centre at Sheffield Hallam University. He is a specialist in the economic analysis of sport and leisure markets. He is co-author (with Peter Taylor) of six books specifically on the sport and leisure industry, and has published over 100 articles in academic and professional journals.

Ian Jones is a Lecturer in Leisure Studies in the Department of Tourism and Leisure at the University of Luton, where he completed his doctorate on football fan identification. As well researching sports fandom, his interests lie in the field of 'serious leisure' and sport and social identity.

Brian Lomax is Chairman of the Northampton Town Supporters' Trust and was an elected director at Northampton Town FC from 1992 to 1999. He played a vital role in the establishment of the Antiracism Working Party at the club, and has been at the forefront of the development of the club's wide-ranging antiracist initiatives. He has contributed to several conferences and seminars on football-related matters, and has recently been appointed Chairman of Supporters Direct, the Government's new Supporters' Trusts initiative.

Joseph Maguire is Professor in the Sociology of Sport at Loughborough University, Department of Physical Education, Sport Science and Recreation Management. He is currently President of the International Sociology of Sport Association and has served on international journals relating to the Sociology of Sport. Professor Maguire is also editor of the serial *Research in the Sociology of Sport*, a fellow of the European College of Sport Science and has lectured widely in Europe, Asia and North America. His latest book is *Global Sport: Identities, Societies, Civilizations* (1999).

Dominic Malcolm is a Research Fellow at the Centre for Research into Sport and Society at the University of Leicester. As well as teaching on the campus-based MA and the distance learning M.Sc. courses, he has a wide range of research interests including cricket and 'race' relations, cricket spectator violence, cricket player violence, physical education and gender and physical education and health. Dominic is a founding co-editor of the journal *Soccer and Society*.

Richie Moran is an ex-professional footballer who played for Fujita of Tokyo in the Japanese League and Birmingham City in England, before quitting the game because of the racism he was subjected to. Since then has become a vociferous campaigner on the subject of racism both in football and society in general, and has contributed a number of articles for national newspapers and books, as well as appearing on television and radio and speaking at numerous conferences. He now works for Portsmouth City Mental Health Services, and is a martial arts instructor.

Bob Pearton is Head of the Department of Sport Science at Canterbury Christ Church College University. An international sportsman in 1960s and 1970s, his research into sport-related violence led to a range of publications, many in collaboration with George Gaskell. His current research interests are mainly in the area of sport globalization. In 1993 he co-edited *The Sports Process* with Eric Dunning and Joseph Maguire and since 1994 he has been Visiting Professor of Sociology, University of Colorado.

Sean Perkins is a Research Associate at the Sir Norman Chester Centre for Football Research, University of Leicester. His work has included annual surveys for the FA Premier League and Nationwide League, and research for the Football Task Force. He compiled the first *National Guide to Facilities for Disabled Football Supporters* (1997), and has recently completed a national survey examining the relationship between Football Clubs and Local Government.

Barrie Pierpoint was Group Chief Executive and a Board Director of Leicester City Football Club Plc, and its Stock Exchange-listed parent company Leicester City Plc. He joined Leicester City as Marketing Director in 1991 from a marketing and publishing consultancy serving the automotive industry. Before becoming Group Chief Executive in 1998, he was Leicester City Football Club Plc's Managing Director. He left the club in January 2000.

Michael Rowe is Lecturer in Policing and Public Order at the Scarman Centre, University of Leicester. His research interests include policing and minority ethnic groups and the politics of racism and public order in Britain. In 1998 he published *The Racialisation of Disorder in Twentieth Century Britain* and he is currently collaborating with Jon Garland on a book about racism and antiracism in football, a topic on which he has written widely.

Alan Tomlinson is Professor of Sport and Leisure Studies at the Chelsea School Research Centre, University of Brighton. His research interests are in the social history and sociology of consumption, and the politics and culture of global sports spectacles such as the Olympic Games and the football World Cup. His most recent books are *FIFA and the Contest for World Football: Who Rules the Peoples' Game?* (with John Sugden, 1998), *Understanding Sport: An Introduction to the Sociological and Cultural Analysis of Sport* (with John Horne and Garry Whannel, 1999), *Great Balls of Fire: How Big Money is Hijacking World Football* (with John Sugden, 1999), and *The Game's Up: Essays in the Cultural Analysis of Sport, Leisure and Popular Culture* (1999). He is the editor of the *International Review for the Sociology of Sport*.

Ivan Waddington is Director for International Affairs at the Centre for Research into Sport and Society, University of Leicester. Previously he was Director of the Sir Norman Chester Centre for Football Research. He has a long-standing interest in both the sociology of sport and the sociology of health and many of his research interests bridge these two areas of study. He has recently completed a major report for the Professional Footballers' Association on the roles of the club doctor and physiotherapist in professional football. His latest book is *Sport, Health and Drugs* (2000).

Neil Watson is Director of the Leyton Orient Community Sports Programme. He studied physical education at Sheffield Hallam University before moving to London in 1983. After six years of teaching in west London and working part-time for Brentford's Football in the Community Scheme he was appointed Community Development Officer at Leyton Orient in 1989. The Leyton Orient Community Sports Programme is nationally recognized as being at the forefront of community sports work and has won a number of national awards, including the Football Trust 'Community Club of the Year' title.

Abstracts

The Peculiar Economics of English Professional Football
Chris Gratton

This piece analyses the 'peculiar' economics of professional team sports (Neale, 1964) as developed in the North American literature leading to a definition of 'the American model' of a professional sports league. Secondly, it discusses the extent to which English football reflects this American model. Finally, it examines the hypothesis put forward by Hoehn and Szymanski (1999) that the present structure of English professional football is unsustainable and that the natural equilibrium for the English and other European countries league systems would be the formation of an American-style European Superleague.

European Law and Football: Who's in Charge?
Ken Foster

This essay discusses the impact of European law on football. It analyses the right of footballers to move clubs freely and the right of clubs to play wherever they wish. It describes the emerging policy of the European Commission in applying European competition law to football. The piece concludes that the Commission will recognize that sporting goals can sometimes only be achieved by anti-competitive measures but nevertheless such deviations from the normal legal rules will continue to be carefully monitored.

'Heads above Water': Business Strategies for a New Football Economy
Barrie Pierpoint

Barrie Pierpoint argues that many top-flight clubs find themselves in a precarious financial situation – barely managing to keep their heads above water. The dangers of being over-reliant on television revenue are addressed, and the need to attract new communities to watching live football illustrated. In particular, Pierpoint stresses the necessity for clubs to develop marketing strategies to entice previously excluded communities, such as minority ethnic groups and women, to watch live football, and evaluates some of the methods that clubs can employ by highlighting the initiatives devised by Leicester City FC. The essay concludes by warning that the nature and amount of revenue generated through television rights will soon change, and that this may cause severe problems for all but a handful of the richest clubs.

FIFA and the Men Who Made It
Alan Tomlinson

La Fédération Internationale de Football Association (FIFA) has had eight presidents since its formation in 1904. The first six were from England, France and Belgium, the seventh and eighth from Brazil and Switzerland respectively. This essay explores the background and philosophes of the presidents, showing how a sports ethos rooted in educational beliefs and idealism has been superseded by a big-business ethos combining global market expansion and personal aggrandizement. The analysis combines scrutiny of documentary sources and organizational records with use of oral history, qualitative interviews and personal observation of FIFA events and congresses. It shows how key powerbrokers are reshaping the future of world football.

The Administration of Football in the Twenty-First Century
Pat Day

Pat Day reflects on likely trends in the administration of football in the twenty-first century. In particular she considers the English FA's attempts to rid the game of hooliganism and the resulting change to the relationship between football authorities and the government, the changing role of supporters in the running of the game, the development of Centres of Excellence, and managing the demands of club and national playing success. The significance of staging major international football tournaments is also examined.

Democracy and Fandom:
Developing a Supporters' Trust at Northampton Town FC
Brian Lomax

Brian Lomax recounts the history of Northampton Town Supporters' Trust, the first such trust to be formed in British football. He attempts to analyse the impact the trust has made upon the life of the Football Club, which was also the first to admit elected supporters' representatives to full Directorships. The benefits have been not only financial, but also social and in terms of community development. The essay concludes by listing the necessary conditions for supporters' democracy and representation to be effective in football clubs generally.

The Changing Face of Football: Stadiums and Communities
John Bale

Football stadiums have traditionally been sources of benefits and disbenefits for the communities in which they are located. Various developments have occurred in British football since the implementation of the Taylor Report, following the Hillsborough disaster. These developments include stadium relocations, *in situ* expansion of stadiums, the diversification of stadium activities and the emergence of the Federation of Stadium Communities. Despite these innovations the negative effects of football (namely, spill-over effects such as traffic congestion, crowding and hooliganism) have not been eliminated.

Exploring Future Relationships between Football Clubs and Local Government
Sean Perkins

The link between football clubs and local authorities is likely to strengthen in the twenty-first century. For the major 'global' clubs it will be a means of anchoring themselves to their immediate community as they seek to expand their support in overseas markets. For smaller professional clubs, whose very survival is, at best, uncertain, effective local partnerships will contribute to ensuring their day-to-day existence. There are several examples of effective multi-agency partnerships which have tackled issues of education, community involvement, sports development, racism, drug abuse and other social concerns. However, Perkins argues that these models are relatively few in number, and that most clubs and local authorities have failed to see the benefits of such links.

Football in the Community: 'What's the Score?'
Neil Watson

'Football in the Community' schemes have been a feature of the vast majority of professional football clubs since the early 1990s. Originally suggested as an interventionist measure for football hooliganism as far back as 1975, their recent growth and development have been extraordinary. It is now the case that community schemes are more mature and sophisticated, are developing sport from grass roots to excellence and tackling serious social issues in partnership with the private and public sectors. This research investigates Football in the Community schemes in this new era, at football clubs which can generally be classified as either big or small. It focuses particularly on their aims and priority areas of work, their relationship with the football club and their sources of funding. It will also examine the changing role of the Footballers' Further Education and Vocational Training Society, the umbrella organization responsible for their development.

The People's Game? Football Spectatorship and Demographic Change
Dominic Malcolm, Ian Jones and Ivan Waddington

This piece takes a longitudinal perspective on the history of football crowd surveys and attempts to draw some conclusions about discernible patterns of change. In particular the common claim that, at the expense of 'traditional' football fans, increasing numbers of women and middle-class supporters are now watching live football is assessed. The essay concludes that there is little empirical evidence to support these prevalent ideas. Moreover, the nature of being a football fan, with the high level of commitment which this cultural practice entails, would suggest that supporter demographics are likely to be rather resistant to rapid change.

The Hooligan's Fear of the Penalty
Jon Garland and Michael Rowe

Football-related disorder is still evident at league and national team fixtures in England. This piece assesses the levels and trends of this disorder, and examines the methods developed to police hooliganism in the 1990s, including the use of close-circuit television, private police and police intelligence gathering. Although these strategies have had some impact in reducing levels of disorder, the number of incidents of violence still occurring seems to indicate that 'solving the problem' of football-related disorder is not simply a matter of concentrating on organized hooligan gangs, as it is contested that much of the 'hooliganism' is unorganized and spontaneous.

Taking Offence:
Modern Moralities and the Perception of the Football Fan
Carlton Brick

The 1990s witnessed a dramatic 're-centering' of the football fan within socio-political discourse. The emergence of fan groups in the post-Hillsborough period has enabled fandom to acquire respectable media and political profiles. But The Football (Offences and Disorder) Act actively expands the concept of fandom as a deviant activity. A key theme in this expansion is the concept of 'safety'. Through the concept of 'safety' notions of football deviancy have been expanded to include acts of speech and offensive gestures. The recasting of football deviancy is representative of an authoritarian transformation of the relationships between State power and the individual.

Global Sport and the Migration Patterns of France '98 World Cup
Finals Players: Some Preliminary Observations
Joe Maguire and Bob Pearton

Elite labour migration is an established feature of the sporting 'global village'. Research examining this migration has established that a shifting set of interdependencies exist which contour the migrant trails of world sport. These interdependencies are multi-faceted and incorporate economic, historical, social and cultural factors. This study seeks to contribute to ongoing research about talent migration in world football through a case study of one area of this migration – the very élite level. In this respect a preliminary study of the sporting origins and destinations of players participating in the 1998 World Cup Finals in France has been undertaken.

Racism in Football: A Victim's Perspective
Richie Moran

Richie Moran reflects on his career as a professional footballer, a career largely curtailed by the racism he faced. Moran charts the forms of racism he experienced, including verbal and physical abuse, and the prejudice and discrimination he encountered. These personal experiences are discussed within the context of the development of recent anti-racist initiatives within the game, and it is argued that, despite some successes, there is still a long way to go in the quest to rid football of racist attitudes.

The 'Letter' and the 'Spirit':
Football Laws and Refereeing in the Twenty-First Century
Sharon Colwell

This essay examines problems raised around football refereeing. Initially, the Laws of the Game are discussed, with reference to their historical development and to the related concepts of the 'spirit' and the 'letter' of the Laws. The contemporary context within which referees operate is then considered, in terms of the media scrutiny of élite level soccer, and the complex relationships between referees, players, managers, fans and media personnel. Finally, proposed 'solutions' to refereeing problems are critically examined.

Index

Other Titles in the Sport in the Global Society Series

Football Culture

Local Contests, Global Visions

Gerry P T Finn, *University of Strathclyde* and **Richard Giulianotti**, *University of Aberdeen* (Eds)

This new collection of essays provides a critical investigation of football cultures throughout the world, examining local and national impacts of the game's new millennial order. The authors traverse five continents, examining the diversity of contemporary football cultures in highly modern and developing societies. *Football Culture* will hold particular appeal for anyone with a specialist interest in football, or for those simply with a genuine love of the world's premier sport.

Contributors: *Gerry P T Finn, Richard Giulianotti, John Hughson, David L Andrews, Bea Vidacs, Pablo Alabarces, Marìa Graciela Rodríguez, Nicola Porro, Pippo Russo, Gary Armstrong, Malcolm Young, John Horne, Patrick Mignon.*

312 pages illus 2000
0 7146 5041 2 cloth
0 7146 8100 8 paper
A special issue of the journal Culture, Sport, Society
Sport in the Global Society No. 16

FRANK CASS PUBLISHERS
Newbury House, 900 Eastern Avenue, Ilford, Essex, IG2 7HH
Tel: +44 (0)20 8599 8866 Fax: +44 (0)20 8599 0984 E-mail: info@frankcass.com
NORTH AMERICA
5804 NE Hassalo Street, Portland, OR 97213 3644, USA
Tel: 800 944 6190 Fax: 503 280 8832 E-mail: cass@isbs.com
Website: www.frankcass.com

France and the 1998 World Cup

The National Impact of a World Sporting Event

Hugh Dauncey and **Geoff Hare**, *both at the University of Newcastle*
(Eds)
Foreword by **Gérard Houllier**, *Liverpool FC.*
With a Contribution by **Pierre Bourdieu**

> '... by beating Brazil, and by having qualified for the Final, France
> had exorcised its demons: the spectre of racism, the headlong rush
> back towards intolerance, the catastrophic image of a country
> hemmed in by fear, hatred and introspection.'
> **Olivier Poivre d'Arvor, *Cultural Counsellor, French Embassy,***
> **London, Director, *Institut français***

The 1998 soccer World Cup was perhaps the greatest international event in
recent French history. This collection examines the effects on the host nation
of the major economic, political, cultural and sporting dimensions of this
global sports event. It discusses issues such as the impact on traditional
French approaches to sport of the commercialization of football, the
improvement of sporting infrastructures, the marketing of the competition,
the role of commercial sponsors, media coverage of the matches, policing
and security during the month-long competition, and the French nation's
identification with the multiracial national team.

The analysis of France '98 is set within the recent history and organization of
French football (the links between football, money and politics; and the
characteristics of the French football public), and more broadly within the
French tradition of using major cultural and sporting events to focus world
attention on France as a leader in the international community.

256 pages 1999
0 7146 4887 6 cloth
0 7146 4438 2 paper
A special issue of the journal Culture, Sport, Society
Sport in the Global Society No. 7

FRANK CASS PUBLISHERS
Newbury House, 900 Eastern Avenue, Ilford, Essex, IG2 7HH
Tel: +44 (0)20 8599 8866 Fax: +44 (0)20 8599 0984 E-mail: info@frankcass.com
NORTH AMERICA
5804 NE Hassalo Street, Portland, OR 97213 3644, USA
Tel: 800 944 6190 Fax: 503 280 8832 E-mail: cass@isbs.com
Website: www.frankcass.com

Scoring for Britain

International Football and International Politics, 1900–1939

Peter J Beck, *Kingston University*

> '*The scope of Beck's book is extraordinary ... Beck, who went to the same grammar school as Des Lynam, has created a history that will fascinate academics, anoraks and fans alike, whether in the library, in the armchair or on the terraces*'.
>
> **Woking News and Mail**

This fascinating book considers the nature and development of linkages between international football and politics between 1900 and 1939, and also provides a history of international football in Britain. It discusses Britain's influence over the development of football as a world game, British footballers as international stars, and the extra-sporting significance of fixtures such as England v. Germany (1935 and 1938). Finally, it illuminates the long-standing sporting debates as to whether professionals representing their country play for themselves rather than for their nation, whether international sport serves as a force for co-operation or conflict, and whether sporting performances affect a nation's prestige.

320 pages 15 illus 1999
0 7146 4899 X cloth
0 7146 4454 4 paper
Sport in the Global Society No. 9

FRANK CASS PUBLISHERS
Newbury House, 900 Eastern Avenue, Ilford, Essex, IG2 7HH
Tel: +44 (0)20 8599 8866 Fax: +44 (0)20 8599 0984 E-mail: info@frankcass.com
NORTH AMERICA
5804 NE Hassalo Street, Portland, OR 97213 3644, USA
Tel: 800 944 6190 Fax: 503 280 8832 E-mail: cass@isbs.com
Website: www.frankcass.com

The First Black Footballer

Arthur Wharton 1865–1930: An Absence of Memory

Phil Vasili
With a Foreword by **Irvine Welsh** *and an Introduction by*
Tony Whelan, *Manchester United FC*

> *'...the most conspicuously absent volume from the library of British Sport ... the extraordinary tale of Britain's forgotten all-time sporting great has finally been told.'*
>
> **Independent on Sunday**

Arthur Wharton was the world's first Black professional footballer and 100 yards world record holder, and was probably the first African to play professional cricket in the Yorkshire and Lancashire leagues. His achievements were accomplished against the backdrop of Africa's forced colonization by European regimes. But while Arthur was beating the best on the tracks and fields of Britain, the peoples of the continent of his birth were being recast as lesser human beings. The tall Ghanaian was an extreme irritation to many white supremacists because his education and sporting triumphs refuted their theories. In the late Victorian era, when Britain's economic and political power reached its zenith and when the dominant ideas of the age labelled all Blacks as inferior, it was simply not expedient to proclaim the exploits of an African sportsman. This shaped the way Wharton was forgotten.

272 pages 25 photographs 1998
0 7146 4903 1 cloth
0 7146 4459 5 paper
Sport in the Global Society No. 11

FRANK CASS PUBLISHERS
Newbury House, 900 Eastern Avenue, Ilford, Essex, IG2 7HH
Tel: +44 (0)20 8599 8866 Fax: +44 (0)20 8599 0984 E-mail: info@frankcass.com
NORTH AMERICA
5804 NE Hassalo Street, Portland, OR 97213 3644, USA
Tel: 800 944 6190 Fax: 503 280 8832 E-mail: cass@isbs.com
Website: www.frankcass.com